Violet *is* Blue

Books by Anne Shaw Heinrich

The Women of Paradise County Series
Book One: *God Bless the Child*
Book Two: *Violet is Blue*

Coming Soon!
The Women of Paradise County Series
Book Three: *House of Teeth*

For more information
visit: SpeakingVolumes.us

Violet *is* Blue

Anne Shaw Heinrich

SPEAKING VOLUMES, LLC
NAPLES, FLORIDA
2025

Violet *is* Blue

Copyright © 2025 by Anne Shaw Heinrich

All rights reserved. No part of this book may be reproduced or transmitted in any form or by any means without written permission.

ISBN 979-8-89022-315-9

To Bret,
my husband, friend, soulmate . . .

Acknowledgments

Every good thing happens when we have the space and grace to consider possibilities. My fortunate path has been forged by my loving parents, Patrick and Ramona, my soulmate and husband, Bret, and our three children, Eleanor, Harrison and Charlotte, who have my heart.

I'd also like to thank some of the best friends in the world a person could have. Fortunately, there are too many to list here.

I'm forever thankful to my editor and friend, David Tabatsky, and to my literary agent, Nancy Rosenfeld. Thanks, too, to Erica and Kurt Mueller at Speaking Volumes.

A Word from the Author

In *God Bless the Child*, the first book in The Women of Paradise County series, you met a quirky cast of characters—lovable, for sure, but desperate to *be* loved, with most of their challenges on full display, especially among the three main women: the needy heavyweight, Mary Kline; her only friend, the vulnerable Pearl Davis; and Elizabeth, the daughter these two misfits had no business raising.

As their story unfolds, reliable figures emerge. Johnson Kuhlman, obsessed with fabric and sewing, is desperate to show Mary that he loves her, and David, Elizabeth's husband, is remarkably patient. But the small town of Poulson has its villains, too. Chief among them is James Pullman, a pastor's son, whose penchant for forcing himself on young girls leaves a trail of pain and secrets that unravels in the worst way in the pages of the second book in this series.

So, welcome back to Paradise County, where people love, hate, and settle for indifference—all in the span of a typical, single day. Crimes are committed. Some go unpunished. Others are pounced on for swift justice. People think they understand your business because they know where you were born and most likely to whom. They know when you arrived and have your place in line saved for you.

In Poulson, some have everything going in their favor while others have nothing but the grimy shirts on their backs, and a special few know all too well how worn footpaths and battered heartstrings connect both of these worlds.

This is where Violet becomes blue.

Chapter One

Margaret Burns

If you are a stranger and you're lucky, this town will chew you up and spit you out. If you aren't lucky, you'll get stuck in its teeth or swallowed whole.

I'm qualified to make this observation because I am no stranger to Poulson. I'm a lifer. I've never left here, or Paradise County, for that matter, for more than a few days. I buy the same groceries from the same store on the same day of the week. I mark time with this town's weddings and wakes.

I've watched new folks come and go, like they do. They arrive hopeful that they will be embraced. They crave a warm welcome and are eager to join you for coffee and pass you the sugar. They volunteer at school and church, bringing fresh new energy, but they don't quite understand that no amount of effort will change a fundamental fact.

They don't belong.

After a few years of smiling so hard it hurts, trying to convince themselves they actually like it here, that they blend right in, these poor fools get bitten. Something happens just distressing enough that they must leave. Bags are packed and they don't bother with farewells. They simply disappear.

These strangers know that the energy they spent had minimal value. They're better off licking their wounds and picking their homes more wisely next time. They should probably keep their eyes peeled for more welcoming towns that don't hold a grudge. They are lucky they have escaped, and they know it.

But others get stuck. They stay just long enough to marry and have children with a lifer. Eventually, they get tangled up in a mortgage or job they think they can't leave. I've seen plenty of these unlucky ones, and the longer they stay where they don't belong, the more damaged they become.

I've liked some of these people enough to take them aside and offer friendly advice. I could've slipped them a note on a napkin, saying, "Trust me. This won't work for you," but these folks won't hear it. They're too charmed by our white picket fences, porch lights and front doors we leave unlocked.

The sweet parts of any small town can only be found in the gooey center, not on the dusty outskirts or ashen underbellies. These strangers look at me and all they see is a lonely old woman with no kin and no pets—someone best ignored.

I just shrug and wait for the truth of this place to show itself. When it does, these strangers will cross paths with me. It's inevitable in a small town. Our gazes will meet, and their eyes will tell me something I already know.

Chapter Two

Violet Sellers

My name is just one letter short of violent. Somewhere between the 'e' and 't' is a silent, invisible 'n,' a tiny letter that makes me do things nice girls shouldn't do. I could become a shrinking Violet, my dark thoughts enjoyed in solitude, but that's just not me.

My descent into the life of an angry court jester began one rainy afternoon when I was thirteen. It would take a while for the truth of that day to come up for air. For a long time, all the ugly bits could do was sputter up smoke signals begging for attention.

Then my parents saw it—a skull and cross bones tattooed right above my bikini line.

"Gloria!"

My father, Skip, started screaming, white with fury.

"It's a goddamned tattoo! It's practically on her privates, Gloria! A skull's head. Have you seen this damned thing?"

My mother had seen it and didn't know what to say.

My parents didn't know what to do as they stared at Mr. Bones, poking out of my panty line, leering with a sinister gaze, taunting them with a mocking grin across his skeletal head. Mr. Bones was my loyal guardian, protecting me, at least in my mind, from invasion. Placing him on the flattest part of my pubescent underbelly meant his twisted face would discourage unwelcome advances.

As we all stared at the hack job graffiti I'd had burned into my own flesh, Mr. Bones looked especially menacing. He was puffy, oozing and red, infected, for sure, and hot to the touch.

Gloria touched him anyway. I flinched and whimpered as she tried to press her finger into my tender, puckered flesh.

"Mom! Stop! Don't touch it!"

"Baby, you've got the chills."

Her usually smooth forehead was furrowed.

I nodded. My wisecracks, the ones I'd taken to using more and more to fend off her mothering seemed out of reach. Skip shook his head and wheezed, not sure what to do. It had been a while since he'd seen me in my underpants, and he was uncomfortable. His neck flushed pink, probably triggered by the sight of my undies, but as he stared at Mr. Bones and the reality of the tattoo sunk in, his face went from screwed up to berserk, bursting into a red-hot rage that made it difficult for my mother to stay focused on the problem at hand.

"Skip, you don't look so good."

My father did look unwell, like he might explode.

"Gloria, for God's sake, call the doctor! Get Todd Ladd on the line, for Christ's sake."

Yes. The doctor. Gloria shuffled off to get the phone, but I knew she would hesitate. What would Dr. Ladd think of the tattoo? What would he think of the *girl* who had the tattoo? What would the dear respectable doctor think of the *parents* of the girl who had this tattoo right next to her pubies? I had to give Todd Ladd credit. Whatever he might think, he'd keep it to himself. But my mother worried about his receptionist. That woman knew who was pregnant before anyone else, friends and family, for sure, and sometimes even the husband or soon-to-be startled boyfriend. She knew whose bones had been broken and how. She always knew how much weight we gained or lost, and which medications we were taking. She knew who had balances paid in full and who did not.

She'd have a wonderful time reading Dr. Ladd's notes about the hideous artwork I'd just had emblazoned forever on my delicate skin. There'd be no keeping that juicy piece of news to herself. That would require a strong and stable receptionist, and she was not the woman for the job. She could file, open mail, answer the phone, greet patients, and make appointments as efficiently as she made coffee, but discretion was not her strong suit.

Gloria and Skip weren't quite ready to reveal our festering problem. They knew that my new skeletal friend was blistering confirmation that their Violet had changed. They should have expected something like this. I'd left them clues that something was about to blow. They had their breadcrumbs.

In the months before Mr. Bones was born, I'd grown accustomed to a new sensation, one I'd never explored but enjoyed immensely. My parents were processing uncomfortable thoughts about their only girl. I had the power to annoy them. My newfound ability to confound them was difficult to leave in a box. I lifted its lid up again and again and again, often taking it for joy rides that left me breathless and scared but feeling satisfied and powerful.

Their resigned sighs and the way they hissed back and forth at each other after I'd lock them out of my room confirmed that I held in my hands a new set of moves that baffled them in ways they had never imagined. I smuggled this rude awakening right into the privacy of my room with its pink walls so I could hatch a plan to make them perk up and take notice.

They would need an engraved invitation to rise from their assigned seats in front of the television and sniff out the source of a deep stink that festered somewhere in the shadows of our house. This new state of affairs would require a level of curiosity they'd never exercised. My folks' collective ability to look both ways before they crossed the street and keep the valuables hidden had gotten flabby, thick in the middle.

The flawless record I held for practicing the piano without a nudge took a considerable hit. While still adjusting to the boundaries I had drawn between us like fingernails on a chalkboard, my mother would gingerly bring it up.

"I really miss hearing you play, Vi."

She would glance my way, hoping I'd catch on to her hint and start practicing my scales. The sheet music from the complex piece I was to perform at the spring recital sat still and crisp on the piano, waiting to be marked up with my pencil and peered at over and over as I tried to conquer the challenge before me. *Chopin's Fourth Ballade* could wait, and so could my hopeful mother.

Gloria longed to wake up one morning and find me and Skip teasing each other at the breakfast nook like we used to. Skip. She hated the fact that I'd started referring to my father by his first name.

"It's disrespectful, Violet."

After thinking it all over, I decided Gloria was right. I'd call him Skipper instead. Gloria loved that as much as she loved the wet towels and ripped jeans I left under my bed, along with my dark eyeliner and my silence, which I could bring anywhere with me and also break out whenever I wanted.

Gloria loved the way I pouted with my arms folded as we sat in our church pew together on Sunday mornings. She and Skipper almost pooped themselves when they discovered that I preferred to sit several rows behind them, snapping and popping my gum loud enough to elicit whispers and stares from the wrinkled old ladies who once admired me from afar. They gathered in the same pew for years to hear over and over how fabulous God was and what a swell time they were going to have once they finally stopped breathing.

I could hear my parents discussing strategy. They whispered to one another just how they were going to collectively respond to the sulking and impossible girl I'd become.

"Just ignore it, Skip. This is normal. Completely normal. It's her hormones. She'll outgrow this. Violet is just testing us. Don't respond. If we do, she wins."

"Don't respond?"

Skip's patience had run dry. He'd had enough of me. This nonsense needed to be nipped in the bud.

"Nip it. Nip it in the bud. Now. I mean, Gloria, do you hear what you are saying? Just how do we 'not respond' to a report card that's all Cs? Our Violet? Cs are average, Gloria. Violet is not an average girl. She's *our* girl. We must respond. We *will* respond. Oh, we'll respond, all right. I'll tell you that much."

Skipper meant business. My abrupt severance of all ties with our grand piano irritated him and gave him a heat rash. But my slipping academic status hit him in tender spots he didn't realize he had. Grades, academic achievements, and accolades were a weakness for my father. He loved, loved, loved a good report card. He also adored trophies and ribbons and certificates of achievement. I'd never made a C in my life, or a B, for that matter, but the report card I'd just brought home had all average marks, and one token D.

I'd done poorly in P.E. because I refused to shower after class. Each day we didn't shower, ten points were deducted from our overall scores. We had gym class every day, so my debts mounted quickly.

I was always good at math. Relinquishing fifty points a week was no skin off my developing body. I wasn't about to strip down and shower in front of all the other budding girls or our fearless, curious, and husky physical education teacher when at that time, I hadn't even broken a sweat.

Just how sweaty did she think we could get by square dancing?

Miss Cornell asked me to sit out the rest of the square-dancing unit. The girls who obeyed and took showers couldn't concentrate with me cutting up like I did. Mastering those do-si-dos and promenades was serious business. The fancy footwork could be best executed with sober calculations, lest someone got hurt swinging their partner round and round in the wrong direction. A foot might get stepped on, or someone could bungle the next left allemande.

Less clever girls might need help to remember how to face their partners and count to four. If things got too rowdy, all the ruckus could cause the record player to skip, and we'd be forced to start all over again. That would never do, at least according to Miss Cornell, who took all of this quite seriously.

I can't blame our souring relationship all on square dancing. It was compromised long before we started preparing in earnest for the next barn dance. I found Miss Cornell's level of physical fitness amusing from the very first day of class. It was hard not to laugh watching my chubby gym teacher, the one charged with inspiring us to take care of our bodies, as she tried her darndest to encourage our appreciation for all things athletic. I could usually squelch a full-scale chuckle by biting my lip, but the afternoon she tried to demonstrate how we should go about a proper squat thrust, I lost it. I didn't say a word, but my laugh needed no translation. It was the first of many trips I made that year to the principal's office.

Mr. Skolnik was tired of me. Skipper and Gloria were tired of me, too. It was not possible for me to care less. Their exasperated responses fueled me. Patricia Cornell deducted points and sent me packing down the hall to the main office, where Mr. Skolnik waited for me in his wrinkled suit, arms crossed, ready to dole out the next penalty. He did so carefully. My father expected special treatment. Poor Skipper. While he bellowed, Gloria tried to whisper. They bickered in front of me, and behind closed doors, but they coped well enough until I upped the ante with my tattoo. Mr. Bones really stirred things up. The temperature shifted quickly from an exhausted, "this-is-just-a-phase" to an urgent, full-throttled alarm. I could hear them trying out new, worried words: *therapist*, *psychiatrist* and *unstable*.

"Is *this* normal, Gloria?"

Skipper was pacing as he huffed and puffed from one end of the living room to the other. Gloria worked hard to keep him calm.

"Honey, calm yourself!"

The desperate sound in her voice told me she was worried that he might have a heart attack, or worse, the neighbors would hear.

"Are you trying to tell me that this goddamned thing on her belly is normal, Gloria? It's just business as usual?"

This growling between them would usually spike before it quickly sputtered, at least until one of them got worked up again. From behind the locked door of my bedroom, I listened and waited, congratulating myself and Mr. Bones for the disruption we'd created together.

Once he healed, I grew fond of Mr. Bones. I imagined him jaunty and fun-loving as I stood with my head cocked to one side in front of the mirror while the two of us gazed at my naked self. From a distance, it looked like Mr. Bones had made himself comfortable on a tidy, soft nest. He rested there and watched the dramatics unfold as my parents' theatrics reached the next award-winning, feverish pitch.

Skipper wanted to know what kind of a person in what kind of a hideous establishment would take money from a child to burn such an awful image onto such a private place. He wanted names and details.

Where did I go? How did I get there? How did I pay for it?

He threw around talk of contacting police and lawyers and wringing necks with his own bare hands. He hounded me to provide him with the information he needed to exact a glorious revenge. One time, he even threatened to spank me, which was hilarious to think about, but it made Gloria nervous.

"Skip, stop. That's not going to help anything. That won't do."

"I don't know, Gloria, maybe that's the problem. If we'd given Vi a crack or two long ago, we wouldn't be dealing with this. Now, we're long overdue. We're letting the child in this house call the shots. She shouldn't be doing that. *I'm* the one calling the shots in this house."

My father would work himself up into another froth while my mother soothed him and confirmed that he *was* in charge.

"Of course, you are in charge, Skip. Nobody doubts that. We just need to be careful and keep this tattoo problem under wraps."

Skipper would huff and puff and finally agree that this mess needed to be managed in-house and with minimal drama.

"Spanking Violet isn't going to fix this, Skip."

As Gloria softly reassured Skipper, I knew I was safe for a while. She'd hand him his newspaper and a whiskey sour and urge him to find his chair and cool off a bit. He'd stomp into the living room, muttering about the benefits of corporal punishment.

"I'm not promising anything, Gloria. You hear that, Violet? You hear me? Gloria, you might come home one of these days and see that I've blistered someone's behind. And I can promise you, it will hurt her more than that tattoo ever did. And when I'm done, we'll have what we need. You can count on that."

Skipper would end his tirades by snapping the paper open with a crack meant to let us know he hadn't made up his mind just yet.

When Gloria wasn't distracted by the bluster and threats to beat me, she was thinking of my wedding night.

"Violet, darling, what were you thinking? It won't come off, you know. You know that; don't you? Vi, can you hear me? I'm telling you,

Honey, that awful thing is there for the rest of your life. What will your husband say, Violet? What will he say?"

My husband, the poor man, would be startled, I was sure, but he'd receive the message loud and clear. He would never be allowed past my iron gates and Mr. Bones. My hysterical mother, infuriated father and would-be husband might finally understand that Mr. Bones was no whim or act of rebellion. He was my protector, and he looked ferocious by design.

Chapter Three

Gloria Sellers

I reminded Skip that Violet's tattoo wasn't my fault. He agreed in theory but couldn't help pointing out that she got it on my watch.

"Honey, when I'm at the office all day, and even late in the evening, Violet's whereabouts are *your* responsibility, not mine. I simply can't keep winning bread for this family *and* taking care of things at home. That's *your* job, Gloria."

We'd been over this umpteen times. I did a good job with Violet, a really good job. Things had been perfect for a long time. I hadn't missed a beat with our child. Immunizations and dental appointments, permission slips, class parties, manners, piano lessons, clean fingernails, regular bang trims, goodnight stories and kisses, homework and thank-you notes were all under my careful management and I took the role as seriously as my husband took his job doling out debt at the bank. And I liked to point out that I did it without an assistant taking memos, making appointments and bringing me cups of lukewarm coffee with two packets of sugar.

"That's not fair, Skip, and you know it. I've told you that I don't know where Violet got the tattoo, or when. After school she walks home, and I can't follow her everywhere. You've said so yourself. She's a teenager now. Isn't that what you've been saying to me?"

Skip could see that he was hurting my feelings. A shift in his tone would be necessary to keep the peace, which is exactly what was needed if he wanted to come home to the dinners he liked so much and to slip into clean sheets each night next to my warm, soft body. If my husband wanted to find me receptive to his frequent advances, a change in tactics would be required.

When he remembers this, his brown eyes soften and his face relaxes as he remembers that he is my friend, and I am his. He takes off his gloves and approaches me, defeated.

"Aw, Honey. I'm sorry. Really, I'm sorry. You *are* good with Vi. Very good. I'm just so angry about that damned tattoo. It's going to kill me if we don't get to the bottom of it."

In that moment, my man let me soothe him. We locked eyes in a way that confirmed our shared understanding. This new problem would be ours alone to master. We could do this if we stuck together.

These truces of ours were sweet, but short-lived. We stewed and fumed about that tattoo more than we kissed and made up. An irritable silence wedged itself between us. My husband's good nature went missing in action. Fun-loving Skip had been replaced by a man no longer sure of himself and easily offended. He was less interested or able to rise to the erotic occasion with his usual skill and determination. When we did try to dance under the covers, it felt mechanical, an act stripped to its rudimentary essentials.

This version of my husband showed no interest in planting any soft kisses along the curves of my shoulders or merging our mouths, hoping to kindle the fires below. The unsatisfying situation took us by surprise. It was such a stark departure from our norm and from the romantic weekend away we'd just taken before Violet started acting up.

Those days alone without our daughter had a premarital sweetness and intensity that we welcomed like a long-lost friend. I'd been worried about leaving Vi and sheepishly realized how silly I'd been to put this adventure off for so long. Skip teased me about it as he ran his hands across my backside, inviting me back into the unmade bed in our hotel room. We were dressed and ready to have lunch in a fancy restaurant, but my randy man surely had other ideas. Cloth napkins and wine were no match for what my husband had in mind as he placed the "Do Not Disturb" sign on the door.

"Don't you think, Mrs. Sellers, that you were a foolish girl, making me wait so long to have you to myself like this?"

I tried to laugh him off, but he wasn't having it.

"Mrs. Sellers. I need an answer straightaway."

I nodded and planted a kiss on his nose to buy time.

"Oh, so you're not sure? I guess, we'll need to remind you how this whole thing got started."

We spent the rest of the afternoon not giving Violet a single thought. She was fine where she was, staying with Reverend Pullman and my sister and their son, probably not even thinking about us at all.

By the time we were obsessing over Violet's tattoo, those sweet moments seemed far, far away. My husband was just a banker again, and I was his worried, careful wife. Our only child took her rightful place at center stage, but now the show was anything but boring. We sat up straight in our reserved seats. Riveted by her performance, we worried and waited for the phone to ring, or for someone to pull one of us aside to tell us they also noticed changes.

Is everything all right at home? What's gotten into Violet? She was always such a sweet girl, but now, with her folded arms, sullen face, and heavy eye makeup, she's almost unrecognizable. Where has the piano-playing, straight-A student with impeccable posture and clean fingernails gone? The good folks wondering such things didn't know about what troubled us most.

That tattoo tilted our world off its axis and robbed us of the strong equilibrium we'd enjoyed for so long. We'd been poor stewards of our good fortune, and our problem would need to be managed in the dark, with the porch light off to turn away nosy neighbors.

Violet's tattoo had the potential to clear our social calendar and ruin our standing in town. Our heads were best kept down. Nothing to see here, folks.

Skip put his energy into sleuthing and seething. His fantasies shifted abruptly from the magic we could make between our sheets to the pound of flesh he was going to extract from that poor son of a bitch who put that vile tattoo just north of our daughter's crotch.

I knew I would not get my charming, lusty banker man back until he made the culprit sorry he'd ever laid eyes on Violet Sellers. It scared me to think about what he would do if given the chance to cut loose with his red-hot rage. He got so worked up I thought I might become the wife of a murderer. Skip would be behind bars, and I'd be left at home with our surly Violet forever. No man would ever want a girl who had damaged herself like she had.

Maybe it was better if we never knew who marked her up. The whole town could know our mess, and I already hated them for it.

Parts of me had to admire my husband for the depths of his rage. It signified a protectiveness that most women want in a mate. Still, we needed him to drop his mission before things unraveled too quickly.

Skip didn't know this town like I did. He didn't know Poulson had its own set of quiet rules that hummed beneath its streets and bled into the soil, trickling into the water we used to quench our thirst and wash our filth down the drain. The "Poulson Rules" had unspoken caveats that could make people one day and break them the next.

While I watched for what my husband would never see, I prayed that Violet would settle herself down. Meanwhile, I tried to show her quietly that I loved her. I kept calm on the surface, but underneath, my heart churned and burned as hot as my husband's.

What had happened to our girl?

Chapter Four

Ruth Pullman

It was high time we had Violet for a stay. I'd offered before, plenty of times, but had always been rebuffed by my older sister. She was a careful one, that Gloria. Prickly. We'd never been allowed to even watch our niece for an afternoon. Not once. It was hardly a high-stakes gamble. I was a seasoned mother myself, and even though I was the little sister, I had more experience. Our Jamie was three years old by the time Gloria and Skip announced they were expecting.

I was not as outwardly attractive or outgoing as Gloria. Still, I was the first to marry and have a child, which took our parents by surprise, especially Pop. He was fond of me, his "Red," and never could resist ruffling my head of unruly curls. I think Pop and Mother understood early on that I would be theirs alone to love from the minute I was born. My hair was shocking, and the freckles took some getting used to.

Despite my appearance, they loved me, or felt sorry enough that they cast a lavish, coddling net over me, which they figured my blue-eyed, blonde sister would never need.

Some babies are just ugly, and their parents know it. Others need the news broken to them. After years as a pastor's wife, and being homely myself, I'd become well versed in such diplomacy. As a child, I heard whispers among the grownups, but even though my little ears could hear the words, the insults never quite landed. Those adults knew just how to deliver their cruelty without anyone noticing.

In contrast, people like my sister, who were authentically attractive, heard no whispering other than from those who were jealous. For lucky cherubs like Gloria, the appropriate truths came forth naturally, but for us ugly ones, people had to scramble to come up with something kind to say.

I'd caught enough of those careful comments whistling in the wind above my little red head that I was ready for anything when I became a pastor's wife, which meant I knew that I was expected to respond to every little baby that came into our church.

"What a clever-looking baby! I wonder what he's thinking about!"

"Well, feel that grip, will you? What a strong one!"

"Will you look at those eyes? I've never seen any so bright!"

"What an alert little thing! My goodness, you are blessed!"

These compliment imposters rolled off my tongue with almost no effort. Keen parents receiving such comments about their progeny will eagerly lap them up but go home and gaze a little more deeply into their babies' homely faces. And then, these mothers and fathers will take the only option they have. They claim it.

"We have an ugly child, and there's nothing we can do about it but pull our child closer to us and negotiate with God."

These poor parents look hard for traits they can focus on instead of their child's mere visual appeal. They squint their eyes, tilt their heads and settle on something, anything, that makes their baby special.

For Pop, my red unruly tresses and freckles sealed the deal. He didn't love me more than Gloria; he was just making up for all the prettiness that the good Lord forgot to pack in my bag before sending me down to him and Mother. Our parents compensated aplenty, leaving my sister jealous and mean for the longest time.

Even as grownups, Gloria eyed me warily, like I was the one who'd relentlessly pinched and poked. It was as if she were ashamed of all her past mean-spirited treatment when we were growing up, but she just couldn't bring herself to officially make amends.

I had let that go and just prayed that my big sister would want to connect with me one day. When Gloria's call came, asking if Vi could stay with us for a few days, I was so excited I ran to tell Richard as soon as I hung up the phone. He was busy with the next week's sermon, but he looked up and smiled.

"Well, isn't that wonderful, Ruthie? It's about time. You'll have a girl in the house, won't you? What a treat, Sweetheart."

I was already thinking about putting pink sheets and pillowcases on the bed in the guest room and imagined Vi sitting right between me and Jamie in church.

Richard could read my thoughts.

"Oh, Mrs. Pullman, I can see by the look on your face that you're already cooking up something special, aren't you?"

I was. Another girl in the house would be a lovely change of pace at the parsonage. I'd make a few special treats for our niece's visit; maybe meringues or finger sandwiches we could have with lemonade on the front porch.

Richard called after me as I went into the kitchen to hunt down some recipes.

"Hey, Ruthie? Violet's visit will be good for Jamie, too, don't you think? Right?"

I nodded. It *would* be good for our son, James. He could practice his good manners and show his little girl cousin a good time. Neither of them had a sibling so they needed to make the most of being cousins who lived in the same town. One day, Gloria would be gone, and so would I. These two might just need each other.

Chapter Five

Skip Sellers

I never did like that kid, James Pullman. His glossy, blond hair and blue eyes did nothing for me. Not a thing. The deep dimple on his right cheek was nothing but a trap in my book. It would be a few years before his pink gums shed that first set of perfect white baby teeth to make room for the jagged, adolescent choppers that would erupt and fight for space. That phase would diminish his cuteness, and when it did, my red-headed sister-in-law and that pompous husband of hers would scrape up enough from the collection plate to pay for a mouth full of metal to put things right.

He was just a tyke when I first laid eyes on him. He didn't need my adoration. He soaked in enough of that from his parents, grandparents and even Gloria.

She was just my girlfriend back then. She had brought me home to meet her folks that first time. I had met my fair share of mothers and fathers, so I wasn't all that nervous.

Before we went inside, I pulled my blue-eyed blonde honey to me. My backside was warm, pressing against the heat of the car, but it was cool by comparison. The source of heat that I tugged toward me pulsed with promise.

This one was special.

It was hard for me to fathom that she'd not been snatched up, as pretty and sweet-smelling as she was. The way her lips fit mine made me want this to be my last family meet-and-greet. I needed to get this one right. I'd need to relocate, but that was something I was willing to do for Gloria.

If we stayed by the car much longer, pressing up against each other, we'd have to cancel dinner. My guts growled. I gave Gloria a peck on her cheek and worked to get my shirt tucked back in my pants. It was showtime. I had some impressing to do.

Her folks were just fine. Her father was on the grumpy side, though, which I expected. The old man was doing the best he could. It was clear that he just wanted to be parked in his chair with his favorite newspaper. Gloria's mother was fussing to get food on the table, followed around by her little sister, Ruthie. She was no looker, not like my Gloria. It was hard to believe the two were even related. I was getting the tastier treat, no doubt about that. We shook hands, all of us, making nice, like *nice* folks do.

Red Ruthie's husband, Richard, put his hand out to grab mine. He had a smile on his face, and strong arms. Good grip. The charisma was evident. I could smell it like it was aftershave slapped on his face. But I wasn't convinced it ran deep. Pastor Man was aloof. He could take me or leave me. I could see that. No worries. The feeling was mutual. I'm sure he'd caught wind that I was a good Catholic boy. The wicked Protestant standing in front of me had thoughts about that. I could tell. I made the sign of the cross with extra relish after he led the prayer, and we dove into the spread Gloria's mother had prepared.

The meal went well enough. I knew I'd be eating at that table again with those people, even the smug bastard married to Gloria's sister. I left the house knowing I'd be back. I also knew I'd never warm up to Richard or his little boy. Jamie. The kid was a brat, through and through. It wasn't until after the wedding, long after the rice was thrown and our brand-new kitchen towels started looking worn, that I divulged to Gloria how I really felt. She was disappointed.

"Skip, what do you mean, you don't like Richard? What's not to like? He's a pastor, Honey. One of the good guys. Could you try harder? For me?"

I nodded, but I didn't mean it. She pressed.

"And how can you not be just smitten with Jamie? That adorable little boy is just a lump of sugar. What's the matter with you?"

What was the matter with me? I couldn't answer that.

From a distance, Jamie looked like a harmless little boy, but when I moved in close enough for that little shit's eyes to meet mine, I could see that he was a surefire pain in the ass. He was a sneaky, shifty little son of a gun.

I seemed to be the only one in the family who had his number. The kid seemed to know, too, that we'd never be buddies. He'd have no doting uncle in me. Nope. That just wasn't going to happen.

I tolerated the brat through holiday dinners and birthday parties, and more times than I liked when Gloria kept him for an afternoon or an overnight while Pastor Man and the red head went out of town.

I just never warmed up to that little prick or his father. They had the rest of the world fooled somehow, but not me.

Chapter Six

Gloria

I remember every moment of the day our Violet was born. She was two weeks behind schedule, and as the weather grew chilly and crisp, leaving frosty designs etched on the windows, my bare feet needed wool socks to warm me up from our icy hardwood floors.

Skip brought them to me, along with a mug full of warm cocoa. We both hoped its sweet, hot goodness would beckon the babe inside me to venture out to meet us. Wasn't this baby curious enough to know the benevolent source of warmth it was feeling?

"What else can I bring you, Your Majesty?"

Skip was such a tease.

I laughed. He had been waiting on me hand and foot every evening, but I had one final request that Sunday afternoon.

"Could you slip my socks on for me?"

My large, round midsection made it impossible to reach my feet.

Skip laughed and came to my rescue. We watched the fire snap, hoping that this would be the day. We were ready. That morning, I'd checked my suitcase one more time. A brand-new pink nightgown, robe and slippers from my sister Ruthie were tucked inside, along with everything else I'd been advised to bring to the hospital. The suitcase was right by the front door, waiting for Skip to toss her in the backseat for our last ride as a married couple with no responsibilities. The return trip would be different once we became parents.

As the fire fizzled, night set in, and we grew sleepy. I heaved my bulky body up the stairs, stopping on the landing to catch my breath.

The skin across my gut was tight as a drum. There was no elbow room left for our babe. Skip helped me into bed and tucked me in.

"Good night, Little Mama."

Skip's breathing kept time with the alarm clock on his nightstand. Well before it was set to go off, our baby-to-be announced its presence with a warm gush beneath me. We fumbled and hustled out of bed, grabbed some clothes and then Skip tucked me into the front seat of the car with a blanket wrapped around me. I shivered in the dark while the car warmed up and Skip scraped frost off the windows. When he finally slid inside behind the steering wheel, he brought a rush of cold air with him, but he was smiling.

"Well, Little Mama, I think this is it. I bet before the sun rises, we'll have ourselves a boy or a girl, won't we?"

I hoped things went that quickly. I turned on the radio and found my favorite station. Perry Como and the Fontane Sisters crooned, "It's Beginning to Look a Lot Like Christmas," even though we were two weeks short of Thanksgiving. Back then, decking the halls prematurely just wasn't done.

Skip laughed and talked back to Perry.

"No sir, Mr. Como. I think you're a little early. It doesn't look like Christmas here. Not yet. We've got a turkey to tend to, and a baby on the way!"

The nurse at the desk helped us sign in and motioned for Skip to stay put. Husbands were not invited into delivery rooms in those days. He kissed me on the cheek and winked.

Now, the heavy lifting was up to me and the stern-looking nurse confirmed that as she guided me down the hall.

Skip looked as happy as could be.

"I'll be right here, Honey!"

That lucky man missed out on the harsh reality that took place right behind the curtain. There were indignities to bear—pushing, grunting, breathing through searing pain, screaming, cursing and more pushing until the final release.

A mewling baby was pulled from me. A girl!

I took one look at her pink face and tiny hands before the efficient nurse whisked her off. The doctor, kind old Dr. Fisk, worked with steady hands to sew me back up carefully. He'd delivered me, and my little sister, Ruthie, too.

"Didn't I just help that red-headed sister of yours a few years ago with her baby? A little boy, if I remember correctly."

I nodded. He looked at me and smiled.

"Congratulations, young lady. You'll never forget this day, will you, now?"

Dr. Fisk was right about that. Every sight, sound, smell, and word that was spoken on the day Violet arrived made a home inside my heart. I leaned into the sweet sequence to help me fall asleep on hard nights and let it anchor me each time we celebrated her birthday.

Violet was cause for celebration.

I baked homemade cakes, anything our girl might dream up. Clown cakes, angel food, and chocolate. Violet's favorite was baked when she was just six. A doll cake. It was something special. The doll stood at the center, with a frosted layer cake as her delicious pink skirt. Vi squealed and happily posed as Skip took a photo of the milestone. Her toothless gap made her birthday smile seem big and beautiful, confident that all the birthdays to come would usher in another dose of annual goodness: cake, balloons, candles begging to be blown out, singing, presents, and friends excited to share her latest soiree.

Chapter Seven

Violet

My mother always said I was a sweetheart. Most who observed me from afar and close up had to agree. I hugged and kissed my parents. I obeyed them.

The good Violet asked permission and waited patiently for it to be granted. She wanted approval. She ate her vegetables before they got cold on the plate. She said *please* and *thank you* and *you're welcome*. She washed her hands after going to the bathroom and turned off the lights when she left the room. Her good posture was consistent and hard to ignore. She pleased others and took pleasure in doing so. There was no sass and no choppy waters. Sailing through life was so smooth the guards could be sent home for the night.

At first, my complacent parents were plenty conscientious. I never had a babysitter, not even on New Year's Eve or for the occasional weekend movie or date night. I accompanied Gloria and Skip wherever they went, much to the chagrin of other adults who were looser and freer with their own children. I sat politely in living rooms with a book or paper dolls as my parents shared cocktails in the homes of their childless friends, and more than once, I snuggled under a blanket on a sofa while they played cards and cackled through the night with couples who'd been wise enough to leave their children at home.

I was no trouble at all.

It wasn't until I turned thirteen that my father convinced my mother it was high time they took a proper getaway, without me. They hadn't been alone since their honeymoon, and it was perfectly reasonable to ask my Aunt Ruthie and Uncle Richard to let me stay a long weekend. My father was adamant about getting away "with his bride."

"Gloria, we've watched that brat of theirs plenty of times," Skip said. "And yes, I said *brat*. I still can't believe a pastor's kid could be such a *spoiled* brat. I think Reverend Pullman must have been nodding off during the 'spare the rod' lesson in seminary. Holy shit, that kid of theirs needs a crack and I'd be first in line to dole it out. First in line, Gloria. Vi will be a walk in the park for your sister. Trust me. A walk in the park."

My mother wasn't crazy about letting me stay with Aunt Ruthie, but I really wanted to, and my father wasn't taking no for an answer. It was time for me to spread my wings a little bit. I'd never gone to sleep away camp or for an overnight with friends. Surely I could survive a weekend across town with relatives.

Skip was convinced as he put my suitcase in the station wagon.

"Violet's not a little girl anymore. She's a teenager, Gloria. It's high time we did this. This will be good for all of us."

My father smacked my mother's behind and gave her a wink.

As my mother kissed me goodbye in Aunt Ruth's living room, I could tell she was trying to swallow a lump in her throat. I'd seen it before, once on my first day of school and whenever the nurse in Dr. Ladd's office rolled up my sleeve to give me a shot in the arm.

My mother was smart. She knew she was kissing the old Violet goodbye. She was right. The girl she picked up two days later wouldn't look her in the eye as she slumped into the back seat of the car. She mumbled and stared at her shoes.

"Violet, Honey, did you thank Aunt Ruth and Uncle Richard?"

Chiding didn't suit my mother, not back then. She fumbled to find the right tone. The poor woman wasn't accustomed to pulling out a reproach. It simply wasn't in her repertoire. The old Violet would never have needed it. But the diminished version of Vi was not serving up any sweetness. I was sullen and aloof, forcing my mother to press me further, hopeful and desperate for her sweet girl to resurface, especially in front of Aunt Ruthie.

"What about Jamie, Violet? Did you thank your cousin? He's shown you such a good time, I'm sure."

My cousin was nowhere in sight. He was still upstairs, dreaming up nasty maneuvers, or maybe he was wide awake and hungry, waiting for us to pull away so he could avoid my gaze and the obligatory thank you hug we'd be forced to share after all his gracious hosting.

"Gloria, it's okay, really," said Aunt Ruth. "She's just embarrassed. This is an awkward time for girls. Don't you remember?"

My aunt walked to the car and leaned into the window with her clean, freckled arms to whisper conspiratorial and feminine sentiments to me.

"Honey, it's all right. Jamie doesn't know a thing, and neither does Uncle Richard. This is our little secret. Just us girls, right? You're growing up, that's all."

She smiled and patted my arm. She smelled like soap.

Aunt Ruth thought I'd started my period. I did not bother to tell her that I'd been menstruating for several months by then. I was no rookie. My mother knew this, too, but nodded as if that explained my atypical surly mood. Surely that was it.

"Are you sure we have everything, Vi? You checked the bathroom for your toothbrush?"

I nodded and closed my eyes. My mother sighed as she slid into the front seat of the car, and we pulled out of the parsonage driveway to head back home.

I had everything—my extra shoes, swimsuit, church clothes, even my damned toothbrush. But I did leave someone behind that day—a girl named Violet. That girl didn't make it out of the parsonage in one piece. She was shattered into fragments.

For weeks, I sat gingerly. Going to the bathroom took my breath away. The August air, thick and sticky, was too hot for long pants, but I wore them anyway to keep the dark, purplish bruises on my inner thighs covered until they faded to mottled light blue, then yellow, then a faint mark, the color of nothing.

By Halloween, the girl I left on the other side of town was too old for silly costumes and no longer frightened by ghouls or vampires, or leering clowns marching in front of the house, ready to barter a good clean joke for one of Gloria's famous popcorn balls. I watched from the living room window, peering into the spooky night, knowing that real monsters existed, and they had tricks, not treats.

Chapter Eight

James Pullman

I didn't start off so smoothly. By the time I worked Pearl Davis over like I did and paid the steep, lifelong price I deserved, I'd come a long way. You don't get good at anything unless you're willing to keep at it. I was committed to refining my nasty craft.

Everybody has to start somewhere. A baby must crawl before he walks and walk before he runs. There will be stumbles and tumbles, but that's how progress is made.

Looking back at the first time I forced myself on a girl, I'm almost ashamed of how amateur my moves were. I left marks all over her and got some myself during the struggle. I hadn't been selective about my target. Pouncing on my own cousin wasn't a brilliant move.

The truth is, I didn't give it much thought. The brutality I unleashed on Violet that first afternoon was not premeditated. My first foray into violence took me by surprise and swept me away. I loved the imbalance of power, how my muscles had an advantage over hers and the way her mouth squirmed with hot, frantic breath under my sweaty hand that covered it.

Reformed as I am after all these years, I must admit that I let myself surrender to my urges on that rainy afternoon when my mother left me in charge of entertaining my younger cousin.

I knew there would be some kind of physical contact. I anticipated nothing different from the usual frustrated encounters I'd enjoyed so thoroughly. Friction with no possibility of release forced me to push past niceties that were getting me nowhere. My body didn't know it yet, but brute force would take me to the next, more satisfying level.

And once I got a taste of that, sugar and spice would no longer suffice. My prey was a better prize if caught off guard and terrified.

That afternoon provided time and space and ideal conditions. My parents, the pastor and his wife, were at the church. Dad was officiating another summer wedding with a reception to follow. Mother scuttled about the fellowship hall, filling the punch bowl, and making sure the fancy dishes with pastel mints and mixed nuts were replenished.

Time was on my side.

I'd need about an hour to make my young cousin comfortable. Piece of wedding cake. We could start with ping-pong, an old movie on the television, even darts or Chinese Checkers. I wasn't sure this girl was sharp enough for chess.

The basement at the parsonage was much bigger than the backseats of cars I'd grown accustomed to. I'd need to get her underdeveloped body in close proximity to my own. A board game would do the trick. Chinese Checkers for the win.

I'd entered the world four years earlier than Vi. Signs of my ascent into manhood were well-established. There was hair down there and on my arms, but not my chest just yet. I smelled like a man, and she smelled like baby powder. Her little lollipop lips and tongue were no match for my practiced smackers. I'd need to show her the ropes.

The bride and groom were cutting the cake right about the time I maneuvered my tiny cousin's sweet frame under me.

"You're telling me you've never kissed anyone yet?"

She giggled at my teasing. It came with friendly tickles at her neck and skinny ribs. She shook her head.

"Vi, how are you supposed to be ready for that first kiss without some practice?"

As I posed this question and moved my face closer to hers, so I was within striking distance of my target, her smile went slack, and her eyes widened. Our mothers are sisters. I should have pulled away, retreated to tickling and giggling, but I did not.

I forged ahead. It took me less than a minute to lift up her dress and rip off her underpants. They had pink flowers all over them. She hadn't graduated to women's undergarments like the older girls wore. The stark difference didn't make me hesitate. It might have even made me go quicker.

There was no sense going for Violet's chest. Nothing there to see. Another minute was needed to get my own eager lower half exposed. I did this with one hand, letting the full weight of my body crush hers as I kept the other firmly plastered to her mouth.

"There we go, cousin. Now, let me help you get ahead of the game. I'll do you a favor. You'll thank me later. You will."

She bucked against me. Her struggle was real. It fueled me and lit my fire. I didn't wait for her muscles or bones to retreat. I dove right in to kiss her hard, but she resisted by clenching her lips tightly. Something about that small revolt enraged me and made me ravenous. I took a bite at her upper lip. I could feel one of my fangs sink into skin. The blood tasted good, and the shock of the bite beckoned a scream from her, which meant an open mouth.

Entry was possible. This was no first kiss. She hadn't settled down enough to let that happen. Not at all. Our mouths mashed and battled. Hers retreated and mine forged ahead with sloppy, determined force until she bit my tongue hard.

I'd not bitten my tongue since I was a child. I remembered doing so falling off my bike. The injury that sent me blubbering to my mother had a different effect on the manchild I'd become. This time, the pain was still there, but I liked the struggle. I had to work harder for this, and the challenge, the rage that it welcomed, was bitter but full-bodied.

The rest of our encounter was less gentle. I lost track of minutes slipping by. It was time enough to terrify the girl beneath me. As I tore into that little wisp of a thing, my plunges weren't loving. Her tears and muffled cries did not move me.

The rain was still coming down, punctuated by thunder and a crack of lightning that was no match for the storm Violet was weathering on the basement floor. I was a savage, with no thought for the days and nights that would follow. My mind was not capable of processing the consequences. Thanksgiving and other family gatherings were not on my radar. I hadn't even considered the next morning at the breakfast table, where my parents would politely ask my battered cousin and I what we did while they were gone.

Violet wept and sniffled as she pulled down her dress. She was surely battered as she crept up the stairs, her hair a matted mess.

"Hey, Vi?"

My cousin turned toward me.

"You forgot these."

I tossed her little girl underwear to her, and she caught it.

"Good catch."

I smiled.

She ran up the rest of the basement stairs and went into the guest bedroom, where a day earlier my mother had put clean, pink sheets on the bed. I collected myself and walked softly to my own bedroom. I stopped briefly to listen for sniffles or muffled crying behind the closed door. Nothing but stillness. Violet must have fallen asleep.

As I closed the door to my room, I congratulated myself on a stellar execution and the discovery I'd just made. This power I had was new. I liked it and knew I would need more. When I looked in the mirror, the master staring back at me understood what had just taken place and smiled anyway. His lip was bleeding. A deep scratch that scored his cheek would need time to heal.

I traced the jagged edge of this souvenir from a brief, but eventful tryst with a reluctant companion who had her own fresh wounds. I smirked back at the devil in the mirror, who gave me an approving nod to remind me we were one and the same. We shared a heart that was still pounding and lungs that were still recovering from our exertion. We shared other body parts that were still in shock that such pleasure could come with brute force.

The wedding was over. I heard my father's footsteps at the front door. My mother was behind him, shaking off the rain from her coat.

"Well, wasn't that lovely, Richard? Just lovely?"

He grumbled but agreed.

"Yes, Ruthie. Yes, it was. How did I do?"

"It was perfect. I think that might have been your best one. I think it just might have been, Reverend Pullman. You have refined your craft. I wouldn't change a thing."

"Well, thank you, Dear. Every time I help someone tie the knot I learn something new. I guess if I could change anything about this one, I might have prayed ahead of time for better weather."

"Oh, Richard, no. Don't you know that rain on a wedding day is good luck?"

I smiled, thinking nothing had changed.

Chapter Nine

Gloria

When Vi turned fourteen, I pretended that a showstopper cake and party would tease out the old girl we missed so much. Whatever had gotten into her, I hoped a good old birthday celebration would chase it back into the dark.

"Vi, Honey, what kind of cake should I make for your birthday this year? Huh? Let's do something extra special, since you're in high school. How about a Black Forest cake? With cherries? Or maybe Baked Alaska?"

She shrugged.

Skip didn't like that.

"Young lady, your mother is talking to you. She's asking you about what she can bake to celebrate your birthday, for Christ's sake. You're being rude."

"Honey, what sounds good to you?"

I pressed. This was supposed to be a fun conversation, which we hadn't had for so long.

Violet stared at me. Our girl was somewhere in there behind the scowl and her rolling eyes.

"I don't want cake this year."

"How about pie? Cheesecake? I haven't made a cheesecake in a long time, but I could sure look up the recipe. It's not every day your girl turns fourteen."

Another shrug from Violet, followed by an exasperated grumble from Skip.

"Hey, hey, I've got an idea," I said. "What about a sleepover, Vi? How about that? You've never done that. We could send Dad packing for a girls-only night. I bet we could fit ten sleeping bags on the living room floor."

Violet squinted at me and curled her lip.

I was grateful Skip missed it. He'd had enough of her sass.

"Let's see, Violet, you could ask Susan Wells, and what about the Jennings twins, April and Jeannie?"

I kept chattering as if my one and only daughter was responding with the enthusiasm I craved.

"And you should invite Mary Kline. Yes, let's invite Mary. That poor girl never gets included. It's just shameful. Louise tells me that Mary has a little friend who is new to town. I think her name might be Pearl. You really should invite those girls, Vi."

That got her attention.

"Davis," said Vi. "Her name is Pearl Davis. Pearl is not coming to my party. I barely know her, and there's something wrong with her. She's slow. That's the only reason she's friends with Mary. Pearl doesn't have a choice. I haven't spoken to Mary Kline since fourth grade. We aren't friends."

"Oh, Vi. How can you say that? Don't you remember all those times the Klines came over to play cards and the two of you were thick as thieves? Skip, you remember that, don't you?"

Violet was unmoved.

"I'm not inviting Mary Kline, or Susan or April or Jeannie. Nope. I'm not inviting anyone because I don't want a party. Do you hear me? I said I don't want a party. What I want for my birthday is for you to stop talking about this. I have one friend. His name is Jules Marks, and our family is too snotty to let him inside our house."

Skip shifted in his seat.

"Oh, Vi. That's not so, Honey. We're not snotty. No, we're not. You know exactly why Jules doesn't come inside. A boy like him wouldn't be comfortable at one of your parties, not the way we do them. He just wouldn't. And if we're doing a sleepover, he would not come anyway. Even inviting Jules to a daytime party would be cruel."

Vi was not convinced. Her tight jaw told me I needed to retreat. If she cocked off with one more ounce of backtalk, Skip was going to forget about his newspaper and come flying out of his chair.

"What about the families, Vi? Can we at least have the family party? Your grandparents will wonder what's wrong with us if they don't get an invite. And Uncle Richard, Aunt Ruthie, and Jamie? We always do a family party, Honey."

Skip piped up.

"Tell you what, ladies. I don't care about a friend party. I don't give a damn about that, but I'll tell you one thing. We're having a family party. We're having family here for cake and ice cream. And Vi, you'll need to shape up for that. Do you hear me? You'll shape right up."

Skip's deep voice had a power to it that was hard to ignore. He'd never raised a hand to Vi, but he'd threatened to give her a pop a time or two. The possibility of it hung heavy enough in the air that she kept her sass to herself as she watched her father stomp out of the room.

"Vi, Honey, what kind of cake would you like for the party? What sounds good to you? Lemon poppyseed? German chocolate? You name it, and I'll make it."

We finally agreed on Black Forest cake with vanilla ice cream. No balloons, no streamers, no friends, just the three of us and two sets of grandparents. Aunt Ruthie and Uncle Richard were welcome, but not Cousin Jamie.

This was awkward, but Vi wouldn't budge.

"No way."

"Now, Violet, how am I going to tell Aunt Ruth that Jamie's not welcome? Why would we not invite him to a family gathering?"

Vi shrugged. I'd have to navigate that one. Feelings would likely be hurt. Questions would be asked. Skip would be secretly pleased. He never enjoyed Richard's company and had never warmed up to our nephew like I'd hoped.

We ate cake with the grandparents, but it was a subdued affair; that's for sure.

Pop kept asking why my sister and her family weren't there. The birthday girl was polite enough, but distant, and asked to be excused after we'd eaten. I could hear my mother and Skip's mother whispering by the fireplace.

"What in the world has gotten into that girl?"

"I don't know, dear. I just don't know, but you're definitely right. She seems blue."

"What's that?" said Pops. "What's the matter with Violet?"

My mother responded louder than she should have to make sure the gist of the message reached my grandfather's compromised ears.

"She's blue, dear. We think our Violet is blue."

I was relieved to retrieve their coats so all four of them could head home before it got dark. I washed the dishes and let them dry on a towel next to the sink. We had plenty of cake left. I covered it and created space for it in the icebox.

I hadn't even tasted the cake yet. I sat at the kitchen table and licked the dark chocolate and cherry mix from the knife. I'd outdone myself.

This was a cake for refined palates. The sweetness was pleasant but it was not overpowering, like a gaudy buttercream confection that would satisfy a child. The dark red cherries had been soaked overnight in kirsch. The fresh whipped cream dissolved on the tongue, followed closely by chocolate shavings and a drunken cherry taste. The tang of the cherry is no match for the bite of bitter liqueur that lingers. You don't rinse Black Forest cake down with a glass of milk, either. Nope. You chase that kind of treat with hot dark coffee served discreetly by someone who hopes you will leave a generous tip.

Skip had gone to bed, and I was ready, too. I'd been waiting all day for things to quiet down so I could close my eyes and retreat to sweeter thoughts that no one could take from me, like that last night in front of the fire before Violet was born, when Skip handed me hot cocoa, Dr. Fisk's hand on my knee as I gave birth, and birthday cakes that met their mark.

The next afternoon, I watched Violet bring Jules a piece of that complex cake to eat on the front porch. Vi was wearing a coat and it looked like Jules could use a new one.

Violet served up the cake on a piece of our good china. This irked me. Did this boy know he was holding a plate I'd selected from the bridal registry at Kline's Department Store back when Skip and I were just a hopeful pair of new lovers?

Jules wolfed down the cake like teenage boys will do. Jules and Vi were not focused on the treat at all, though. They were huddled and swapping secrets like they'd been doing for months out there. This dirty boy could do something for our girl that we could not.

Jules was born just one day before Violet. Perhaps they'd made some kind of unofficial baby pact in the nursery when his mother, Lee, and I weren't looking.

I wondered what kind of birthday celebrations Jules had been given since Lee and I parted ways on that same porch. This kid would have definitely been satisfied with buttercream served on a paper napkin.

Thinking of it made me downright angry and filled me with shame for my superior thoughts and for getting involved with his mother in the first place.

What was I thinking when I essentially adopted her and took her under my wing?

Was it even possible that Lee considered her boy to be a cause for celebration? Was she capable of savoring a good thing?

Chapter Ten

Violet

Gloria was never fond of Jules. No way. This made him an ideal friend for me.

Jules wasn't a bad kid. Not really. But everyone knew that the Marks children were always, without fail, the first ones at school to be tapped out of class for head lice, year after itchy year.

Gloria said she started itching and scratching just thinking about it. Jules was the oldest of the clan, and sadly, the most aware of the shame and the creeping, crawling stigma that attaches itself to a family known primarily for the tiny bugs that keep landing and hatching eggs on their unlucky scalps.

After a head lice check, the entire Marks brood, all six of them, would wait in the office for their mother, Lee, to take them home for a couple days of nit-picking and scouring. Sometimes, she wouldn't show up fast enough to suit the principal, and the disgruntled school nurse would pile them up in her car and deposit them at the end of the dirt path that led to the patch of scrappy houses where they lived. The kids would come back to school with shaved heads, even the girls. It was hard not to stare.

I heard Gloria telling Skip during dinner once that Cookie Leeds, a PTA mother, dropped off a grocery bag filled with shampoo and soap on the doorstep of Jules' house. My mother had seemed to approve of the gesture.

"Soap and water are not that expensive, so there is no excuse for being filthy."

Skip grunted and raised his eyebrows over his glasses at my mother. He cleared his throat to make room for a comment to squeak by, but Gloria stopped him with a shut-your-mouth glare and terse request to pass the salt and pepper.

The Marks family's problems were not as simple as a bar of Ivory soap. The family and their bugs lived in one of the dusty trailers that stood in a cluster of shacks at the south edge of town. The spot was known as Shakey's Half, and everybody knew that those kids got free lunch and smelled like pee. You didn't want a Marks kid to draw your name for the Christmas party gift exchange. That guaranteed nothing but disappointment. While the rest of the class unwrapped goodies that fifty cents could buy from the dime store uptown, like new sets of jacks, bags of green soldiers or marbles or even a pack of new hankies, a gift from one of the Marks meant one thing and one thing only—a tiny box with two chocolate-covered cherries, provided by the principal's office.

Gloria always said that children from Shakey's Half had rotten teeth, another tell-tale sign of their unfortunate address. The kids from that part of town never smiled. But once in a while, when they could forget their itching heads and their odor and their shame, a smile might creep up on one of their dirty little faces. If you got a quick glimpse into the insides of their mouths, the experience wasn't pleasing like a smile from a child should be. Smiles from Shakey's Half kids were haunting and left a hollow feeling that couldn't be rinsed and spit away.

"Violet," Gloria said, not long after Jules and I had struck up our unlikely friendship, "I'm sure that Jules is a very nice young man, but head lice can hop as far as three feet."

"You are ridiculous, Gloria. I'm not sharing hats with him and we're hardly playing beauty shop, so calm down."

"Violet, if that boy brings head lice into this house, it will take me a week to boil and scrub everything down. I won't have an infestation, Violet. I won't have it."

By the time I'd befriended Jules, Gloria had become quite a bit more comfortable sparring with me. I had given her ample room to practice. I won some rounds, and she won others. We wounded each other, but each skirmish seemed worth it.

We finally agreed that Jules was a fine enough friend—*if* he stayed on the front porch. He was never, not ever, to come inside the house.

Honestly, my mother's concession for front porch visits from Jules took me by surprise. Gloria was worried about head lice, but those itchy critters could be picked and scrubbed away.

My mother was far more worried about me associating with someone from Shakey's Half, and right out in the open. People would talk. Someone would take note right away and have something to say. That would bug Gloria more than Jules' bugs. To be honest, her willingness to negotiate took the steam out of this particular victory.

I liked Jules. He was clever enough. He smirked at my jokes. He rarely surrendered to a full throttled, toothy laugh, but I suspected he had thirty-two rotting reasons for that. We caught one another's eye, and despite his dusty, dingy outsides, I was drawn to him.

The new and improved Violet, the one still trying out her dark side for size and style, wanted his approval. We'd been in school together since kindergarten, but I'd never given him much more than a second glance. He had cooties. Before I even knew what cooties were, like everyone else in our class, I knew enough about them to know they were dangerous. All efforts to steer clear of them were acceptable, no matter how cruel.

My own descent to the dark side, to do what I could to irritate my mother, elevated Jules Marks to a spot of distinction. Jules fortified the arsenal I was building to confound Skip and Gloria, my fat gym teacher, the principal, and the old bags at church who gave me the side eye. Gloria protested, but weakly. She waved her surrender flag, white and high, much earlier in the battle than I anticipated.

"Jules Marks?" she said. "Violet, what could you have in common with that boy? I can't think of a thing."

"I like him. He's funny, and he said you know his mom."

Gloria got quiet and busied herself poking the baking potatoes with a fork and wrapping them in foil.

"I do know his mother, yes, I do know her."

"Well then, it's settled. If you can know someone from Shakey's Half, then I can, too."

Gloria sighed and waved me off.

"Fine, Violet. Fine. But that young man stays on the porch. You hear me? On. The. Porch."

Skip, who could usually be counted on to have an opinion and was still within earshot, didn't contribute anything to our stand-off. I filled my glass with tap water at the sink and saw that his eyebrows were raised. He was delivering a cryptic message to my mother with a secret code they shared. She let her own eyebrows respond in kind, shushing my father to save whatever he had to say for later.

"Porch, Violet. I mean it. No further than the porch, young lady."

Chapter Eleven

Jules Marks

I've scratched my head so hard it bleeds.

Momma's cure was to cut our hair to the skull and dump a can of kerosene on our heads. It hurt like a bitch, as if someone was peeling my skin right off, which I guess Momma did. I cried so hard the first time, but even harder when she used the same remedy on my sisters, especially little Kitty. That baby doll cried so hard she threw up.

I always figured a better way to cure our lice problem would be to have us all scalped, like the Indians did to the cowboys. Momma could rip away everything so there would be nothing left for the cooties to latch onto and lay their nasty eggs.

No such luck. Shaving and kerosene was the only cure Momma ever considered. After my head stopped feeling like it was on fire, I was relieved and then I was mad. What was so damned tasty about our heads? Why couldn't those creeping, crawling bastards leave me and my girls alone?

Every time we got tapped out of school, I hated the lice, the school nurse, and Momma for making Kitty and the girls cry and having them end up looking like dirty little boys with crew cuts.

My hatred was big and bad with nowhere to go. I stayed stone cold quiet and pretended I couldn't hear all the talk about jumping cooties. I pretended I didn't notice even the kindest adults who always kept their distance when they walked by.

The older girls took my lead. My sisters, Peg, Suze, Patty and Lolly, had faces that were wide and wise. Their bodies were stringy and ready for combat, but not our Kitty. She was a pretty thing with a wispy face and body that looked like it was put together with spit and feathers.

Kitty's middle name was Catherine, so sometimes the other girls and I would tease her and call her "Kitty Cat." At first, she liked it. She'd get down on all fours and meow her little heart out, letting us pet her behind the ears. But later, after she'd been sent home in shame along with the rest of us because we were all crawling with lice, she didn't want to be teased anymore.

By the time my sweetheart was six, she stopped pretending, even when we begged. She'd just turn her raggedy head toward the window and plop her thumb in her mouth. She'd suck and suck until it was red and sore. She worked that thumb hard. The girls took turns trying to stop her by pulling it out of her mouth.

"You're not a baby no more, Kitty."

I shooed them away, letting her suck if she wanted to. It was her thumb and her mouth. She could have her own bit of peace and some kind of comfort.

It was okay with me if Violet's mother didn't want me in her house. I could understand that. But if my little Kitty Cat ever wanted to come inside that pretty house and Vi's mother told *her* to stay out on the porch, I'd pick a fight. I would. My little kitten could not scratch and fight to survive like the rest of us. She needed a dish of warm milk and a quiet place to curl up and rest in a patch of sunlight.

I think Violet would have agreed.

Chapter Twelve

Margaret Burns

I can tell you all you want to know about Shakey's Half, but most people prefer to pretend that it doesn't exist.

Knowing a place means you've been close to it, and proximity can assault your senses. I said *assault*, and I mean it. Your sense of smell takes the first hit. Skin that's not rinsed fresh with hot water and soap holds the stink. Sweat compounds the odor, too, and God forbid the stench gets in your blood.

Cigarette smoke doesn't help. The odors of spilled beer, dirty dishes, smelly diapers, burned trash, and unwashed clothes just mix and mingle and stir up a thick stench that hangs in the air so thick and heavy it burns your eyes. Soap and water have no power here.

The sights will numb you. Rust and dust and unpulled weeds. Ashy burn piles and cigarette butts, beer cans, old food wrappers, rusted bikes, tired old tires, scrappy racoons, skinny dogs, and feral cats. Any one of them would be enough to make you toss and turn, but not many are brave enough to take it all in at once.

If you stay long enough, you'll see tired, stringy women who don't come outdoors much. You'll see children so exhausted by living in dirt that they've gone unnaturally quiet.

The littlest ones will get you, for sure, but the older ones will, too. They've ventured out from Shakey's Half to go to school, where they can breathe clean air and imagine a better and brighter future until they realize it is not theirs for the taking.

Those kids will break the hardest of hearts.

Chapter Thirteen

Violet

Jules and I like to mess around, but it's not what you think. There's no mashing and grinding, nothing like that. Jules taught me how to cut myself. One day, I watched him thread a long, thin needle through the skin of his thumb without producing even a drop of blood.

I was impressed.

"How can you do that?"

Jules shrugged.

For weeks, I watched him probe the tips of his fingers with pins and needles he fished out of his jacket pockets.

"Wanna try, Vi? It doesn't hurt, not really."

He handed me a safety pin. I pricked and poked gently at the skin on my thumb, applying varying degrees of pressure. I worked the entire shaft of the needle through the outermost layer of skin as Jules looked on, surprised I was willing to try.

"See. I *told* you it didn't hurt!"

He looked right through me without a smile.

I was disappointed. I'd hoped to feel something. Jules must have detected that, and he wasted no time reassuring me.

"It *could* hurt. If you *want* it to."

He glanced back at the house to make sure the coast was clear and gave me a nod. I nodded back and pricked my finger again. This time, a red blood droplet bubbled up. I licked it with the tip of my tongue. My blood tasted almost sweet that afternoon.

Jules went home. I went inside to have dinner with Skip and Gloria. Later, I crept into my room and found a stupid sewing basket I'd received one year for my birthday from Aunt Ruth and Uncle Richard. I'd never opened it but felt a surge of pleasure when I discovered a stash of weapons to puncture and pierce my skin: pins, needles, and a tiny pair of scissors. All mine.

Later, after Jules and I discovered our shared penchant for hurting ourselves, my comrade found me worthy enough to suggest variations in weapons: razor blades from Skip's shaving kit, Gloria's nail files and a small paring knife from the kitchen.

I brought my cutting kit with me everywhere I went, and on the few occasions I forgot, I found tools that would do the job. Jules taught me to be on the lookout for sharp edges, which cropped up everywhere.

The act of puncturing kept my world turning. Jules understood that. He knew cutting was necessary to reach those treasured, mysterious places covered by skin.

Toothpicks from restaurants worked well, as did my spiral bound notebooks, but there was more to learn. Jules showed me how to use notebook paper to make tiny, delicious cuts to the webs of skin between my fingers. It was a subtle trade secret I took seriously.

"Now stretch your fingers out, Vi. Stretch them and spread them so far you can feel the cut tear open more on its own."

He coached me with a voice so low and husky it sent thrilling waves down my spine. He instructed me to run inside and get the bottle of lemon juice from the refrigerator.

"Get a plate, too, Vi. We'll need it."

He poured the juice onto the plate and took the hand I'd just sliced with a piece of paper.

"Stretch it so you can feel the cuts opening up."

Jules smiled as he helped me place my hand onto the plate of lemon juice. I bit my lip as the acid stung the tiny cuts and slivers I'd made in my own skin.

Cutting up with Jules was a private act between us that yielded joy, bubbling to the surface with rich, red rewards. I liked the way Jules smiled at me when a rush was especially sweet, how he nodded with approval when I pushed a little bit deeper. I could tell that he liked me watching him wound himself. He was good at it and resourceful.

Our sessions didn't last long or happen frequently enough. I was greedy. I wanted more cutting than Jules could provide. It would be necessary to satisfy myself.

Chapter Fourteen

Jules

Vi was cool. I could tell her about my first cut.

Little Kitty Cat was just a brand-new baby. Momma brought her home, looking clean and fresh, like she couldn't be ours. The little pink blanket that came wrapped around her smelled so fresh and sweet, but instead of making me happy, it made me angry.

I knew that our little kitten wouldn't stay clean and sweet-smelling for long. She'd been given the same fresh start we all had, but in a matter of days, her perfect baby powder smell would vanish. She'd smell like piss and sweat and spit up. That blanket would never ever be washed. I started to wonder how anyone could look at Momma and then at us and still hand her another baby to bring home.

It was cold outside the day Kitty came to us. Poor thing had no idea. The girls were excited, but I knew better. This new life of theirs was nothing to celebrate.

That first night, Momma slept deep and long in the back room. She asked me to change Kitty's diaper and keep her fed with the formula and bottles the hospital had given her in a paper bag also filled with diapers, lotions and soap.

Tucked in the bottom were two diaper pins we wouldn't need. I put those in my pocket. I may be just a snot-nosed kid, but I can change a diaper, even on a brand-new baby, like this one.

I handed her back to Momma, who didn't even say thanks. I went back to my mattress on the floor in the big room, where we all slept together in the winter to stay warm.

I listened for Kitty's newborn grunts and squeaks because they would be ignored without me. The girls were tangled tight against one another, breathing heavy next to me. I hoped they were dreaming of long hair to brush and pull back with pretty ribbons, and clean, pressed dresses, and the brand new, black patent leather shoes they deserved to have on their feet.

I took a diaper pin out of my pocket and pushed it with my thumb, springing the sharp point out into the open. With the moonlight coming through the living room window and my breath steaming out in white, frosty circles from my mouth, I stuck my thumb over and over. Tiny blood bubbles rose to the surface and trickled in streams down my hand and onto my arms. My thumb hurt, but there was relief, too. I could choose where the pain started, how deep to cut and how long to let the blood drip. There was no man in our house but me, and I was powerless. All I could do was wait for the next barb to roll in, from any direction.

Starting a cut and finishing it made me the king of my castle.

Vi was the only person who knew about my cutting powers. She'd been teasing me the last few days, sure she had a leg up on me. I wasn't convinced. She was one tough cookie, but she had soft roots.

You don't come from a house like hers, with a mama like hers and a father, too, without possessing a softness deep inside.

Vi was never hungry or dirty for long. Her house had hot water, clean towels and cold, unspoiled milk. Her lunches came packed tight and tidy in a metal lunch box with a matching thermos that sometimes had hot, steaming soup inside it.

If she decided to buy lunch, her ticket would be green, not yellow. When Vi went home from school it was because she had a fever or a bad cold. Vi had softness closer to the surface than she knew. If she had a story harder and dirtier than mine, she'd need to prove it.

"How about you, Vi?"

"Can't show you here, Jules. We have to do this somewhere else."

I liked this girl. I'd just told her I slept on a filthy mattress in our living room, and she still wanted to be with me and share a secret.

"Vi, come on. You know I can't be in your house. Just tell me. Right here. Come on. Fair's fair."

She shook her glossy head of hair, grabbed my hand, and led me to the back yard, behind her father's shed. She pulled me so fast with her long legs that I was panting to keep up. She leaned her back up against the metal shed and dropped her jeans.

"Vi! My God! What are you doing? Vi, put those back on! Jesus!"

But she didn't. Instead, she pushed down her underpants until they were just beneath her hips, lower than I should be seeing. She kept pushing until I could see a big, ugly tattoo, a skull, right there, exposed to the air and my gaze.

"Jules, meet Mr. Bones. Mr. Bones, meet Jules."

I reached out with my scabby hand to pet Mr. Bones. I was stunned. He was a pirate up to no good.

"Do your parents know about him?"

I knew full well they couldn't, but she nodded.

"They know."

She was trying to act casual, like what she'd just confessed was no big deal to her or her folks. I was stunned.

"Did it hurt, Vi? That must have stung. Tattoos hurt. And right by your, uh, you know, right above your, you know. That must have been a rush. A real lemon juice rush."

I stared at my friend's lower belly. What Violet had done to herself was impressive. It was scary enough to leave me speechless until I came to my senses.

"Get those pants up, Vi. You shouldn't be showing me this. You just shouldn't. If your mother finds out, she won't let me on your porch ever again, or even your yard."

Vi pulled up her jeans. Something was different now. I didn't think I should be with her behind that shed or even on her porch. I started walking home. She zipped up her jeans and followed me.

"Hey, Jules, what's the matter? You didn't let me tell *my* story. I was just getting started."

She was mad, but I didn't look back. I just kept walking with my hands in my pockets.

"Jules Marks, you come back here! Come back! I listened to your stupid story. Jules! Get back here! Damn you, Jules. What happened to fair's fair? Huh? You're just scared! Well, look at that. You're afraid of Mr. Bones!"

I turned back.

"Need to get home, Vi. Just need to get home."

"What's the matter with you? Oh, I know. I know your problem. You're afraid my story might be uglier than yours, aren't you, Jules? That's it. You don't have anything on me now! Go ahead and leave! I want you to. Why don't you go home and cut yourself! This time, make it count, Jules! Cut yourself hard! You can't beat Mr. Bones!"

Her screaming stopped and I heard the front door slam. My friend was in her mother's kitchen, looking for a new weapon, something dull this time, so her clean skin would resist. She wanted to work for the pleasure of her next cut.

She was right. Vi just beat me with Mr. Bones and she had more to tell me.

Chapter Fifteen

Violet

There were so many delicious and vulnerable places on my body I could wound. I made tiny cuts where nobody could detect them but me.

Skipper and Gloria kept up a close watch, so I had to be selective, picking spots behind my knees and between my toes. Tiny slices inside my mouth produced red bubbles of blood and fresh slits of misery they would never see.

My parents didn't have it in them to process what I was doing. Once Gloria was satisfied that Mr. Bones had healed sufficiently, she pulled me aside to remind me that keeping my new friend under wraps was of utmost concern to her and Skip.

"Violet, it's important that we keep this whole thing to ourselves and not start all kinds of talk in town. None of us need that. You didn't think about that, did you? I know it's hard for you to fathom, but not everything is about you. Your father and I have a good reputation in this town, and you've jeopardized that now, young lady. Not a word to anybody, you understand?"

I turned toward the staircase to get away from her, but she grabbed my arm.

"Violet, this isn't over. You could make it a lot easier on your father if you told us where you got that thing. Have you seen the dark circles under his eyes, young lady? Have you? One way or the other, he is going to find out who did this to you."

I shrugged and trudged up the stairs. As I reached the top, Gloria was still talking.

"You know, Violet, we might need to take away your privileges if this goes on much longer. That might be our next step."

My mother sounded shrill, but I had the upper hand, and we both knew it. I closed the door to my room and clicked the lock. Gloria was exhausting. No wonder Skip had dark circles under his eyes. I wasn't about to get blamed for that all by myself.

I had an hour before Skip came home for another one of our quiet dinners. I dug through my sewing basket and pulled out a seam ripper Jules and I found at Phelps Fabrics. The discovery made Jules smile like a kid in a candy store.

"Vi, that place probably has all kinds of sharp stuff!"

As we scanned the aisles, we were in heaven from all the gleaming metal winking at us with sharp, metallic possibilities. Jules spotted the seam ripper, pulled it off the rack, and declared it had real promise.

"I've got some money," I said. "Let's get it."

My partner in crime nodded and we made our way to the counter. I had just enough to cover it. I shoved our new purchase in my front coat pocket. We didn't say much on the walk home. When it was time to part ways, Jules called back to me.

"Vi, wait for me to try it out."

I nodded and waved him off, knowing full well I would not keep my promise. Our seam ripper was so deliciously threatening that I knew I couldn't wait to share our treat. I didn't owe Jules anything. Since I paid for it, this tiny torture device was technically mine. Jules was lucky I was willing to share it with him at all. He'd get over it.

Once I locked myself into the safety of my own room, I slipped under the covers and hunkered down for the rest of the afternoon. I had seams of skin to rip in delicate places.

Chapter Sixteen

Jules

I needed to think about Violet, so I took the long way home to Shakey's Half. We hadn't been friendly that long, but she'd grown on me. Violet was deep. She was willing to sit next to me. We sat close enough sharing cuts and secrets that our heads touched. She even let me touch her hands as we cut together.

She smelled nice, too, even though she refused to take showers at school. Not me. Each day after gym, I didn't care who saw me without my clothes. I stood there and let the lukewarm water wash over me until the teacher barked that the bell was about to ring. Having clean skin was a luxury that made it worth being marked tardy for my next class. Being squeaky clean made me curious and courageous.

As I turned onto the dirt road at the top of Shakey's Half, I knew exactly where Vi and Mr. Bones found each other. Her tattoo wasn't signed, but I knew the artist. It was Lem. I was sure of that.

Lem came and went as he pleased. He and Momma had some kind of mysterious deal between them that kept him dropping by when he wanted without even knocking first.

He knew better than to come empty handed. Sometimes, he'd throw a wad of cash on the kitchen table. Momma would snatch it up and start counting. If it seemed light, he'd probably spent money on something stupid. A lizard, wild birds, fancy dogs he couldn't feed, a new saw or some miracle gadget that would make us rich. After one of those moves, Momma would toss him out for a while, chiding him like he was one of us kids.

"Lem, you fucking idiot, what am I supposed to do with this? Trade it at the grocery store for cheese and bread? You need to leave and don't come back until you got something I can use. Jules has more sense than you, Lem. I swear he does. We got ourselves hungry kids to feed, Lem. They're yours, too. Don't you forget that. You hear me? And take that crazy-ass bargain of yours with you."

She was right. Me and the girls belonged to both of those fools, but we were never properly claimed. I was smarter than Lem. Smarter than Momma, too. I had more going on upstairs than both of them. My eyes took things in and kept them stored away. My ears did, too. It wasn't until I went to school that my nose got wise, picking up the difference between fresh and stale, sweet and sour, clean and foul. My stained shirts didn't smell nice, which meant I didn't smell nice, either.

My first teacher, Miss Lend, didn't seem to mind. She helped me trace my grubby hand with dirt under my fingernails with a fat, red crayon. Hanging on the wall like that, my hand looked no different than the others.

"Now, Jules, that's a nice hand you've got there."

Miss Lend patted me on the back real soft.

"Well done, Jules Marks. Well done. You'll be writing your name before you know it. We're going to do that soon."

She doled out the same smile for me that all the other kids got, but I liked it more. I know I did. I liked her white teeth and pink lipstick and how she could see that I was good, too, even if my teeth were brown and my lunch ticket was yellow. I liked applesauce with cinnamon, and fruit cocktail, buttered bread, and my carton of cold milk. I liked books with pictures of trucks and animals and clean boys and girls.

I used to touch the pictures with my grubby hands and wish I could be like that. Still do, I guess. On the playground, I sucked in fresh air and enjoyed the warmth of the sun. During rest time, I closed my eyes on my mat, gobbling up the sounds and smells of school until it was time to go home, miles away from yellow lunch tickets and fat crayons and Miss Lend's gentle voice, reminding me that I was a little boy worth paying attention to—a deep departure from how it was at home.

As the school day wore on, my throat would tighten when I realized I would soon be home with Momma and my sisters in Shakey's Half. Miss Lend wouldn't like it there, either. I never wanted her to see me there, blending in with the stench that hung by the door on your way in and out.

Once we all learned about the days of the week, I grew to love Mondays because they promised five days of grace when I could be honored just because I was in kindergarten, where I always had a seat and a snack and my own place in line.

Miss Lend learned right away that I responded well to her kind and gentle touch. Even when she was talking to everybody in the room, I felt like she was addressing me personally and her soft words arrived by special delivery.

"Jules, Honey, go grab a tissue from my desk. We need to wipe that button nose of yours."

"Jules, you are a wiggly one! If you need to use the restroom, you certainly may. No need to be uncomfortable."

My nose always needed to be wiped, and using a clean bathroom felt so nice. On top of that, someone was watching me close enough to notice and made sure I knew it all day long.

The first time I was sent home from school with cooties bruised my heart. It was the day of our Valentine party. Miss Lend had helped me cut out red hearts during recess and sign my name on them for my classmates. She even helped me paste together a Valentine box made with construction paper, something she must have figured that Momma would not manage to do. My teacher seemed to know things about me and my world that I also knew but had no way to say so.

There were pink frosted cupcakes in the corner, and we were going to drink apple juice, play games and deliver our valentines right after lunch. All morning, I could smell the cupcakes with their promising sweetness. I'd never tasted one. Knowing that I would have a box full of valentines with my name written on tiny envelopes made me feel light-headed with something that must have been joy.

To: Jules. To: Jules. To: Jules.

I existed.

I felt Miss Lend's gentle hand on my shoulder during lunch. I'd just finished my milk when her soft whisper tickled my ear.

"Jules, Honey, they need you down in the nurse's office. Let's take your tray up. I'll take you down the hall."

She held my hand as we passed the noisy classrooms where first, second and third graders lined up for their lunch. They seemed giant and sure of themselves. The larger ones looked capable of drinking two cartons of milk.

As we turned the corner into the principal's office, the milk in my stomach soured. Was I in trouble? I'd never been in trouble at school. We made a sharp left toward the nurse's office. She was expecting us.

"I'll wait out here for you, Jules," said Miss Lend.

She was wearing a pink dress with a gold heart pinned to it.

The nurse wasn't unfriendly, but she was all-business, pulling me by the arm toward a big metal light she adjusted to see my scalp. She moved through my hair until she found what she was looking for and then turned off the light and pulled me into a chair against the wall.

Miss Lend looked serious and sad. I could feel my heart thumping hard as she looked into my eyes.

"Mister Jules, it looks like we have a little problem. We're going to have to send you home early, so your mama can give your hair a scrub. It's no big deal, but we have to take care of it right away. The nurse is going to call her now, so she can come and get you."

I was a good boy and a serious big brother, but hot little boy tears stung my eyes, and my nose started running again.

"Oh, Sweetie, it's going to be all right. Trust me, it will be just fine. I know you're disappointed. Wait here."

I heard the nurse talking to Momma. While I waited to be picked up, Miss Lend came back with a brown bag.

"Here you go, Sugar. You can still have your cupcake from the party. Take it home. We'll have your valentines in your cubby when you come back."

She patted my hand and gave me a little wave before she headed down the hall. I could tell that she believed it really would be all right. My cupcake would taste delicious, and Momma would swoop right in and save the day, full of apologies that I missed the party.

I watched the clock on the wall. We had not learned how to tell time. That would not happen until first grade, but I knew that Momma would not show up any time soon. In fact, I was not surprised to see Aunt Clarice show up to save me. She was still in her waitress uniform, but she pulled me to her and patted my back. She hustled me home, where the stink was ripe to greet us. I ate my cupcake alone in our dusty kitchen and listened to my aunt wheeze and sigh while Momma yelled at her until a door slammed outside.

I licked the frosting off the cupcake and held it in my mouth to dissolve as slowly as possible. I trapped the sweetness with my tongue to the top of my mouth, knowing it would be a long time before another cupcake would find me.

The real truth of my situation did not surprise me like it might have affected a clean girl or boy, or the lovely Miss Lend. I understood it like I understood Lem's empty comings and goings and the hollow, dirty differences between my world and the one that had parties and pretty valentines.

Chapter Seventeen

Sally Lend

Nobody ever bothered to tell me that I would need to harden my heart to teach kindergarten.

I knew that I would need to like children, be patient and organized. Check, check, check. I loved books, and those magical moments when you could see that first flicker of understanding that signified a little one was no longer mystified by the alphabet but understood it for the code to the universe that it was. Check.

Mastery of shapes, colors, the weather, days of the week, months and childish songs? Check. Wrangle small bodies into formations, straight lines for trips down the hall, seated circles for story time, heads on desks for quiet time and rumps in the air for tornado drills? Check. A bell on my desk and a shining whistle around my neck to beckon my chicks back to me when recess was over? Check.

No matter what was required, they were ready to please me, easily cajoled and fooled into believing that stringing colored beads would lead them to bigger, better things, like balancing their checkbooks, making change and doubling the recipe.

By the time Jules Marks darkened my door with his deep dimples and ashy blonde hair, I was a seasoned teacher, sure of my place in school, our town of Poulson and the universe.

I'd coached kiddos through accidents in their pants, wiped runny noses, and cleaned up puddles of throw up without a second thought. My gag reflex was hardy. I'd even held one child's hands to his sides and sung in his ear while a doctor carefully stitched up his bloody chin in the emergency room. I never should have let him hop on the teeter totter with a third grader three times his size.

I've rounded up plenty of lost mittens and gloves and sent notes home to parents, knowing full well that the resulting punishments would outsize the crimes committed. I thought I was tough and ready for anything.

Then I met little Jules. He broke me in half. He wasn't the first darling boy I'd welcomed into my classroom. Most of them were cute at this age. They could be a little grubby or scrappy, but you had to chuckle at their antics and their inability to keep their hands to themselves. The way they stuffed their front pockets with trash and treasures amused me. I caught myself trying to imagine these tiny little masters as their grownup selves—bankers, real estate agents, firefighters, lusty ditch diggers gathered at the end of a bar, throwing back a few before stumbling home to paw at their tired wives.

What Jules might become haunted me. He was quiet, carefully watching all that swirled around him. He followed my rules and seemed hungry for what I would say and do next. His eyes did not leave my face. It made me self-conscious, as if he had been sent there to observe me, to dissect my words and the way I delivered them.

You couldn't fault him or any little boy for dirty hands and fingernails. That came with the territory. While those traits might have bonded him to the other boys, he held back, seemingly unaffected by their impulsive fidgeting and restless spirits.

Jules could be still. It made me wonder if anyone had taken pictures of him as a baby and if his mother had saved a piece of hair from his first haircut or tucked away the baby bracelet that was around his wrist when he left the hospital.

I wondered how a child like this had been granted such a dignified name: Jules Martin Marks. Impressive? I'd say so. That kind of a name held weight. It belonged to a proud, wide-chested man who probably could afford to have his suits tailored at Kline's Department Store and a wife at home waiting to starch his shirts and lay out his cuff links. This waif shouldered a name that seemed too heavy for him to carry.

I'd sent children home with head lice before. It was always a sad business, but it was as much a part of a school's inner workings as emptying pencil sharpeners, pounding out dust from chalkboard erasers or discarding dried up bottles of paste. But I had never sent *this* little boy home with cooties right before a class party, after I'd watched his soulful, brown eyes stare at the cupcakes all morning.

His hot face, bewildered and loaded with agony, begged me without words to save him, and that shook me. I gave him a little wave and smile that he usually gobbled up like a thirsty puppy. But this time, he sat there, trying to manage his little shuddering body until someone came to rescue him.

That day, it would not be me.

During the party, I almost resented the other children for their squeals of joy and for not missing Jules. I was relieved to finally send them home. When the last oblivious brat walked out the door, I locked it and sank to the floor in tears. I was ashamed of my helplessness in the face of such a cruel and capricious world.

All I could do was gather the Valentine's Day box I had made for Jules and make sure it would be safe and sound when he returned, stuffed with cards and chalky conversation hearts with their misleading messages of affection.

That was the last year I taught kindergarten. A position teaching home economics at the high school opened. I applied right away, even though I had no idea how to teach cooking or sewing, let alone the birds and the bees.

Even so, I welcomed the idea of a room filled with ovens and sewing machines. I knew I'd miss those darling children with dimples and deep brown eyes who counted on me to save the day, wipe their tears and protect their fragile hearts.

I convinced myself that boys like Jules Martin Marks would grow up just fine without me.

Chapter Eighteen

Gloria

I didn't need to be so extravagant with Lee or her children. I stuck around for Jules, then Peg, then Lolly and Patty. Lee birthed two more girls after them, but by then I'd bowed out of that mess. Skip had warned me for the longest time, but I kept at it, sure that my instincts were right. Deep down, I knew better.

Educated women like me who are loved and enjoy anything we could ever want in life don't fall for just any old trick. We're savvy about quite a bit. We can see when we're being snookered. We can sense when we're being used. We can back away from the fire. Chances are, we've been burned a time or two and can tell when it's about to happen again.

Uneducated women, those who are not loved enough and must scrape and scratch for what they need and want, don't fall for just any old trick, either. They're savvy in their own way. They can see when they're being taken for a ride. They get wise. They know when they are being used. They can also back away from a fire. Chances are, they've also been burned.

So, what's the difference? One woman has everything to lose and the other is already in the hole. The one who has nothing, and nobody, has already learned that she stands to benefit by sticking as close to the fire for as long as she can, as long as it keeps her warm. She's figured out that fires come and go, and so do friendly faces. She'll take her warmth where she can get it. She's not particular. A fire's a fire. A warm body's just another warm body. Fires and warm bodies are simply fuel to be consumed.

Lee and I weren't friends. I was using her to fill up parts of my tank that were empty. My voids were none of her concern. We givers are no better than takers. All we care about is the delicious rush we get as we battle and slay every dragon that comes into that poor taker's life. We are heroes who save the day because it suits us. But make no mistake. Those who give to excess are just as sinful and flawed as those who take with abandon.

We're definitely getting something. That is one thing I learned from Lee Marks.

It took me far too long to see that Lee was choosing her lot in life all by herself. Her initial needs were genuine. But with Lee and her kind, the lessons miss their mark. The teacher is wasting time with learners like Lee. They can ace a test if they want to. Of course they can. But a gold star that comes with a high score leaves them hungry.

Learners like Lee would rather watch the teacher. They want to know where she keeps the gold stars. They want to know how many copies of the test she's made and what's rolling around in the top drawer of her desk. They want to know where the teacher goes to get more stars when she runs out.

Once I started to figure that out, and was willing to admit that Lee could take me or leave me, that she might just open up her cavernous mouth of teeth and eat me alive one day, I started to feel frightened and trapped by the person I'd championed for so long.

I threw Lee's story on my back as if it was my own. I carried her sad little tale around with me like it was a heavy load. Every time that something good came my way, any good fortune of even the smallest consequence, I couldn't allow myself to enjoy it. Instead, I compared my bounty to her lack of everything and ended up succumbing to a sad existence that wasn't even mine. I had it good, better than I deserved, but for the longest time, I could not bring myself to enjoy it.

If I make it to Heaven, and God takes me aside to review my file, questions are bound to come up. My Lord will certainly want to know more about the hard heart I held for my little sister, Ruth. He'll have the number of pinches and pokes and other unkind acts I unleashed on her tallied up. I'll have to answer for that.

He might have questions about Lee, too. He might point out that it wasn't kind of me to invite myself into that little thing's life, to let her get comfortable with all the differences between her life and mine and then call it all off once she made choices I thought were unwise. She didn't need my approval.

Somewhere in the New Testament, there's a story about Jesus that I've always found appealing for its easy out. Jesus and his followers encounter a bad woman. She is so vile and despicable that the men in her village take it upon themselves to throw jagged rocks at her until she's dead. But good old Jesus stays their hands. He points out that they are only entitled to hurl objects at the whore if they are completely without sin themselves. To the woman's relief, none of her would-be executioners qualify for the honor of bludgeoning her in the street.

I like this one. I've clung to it like the half-baked Christian I can be. My red-headed sister could teach me a thing or two. As I see it, Jesus' rescue of the whore who was just a stone's throw away from death gives me an out.

It was never my place to judge others unless I was free of blemishes myself. My selfish, jealous past went back so far that I couldn't even remember my first evil deed or thought. I was covered for sure. I didn't need to take a stand on someone else's behavior because I was just as rotten as they come.

I watched my sister meld so seamlessly from a homely, picked-on child into her new role as a pastor's wife that I started to wonder about heavenly protocols, procedures for classifying martyrs.

Violet *is* Blue

There were degrees of suffering to consider. Some martyrs really enjoy the prolonged agony they endure before their hearts stop beating. We all know the type. They let their hard-headed principles lead them all the way through the blood-thirsty crowds to the stake. They don't even break a sweat as the faggots are piled up around them. They keep it together as the fire is lit and gets hotter and hotter. They might moan as the flames start to lick at their skin, but they hang on. Their bodies roast, and pop and sizzle until they feel a surge of pleasure that's not exactly erotic but might as well be.

The turn-on for these souls is the public nature of the spectacle. They like being admired. They love the fact that someone is watching their suffering. The only thing better than being noticed would be if someone, anyone, would thank them in earnest for their sacrifice.

Ruthie and I shared a mother, grandmother, and great-grandmother before her, who were all sticklers about thank-you notes. It was just the proper thing to do. I am also a stickler. I always like my gifts to be acknowledged. It's just the right thing to do.

Our kind will say that the thank-you note is not so much about gratitude, but a simple courtesy letting the giver know that the receiver has received, and that the receiver is aware of the giver's generosity and good intentions. Good intentions, my ass. People want thank-you notes because they want to be thanked and appreciated, and we want it all properly documented.

Coming from a long line of thank-you note militia, I was able to exempt Lee from this etiquette for one charitable reason: she simply didn't have the same kind of upbringing. She was so ignorant that she could not be held responsible for norms she'd never been exposed to.

I didn't need a thank-you note from Lee, did I? I must have wanted something, or I wouldn't have stuck around for as long as I did, pouring myself into her, ignoring Skip's repeated requests that I cut her off.

I'm sure that Lee and her big sister, Clarice, would say that they didn't need me or any other goody-two-shoes breezing through their tough lives. They didn't ask me for any of it. All the kind gestures that bound us were initiated by me. Clarice protested more than once. From their dingy corner of the world, it must have felt like I was the one who'd come barging in, demanding something. It might have felt like I was the one thrust upon them. They were not as well off as I was, not even close, but they were within their rights to perceive me as a damned nuisance, and it took me forever to change.

Chapter Nineteen

Clarice Downs

Every time I think about my half-sister, Lee, I feel sick. It's the kind of sick that a saltine cracker can't fix. This brand of sick makes your upper lip tremble and turn white and pasty like you just stepped off a carnival ride on a hot summer day. You need to find a shady corner to let your guts calm down, but sometimes they just don't, and you dread that moment. It's unmistakable. You fight it. You try to make friends with it, but you can't. You're just stuck. Nothing else can happen until you empty what's churning in your guts into a hot pool on the ground beneath you.

That's no way to talk about your little sister, even if all you share in this world is a mother. But my brother, Larry, and I agreed, after years of helping, fixing, begging, pleading, and plotting, that we did what we could for Lee.

Larry and I were glad to have the last name Downs while our little sister was known as Lee Marks. To those who didn't know better, we weren't related to each other at all. A nasty soul might make it their business to connect the dots for the curious or mention it in passing as I took their order in Slapp's Diner, just to remind me of my place, but I could shrug that off and smile. Larry and I had nothing to be ashamed of. We made the most of our lot in life. We had honest jobs and earned our way fair and square.

I waited tables proudly. I kept my uniform clean, with the collar starched. I was good at taking orders and smiling and being on my feet all day. I didn't mind wiping Slapp's long red counter a hundred times a day, and filling tired truckers' cups with hot, black brew. I could be counted on to rattle off the specials and knew when we were about to run out of pie.

"Clarice, girl, that's a mighty good job you got."

That's what our mama told me on my first day. She looked me up and down and motioned for me to turn around so she could see my new uniform from the back.

"Nothing to be ashamed of, Girl. Everybody has to eat, and someone's got to bring them their plates. That's the truth, Honey. Good for you, Sister."

Two years later, she told Larry the same thing. He had nabbed a janitorial job at the high school. Our mama was especially proud that he'd be working on school buses, too. That sweetened the deal for her.

"Not everybody can do *that* work, Larry. You remember that when you're scrubbing shit streaks out of toilets. They picked you for this job because you can work on engines, too. They don't let just anybody do *that* work. Those buses, they carry people's babies to school and back in all kinds of weather. Don't you forget it, Son. That's something to be proud of. Your daddy would be proud of you. He was good with his hands, just like you."

My handsome brother nodded. He believed her. He was pleased enough. Our daddy had passed away years before, so we'd have to take Mama's word for it. She was proud of us. That was her right. We didn't have the heart to tell her we were nothing special. We'd both managed to graduate high school. It was a step further in life than she or Daddy ever took. It was something. It was good enough.

Back then, you didn't need so much money to get away from home. That was something Larry was ready to do, and so was I. We'd had enough of Jim Marks. Mama married him mostly to keep the lights on and food on the table after Daddy passed. Jim was harmless at first. He smoked too much though and never helped enough.

By the time Larry was in junior high, he was the man of the house for anything that needed to be fixed or lifted or jimmy-rigged to fend off an expensive new purchase or repair. Jim was no good for any of that stuff, but Mama put up with him anyway.

While things were still half-way good, she wound up pregnant with Lee. At the time, we both knew how babies were made, so we tried not to think too hard on that. It was hard enough conjuring up the details with movie stars in our minds, much less our tired old mother and cranky, smoky-smelling Jim Marks. He was already starting to brood and take in too much beer by the time of the big announcement. I was old enough to babysit by then. I figured I'd be needed for that and a whole lot more and I was right.

Mama constantly called on me to do her errands.

"Clarice, Honey, can you run down to the store and pick Jim up two packs of cigarettes? We need a carton of milk for the baby, too."

I'd make the run, praying the whole way there that the money I fished out of her purse would be enough. Even though he was her daddy, Jim didn't like it when baby Lee's milk habit trumped his needs.

The rest of us loved on Lee. Her start wasn't much better or much worse than what we Downs kids had; that's for sure. It's fair enough to say that she was a spoiled pet. She didn't take kindly to anyone saying no to her and was sneaky from the start. We had ourselves a brat who dished out sass that we never would have been brave enough to try.

But things surely took a turn when Mama got sick. Larry and I had moved on by then, stopping by on most Sundays to check in. Jim would be nowhere in sight, and Mama's cough went from raspy to juicy to downright scary.

Lee was pesky and demanding. She needed tending that Mama couldn't usually provide. I brought food from the diner most nights, and packed lunches for Lee until Mama just gave in and let me sign her up for free lunches at school.

Lee pitched a fit. Couldn't blame the little imp for that.

"Lee Marks, you listen to me," I told her. "Getting lunch up at school is the best way you can make things easier for Mama. Those lunches are fine, so no more bellyaching. I don't want to see any more crying and carrying on out of you about that. You hear me?"

Lee kept on pitching her fit.

"I don't want a damned yellow ticket for my lunch! Yellow tickets go last in line. There's no chocolate milk left by the time the yellow ticket kids get up there. You know what? I'd rather be hungry than eat on a yellow ticket."

I certainly did feel for her. Why on Earth did the free lunch kids have a different color ticket than the paying kids?

I still needed her to just eat the free lunch.

Jim came and went as he pleased. It was easier getting things done if he was gone anyhow. Larry swabbed the decks with all his janitor know-how, but no amount of professional scrubbing was going to get the brown smoke smell out of that house or out of Mama's lungs. The tar from Jim's nonstop smoking had a staying power.

I tried, but he paid me no mind.

"Jim, it would be much better for Mama if you would smoke those things outside."

Sometimes, out of sheer meanness, he'd light up, inhale, and blow a stream of white smoke between us to make his point. I always left those visits feeling uneasy, like I should turn back and be there to keep Lee from wearing Mama out with her sass, and to keep watch for the next problem that always seemed to pop up.

Lee needed this or that, groceries needed to be brought in, and the toilet kept backing up. We needed Larry for that one. He came in handy when Lee's parakeet left this world, too. That was a long afternoon, and Lee had a fit bigger than when she was stuck with a yellow lunch ticket.

Larry borrowed the school truck to bring Mama to the doctor with me. Her lungs were tired and too full of brown, sticky tar to take her cough away.

One Sunday, we had to take her to the hospital, where they found a tumor fighting for space like she was fighting for air. A nurse kept Lee busy with crayons and lollipops while we watched another nurse find a vein on Mama's arm to give her morphine.

"This will calm her down," she said.

We watched her place a gas mask over Mama's sagging face, and it didn't take long before that cough of hers got sleepy, too.

"Larry, you wanna give Jim a call? To let him know?"

"Nope. That son of a bitch would be here if he gave a shit."

I watched my brother wipe away angry tears before they slid down his face. That wasn't manly, even for a man about to lose his mama, so Larry turned away and I let him keep his pride.

Mama didn't have the best luck, but at least her way out was clean and orderly. She didn't linger like you sometimes hear about. She took one more dose of morphine and slipped right out of this world. Her tired face went slack, and her mouth hung open. She didn't look like our mama at all.

Larry took me and Lee to my little apartment for the night. He stayed on the couch, and I bundled my scrappy little half-sister into my bed with me. She was weepy, and so was I. Poor kid. As I held her bony body, her hair and clothes smelled like cigarettes and made my throat sore. At least for that night, the good Lord let us sleep.

The next day was brutal, and the days after that, too. We needed to get Mama buried. We'd need to manage Jim somehow, and we had ourselves a little girl to think about. She was only eight years old and getting gangly. She had no mama, a shiftless sack of shit for a father, and her next of kin, me, and Larry, were just poor kids who had become adults, but just barely hanging on. I got really good at being a waitress and Larry was one good janitor, but we had no idea what to do.

I didn't know it at the time, but that night would be one of the last times I held Lee close. She went back to her daddy and ran wild, which I guess she preferred to what we could offer.

We coaxed and begged and pleaded. Larry and I watched from afar and shook our heads. We gave money. We dropped off food and clothes. As Lee got older, she'd take what we had to offer, but only from a distance. Jim had his neglectful hooks in deep and it seemed like Lee had no rules or restrictions.

She never thanked us for our efforts but took them just the same. She didn't seem to care that we had the same mama. Those parts of Lee just didn't work.

We tried not to think about all that went on over at the house with Jim and Lee. I'd catch wind of bits and pieces at the diner, and they weren't good.

When I heard that Lem Hauser had moved in with them, I tried to believe I'd heard wrong. On any given day, Poulson circulated its share of half-truths and outright lies. This rumor didn't seem possible. Jim wasn't nice enough to let someone move in with him. But the second time I caught wind of it, I guessed the gossip mill must have landed on the right spot.

Lem usually lived in a tent in the woods, back behind the school. He'd been in and out of jail, even though he was only slightly older than us. He didn't finish school, so it was hard to keep track of him.

Larry stopped by toward the end of my shift one night to give me a lift home.

"Did you hear who's moved in out at Jim's?"

My brother shook his head. He looked tired. His hands were still dirty from scrubbing up other people's messes. I shared what I knew.

Nothing good was going to come of this. Not one good thing. My hungry brother didn't dive into his hot sack of food like usual. He was sick to his stomach, too.

Chapter Twenty

Margaret Burns

People feel sorry for you when you live alone. That's nice of them, but the truth is I don't mind a bit. When it's just me, things are simple, and I like it that way.

Aunt Helen used to tease me something fierce about how easy I am to please. She was eager to show me the finer things in life—dresses with a bit of lace and ribbon, boots with brass buckles, and a hat and muff to match my winter coat. She offered chocolate pudding, but I was satisfied with vanilla. She tempted me with a brand-new dolly when all I wanted was the stringy old blanket I'd been clinging to on the day they took me home with them. It smelled as bad as I did, but Aunt Helen got us both scrubbed up with warm soapy water.

Those first mornings after I'd been saved, my sweet-smelling aunt offered doughnuts, then pancakes with crispy bacon, then a sticky hot cinnamon roll. I clung to her in the kitchen as Uncle Teddy wolfed down whatever was put in front of him with a gusto that made food seem appealing and plentiful, but I was too nervous to eat.

This was all new. Aunt Helen was slow and patient as she coaxed me to consider the new bounty that was suddenly there for the taking.

"Child, we've got to find something you'll eat," she said, planting a soft kiss at the back of my ear. "What can Aunt Helen find that this little bird will like? There must be *something* we can put in that belly of yours."

Little bird. I'd only been with them a few days, but already I was her little bird. She smiled and pressed her powdered cheek to mine when I took two bites of scrambled eggs and nibbled at the edges of a triangle toast dusted with sugar and cinnamon. She offered them on a tiny fork, clucking her tongue sweetly at me to tempt me into opening my mouth.

"Well, look here, Uncle Teddy. Will you look at this? Our little bird likes scrambled eggs. Yes, she does. And cinnamon toast. That's what this sweet thing likes."

My uncle beamed at us and reached over to touch my face with his thick, gentle hand. His lips were pink against a dark, neat beard.

"Well, well, Aunt Helen. We're going to fatten this girl of ours right up, aren't we? You make this girl another piece of toast."

His eyes twinkled, and he gave me a wink. Even though my thumb was firmly planted in my mouth, I smiled at him shyly.

"There she is," he cooed. "She's coming around now, isn't she?"

I sure did come around. These lovely saviors coaxed their little bird into a nest feathered with comforts, big and small. Small suited me best. It always has. I still eat scrambled eggs and cinnamon toast for breakfast each morning. I'm satisfied with broth and noodles, black coffee, and plain sugar cookies. I liked clean wool socks and sturdy shoes. I liked helping Aunt Helen strip the beds on Saturday mornings to wash the sheets and replace them with clean ones stacked high in the linen closet. I liked helping her bring groceries home and emptying canned goods into the pantry. I liked sweeping the porch and drying the dishes. I preferred setting the table to playing with dolls like other little girls my age.

"Miss Margaret, you're a cheap date, my little bird. You let Aunt Helen know when you're ready for something fancy. We'll set you right up. Yes, we will, love."

Fancy was within my grasp, but I wanted none of it.

I was satisfied with light instead of dark. I preferred clean to dirty and warmth to cold. I liked the smell of soap, and Uncle Teddy's aftershave and shoe polish. I liked having a clean pair of underpants to slip on each night after a bath.

Our days were predictable and gentle, and I clung to the rhythm we three shared. I was doted upon and loved. This was enough for me and more than enough for them.

There was little talk about why I'd come to them in such a state. At night, after I'd been tucked into bed and kissed, and allowed to leave my night light on, I heard them talking softly. Sometimes, they laughed. Aunt Helen asked questions with her soft voice that made me want to spring from my bed and rush down the hall into her arms.

"It's a miracle that little thing survived, isn't it?"

"She's come a long way since then, hasn't she?"

"We're keeping her, Teddy, aren't we? Tell me she can stay."

To each of these questions, I could hear my gentle giant of an uncle say what my aunt wanted to hear most.

"Yes, Love, it is a miracle. You're right about that."

"Yes, she has come along nicely. She sure has."

"Of course, Helen. We're keeping her. She has nobody to come along and take her from us. You don't have to worry about that, love. We're keeping our little bird."

I could not see them from down the hall, but I'd come to know these lovelies for the sweet talk between them. Uncle Teddy's growl was deep and throaty enough to scare away intruders, but Aunt Helen and I knew better. We were his girls. For us, he reserved his husky love, a smile, and crinkling eyes that twinkled and winked in our direction.

He had names for us. Aunt Helen was Helly, and Love, Sweetheart, and his Beauty Queen. I answered to Margaret when he was serious, but more often Little Bird, Ragdoll and Tiny One.

He touched my face and tousled my hair. The longer my braid grew down my back, he liked to tug at it and kiss me goodnight right on my forehead, like he was my father.

His touches for his Helly were not fatherly, but lovely to observe from across the room. He pulled her to him with his hand on her waist, and planted kisses at the back of her neck, a spot he was adept at finding with his strong hands and smiling mouth. She'd protest at first, but quickly surrender, letting him gobble her up, even if I was right there, watching and giggling.

Aunt Helly was also his girl. They did not hide what they shared between them from me. Still, there were exchanges that left me, even as a child, understanding that the two of them existed before me, that they were happy before I arrived—so dirty and needing everything.

"You're frosting on our cake, Little Bird."

I liked the thought of this.

Aunt Helen considered me a final flourish to something that was already sweet and solid without me.

Chapter Twenty-One

Clarice

Lem Hauser had no business hanging around Lee. She was fifteen years old, and that no-good daddy of hers should have been there to protect her. Our mama was surely turning over in her grave from all that was going on over there.

Larry agreed with me. We sat at the far end of the counter at Slapp's, stewing. Dinner hour was over, and business was slow, so there was time for chit chat.

"You want a sandwich?"

"Sure."

Larry knew I'd sneak him a burger and fries, or whatever was on special that day. He was my little brother, and even though he was a grown man, turning thick at the waist and through his arms and neck, all I could see was the scrawny little boy he used to be. He still seemed hungry for whatever was put in front of him.

"Coming right up," I said. "I'll even throw in a chocolate malt and chips if you get yourself to the men's room and wash those hands. Little brother, those things are a mess. Mama taught you better than that."

I said it with a smile, but I meant it. We Downs had enough people looking down their snotty noses at us. They didn't need any more fuel for their fire. We were poor, but we weren't Shakey's Half poor. We never sank that low and we weren't about to, not on my watch. We needed to keep ourselves clean. That was no problem for me, but Larry, working on those engines and who knows what else, seemed to have dirty hands all the time.

"Alright, alright, Sister. You got me. I'll do the best I can."

He headed toward the washroom for a good scrub, but he couldn't help himself from throwing me sass.

"You know, you can tell your snotty friends that come in here that my hands might *look* dirty, but they get dunked in hot, soapy water fifteen times a day. I bet my hands are cleaner than most people in this stuck-up town."

He was right about that. But we both knew, deep down, that what mattered most was how things looked.

"Hush Lawrence. Hush up and I'll throw some extra chocolate into your malt."

I closed out the last customer, locked the front door and let the good people of Poulson know that Slapp's Diner was closed just by simply turning the sign that said so. I loved that part of each day, when it got quiet, and I could add up my tips at the counter before I scooped them into my front pocket.

"Don't spend all that in one place, Sister."

I placed two baskets with club sandwiches and chips in front of us. It was the best I could do that night.

"One of these days, little brother, I'm going to have a place of my own. No more renting for me. I'm gonna have my own cute little place someday. You just watch."

Larry smiled and shook his head at my big, impossible plans.

"Well, aren't you something, Clarice? Don't get too big for your britches, Sister. Don't forget your dirty janitor brother once you get those keys to your castle."

I smiled. Larry didn't think I could do it, but he could sit by and watch me, like everyone else in town. I would have me my own place one day. One shift at a time, I'd save enough for something small.

As we ate, we hashed out the latest bad news from Jim's.

"Oh, goddamn," said Larry. "Are you sure about this, Clarice? Not everything you hear in this damned place is the honest to God's truth."

"Don't you think I know that? I'm sure it's true. We can't just sit around and wait for it to get worse than it already is."

"Will you calm down and let me think?"

"Well don't shoot the messenger. Would you rather I keep this shit show all to myself?"

Larry slurped up the last of his malt. I knew this would happen, and so did he. Lee, our wild little half-blood sister, was pregnant. The proud papa was Lem. That shiftless bottom feeder liked his new set up with Lee Marks and our stepfather, Jim. It was sure better than his makeshift tent and taking dumps out in the woods. He had a warm cot, plenty of smokes and most nights he enjoyed access to a wild, foolish girl.

My brother and I sat there in the quiet, letting that truth sink in.

"What would Mama think?"

"She'd want me to pay a visit to Jim, that's what."

Larry's lips were tight and determined. I put my hand on his, which still looked dirty.

"Let's think about that, Honey. That might be dangerous. We know Jim's been drinking."

There was no doubt about that. We were both sure that Jim never raised a hand to Lee. We'd never seen that in him. The worst harm he did didn't come from his fists or dirty boots. His damage was done by saying nothing, doing nothing and letting the wild world around him spin hard without putting up even a hint of a fight.

We couldn't say the same about Lem. We didn't know much about the man from the woods, but we knew enough. Any grown man who could wind his way to the likes of Jim Marks for safe harbor and stay long enough to make moves on our scrawny kid sister had low standards. We might just find him warming his belly on the ground, or if we were lucky, he'd have slithered back into the woods.

We cleaned up the dishes and Larry gave me a lift home. As we watched our breath make smoke in the cold air, we hatched a plan to pay our stepfather and his houseguest a visit. We wouldn't be there to make friends. Our business was easier than that.

We weren't going to leave without Lee. We owed at least that much to Mama, the baby on the way, and even to Lee, that little fool.

Larry pulled the truck up in front of my apartment. I was too tired and worked up to invite him in.

"See you in the morning, right?"

"Yes, Ma'am. Just one question. Are you sure I can't throw a punch, maybe two?"

"No punching, Brother. We're going there to rescue that kiddo, and that's it."

I watched Larry drive off to his place, the top half of an old house on Jackson Street he shared with a handful of bus drivers and friends from high school. I'd never set foot inside it, but it sounded like quite a set-up. The whole lot of them were pleased with themselves that they'd talked the landlord into putting a new plywood door on the bathroom. It even had a hook and eye lock.

Still, I was proud of that kid. That was my job. He needed his big sister to throw him a bone every now and then.

Chapter Twenty-Two

Margaret Burns

One summer night, after Aunt Helly and Uncle Teddy cheered me on from the porch swing as I caught one firefly after another, and after I'd been tucked into bed, I heard them talking quietly and laughing out on the front porch. The laughter subsided, and so did the talking, but their soft murmurs and the quiet spaces that floated between those sounds made me happy enough to scamper down the stairs in my bare feet. Standing just out of their sight in the frame of the front door in my white cotton night gown, I was treated to proof that these two did not need me, but they had *chosen* me.

Aunt Helly was wearing a white nightgown, too. Her feet, small and ladylike, were bare. I'd never seen my aunt without shoes. Her dark brown hair had been released and hung long and wavy down her back. Uncle Teddy stood behind her. The sleeves of his shirt were rolled up, exposing strong, thick arms. He had her hairbrush in his hand, the one she kept on her bureau next to a hand mirror and a jar of powder I was sometimes allowed to dust my neck with after a bath.

As Uncle Teddy slowly pulled the brush through Aunt Helly's hair, dragging it gently from the top of her head all the way down to the base of her back, her hands rested in her lap and her eyes were closed. He only paused to pull her hair to one side so he could plant a kiss lovely enough to make his Beauty Queen open her eyes and encourage him with a slow, knowing smile.

Their secrets were not meant for me to know.

"Someday, Little Margaret Bird, you'll have your own husband and your very own house. You just wait and see."

"Oh, no she won't, Aunt Helen. No, she won't."

Uncle Teddy winked.

"Margaret and I made a deal, didn't we?"

He was right. We had a deal. My uncle was always asking me to keep an impossible promise, and before I knew better, I'd crossed my heart and agreed. Even thinking about it now, as an old woman, I start to melt.

"Little Bird, I need you to promise me something."

Uncle Teddy always came up with something silly for us to think about. But he looked serious this time. He took my cheeks into his hands and pulled my face close to his.

"You've got to promise me that you're going to stay five years old. You're perfect just like this. Will you do that for me, Margaret? Do you think you can manage to stay five forever and ever?"

That sounded easy enough. By the time I'd turned five, things were good. I didn't want to change a thing.

I nodded vigorously, which earned me a sweet bear hug and his deep, delighted laugh. With each birthday, or every time I needed new shoes or tights, my uncle would tease me, but it soon became clear that I was not keeping my end of our deal.

"Now, Margaret, we need to have a little chat. Didn't you promise me that you were going to stay five? I'm sure you did. And look at you. Already turned seven and needing bigger shoes! What happened?"

He chased me around the room, which I loved, especially when I could stop and hide behind Aunt Helen.

"Now, don't you protect this girl, Helly! She deserves to be tickled, so let me at her!"

Year after year, I broke our promise until I was almost as tall as my aunt. The three of us made our own world. We didn't need anyone else to complete us and that warmth continued for years and years.

I was of marriageable age when Aunt Helly got sick. Finally, I was needed, in this case to nurse my beloved aunt. I wiped her brow and kept her long hair brushed. I changed her sheets and coaxed her to eat to keep up her strength, just like she'd done for me.

Watching her body diminish made me feel like a scared child all over again. The sweat, her dry lips and her prominent bones that looked like they could snap if I handled her too roughly made our goodbye long and hard.

Poor Uncle Teddy with his bear hugs and delightful swagger, kept insisting that it was all just a rough patch.

"We'll have my Beauty Queen patched back up in no time. Yes, we will. You watch."

He'd flash a bright smile even as his eyes glistened with tears.

I thought Aunt Helly's passing would become our hardest thing to endure. It was plenty hard. Sitting there with her while we waited for the funeral home to take her body shook me. Opening her wardrobe to find her best dress, slip and stockings for the funeral made me weep, as did the funeral, the gravesite, all the visitors, and the empty house.

But it wasn't those things that hollowed me out. That came days later, after people stopped dropping by with food. For everyone else in Poulson, our sad event was over.

The floor slowly gave way as I watched Uncle Teddy diminish. I'd grown accustomed to seeing this giant, loving man cry, but it was other sights and sounds that haunted me, like red-rimmed eyes, sniffles, weak smiles, staring out the window, food not eaten and endless quiet.

I felt such a strong desire to comfort and protect this man, as if he were my real father and Aunt Helen had been my real mother. I owed them everything.

As time passed, my uncle and I took care of each other. After a while, we were even able to talk about Helen without crying.

"That's good, isn't it, Little Bird? Aunt Helly would be proud of us, wouldn't she?"

I smiled and gave Uncle Teddy a hug.

She would be proud of how we carried on. But there was one thing Uncle Teddy would never know. One night, several weeks after Helen passed, the sounds I heard coming from that great big bear of a man scared me.

His sobbing and high-pitched moans as he called out for his Beauty Queen made me wonder for the first time what this kind man must have looked and sounded like as a little boy afraid of the dark. The separation from her cut him to the quick. I listened from down the hall, knowing he would be ashamed if I saw him like that.

I realized then that I would never allow myself to have something so wonderful as they had. The loss of a love that big could leave me wailing when it was gone.

Chapter Twenty-Three

Clarice

God love him. That little brother of mine is a funny one. Solid. Larry is a fixer. He knows his way around tools and can rig up anything just using what he finds around the house. The truth is, he was smarter than the boys in his class. I'd rather be stuck on the side of the road with Larry Downs than any one of those preppy pricks.

He's not afraid of the dark, hard work or any of the elements. He doesn't mind being too cold or hot. He'll kill a spider for you, tackle a hornet's nest, or coax a raccoon out of the attic—if you ask nicely. He'll try new foods, and he never special orders anything at the diner. He likes chocolate ice cream the best, but vanilla or strawberry make him just as happy, if that's all you got in the freezer.

I would say that my brother is fearless on nearly every count, but one dirty trick in this world makes him all dainty. If a good-sized bird gets near him, he'll run for the hills, squealing like a little girl. Any critter with feathers and a beak that's bigger than Lee's little parakeet's terrifies my big and burly little brother.

The boy who picked up black snakes out of the backyard barehanded without blinking and threaded worms on hooks before he could tie his shoes will shudder and jump when the geese come up from the lake at the park, looking for bread. He'll go sit in the truck while we finish throwing them scraps. Chickens scare the shit out of him. The owl that perched outside the window of my first apartment made him nervous enough to insist that we close the windows, even in summer.

"Clarice, close that damned window or I'm leaving!"

"You're kidding me, right? It's hotter than hell and we need a breeze up here."

"Sister, that owl out there is a bird of prey. It has claws sharper than a tiger's teeth. Close the window right now, or I'm taking my iced tea and leaving."

Larry didn't ask for much. I closed the window and chuckled. That was the least I could do to keep him safe from the birds.

When we headed over to Jim's to get pregnant Lee out of that house and away from Lem Hauser, we decided to arrive bearing gifts. We needed to butter Jim up with a box of doughnuts. Lee would like them, too, and she could be talked into things if there was something extra in it for her. In addition to the doughnuts, I tucked a Sears catalog under my arm, prepared to let her pick out a frilly bedspread and pillows for the bedroom in my apartment. Any color she wanted, and I might throw in a matching lamp if I could get her to leave that nasty place and those two stinky men behind to stay with me.

The house stood at the end of the lane; its path lined with pine trees Daddy had planted long ago. They needed a good trim. The leaves in the yard hadn't been raked in years. The shutters looked scaly, in need of a good scrape and a fresh coat of paint. Jim had let all kinds of scrap metal clutter up the side yard. Our old tire swing was hanging at the end of a tired yellow rope that had seen better days.

"Looks like somebody's home," said Larry. "Let's do this."

He grabbed the doughnuts as we hopped out of the truck. Mama's concrete goose was still by the stoop, peeking out from the weeds.

"Give it a knock, and smile, Sister."

I knocked and we waited. Then, I knocked a little bit louder, but nobody stirred.

"I'll check the back door," said Larry. "Hold the doughnuts."

He made his way toward the back, pushing a pile of rusty bikes out of the way. I steeled myself to face Jim. He was such a piece of work that I wanted to get this part over with. I wished Mama had never met the fool. I was prepared to give him the facts and make our demand sound more like an offer.

The box of doughnuts had his favorites: jelly, long johns, and fresh bear claws he always liked. I didn't know what kind Lem liked. He was such an odd one, he probably never even had a doughnut. He struck me as a beef jerky man.

I heard a curdling, girlish scream from the back. Was someone dead? For about two seconds, I hoped we'd find Lem and Jim keeled over in the backyard. I ran through the dried leaves across the front yard as fast as I could.

It was Larry, and his screaming sounded very serious. As I turned the corner, I saw my burly little brother on top of an old picnic table, balancing as best as he could. He was shrieking for help, like a big old sissy boy.

Standing less than a foot away was the biggest male peacock I'd ever seen. Larry must have startled the thing. Its beautiful plumes were on full display, spread as wide and high as they would go. The wind pushed at the plumes gently, but they stood erect and alert. This was a standoff. No doubt about it. The bird was majestic, sending my brother a beautiful warning. All spread out like that, its feathers nearly spanned the length of the table and would have reached as high as my neck. That bird was standing his ground.

"Clarice! Get my gun! It's in the box at the back of my truck. Go, Sister! Go!"

He was frantic. His wild gestures made the bird nervous, and it took another step toward the table and Larry.

"Goddammit, Clarice! Get my fucking gun! What are you waiting for? This thing is coming after me!"

"Oh, Jesus Christ, Larry. Come on! We're not going to kill this bird. Calm down. Carrying on like that is scaring him. Calm yourself and let me think."

"I won't calm down. You get my gun or get in the truck and bring back the police! Do something. Don't just stand there!"

The police. Good idea. It didn't seem like Jim, Lee or Lem were anywhere to be found. If they were asleep in the house, all the noise would have surely brought them outside. Knowing what I knew about Lem, they were inside watching the show. I turned to make a run for the truck.

"No wait, Clarice. Wait! Don't go. Don't leave me here alone with this thing!"

I kept my chuckles to myself. This was ridiculous.

"Larry, just hop down and walk past the bird."

He shook his head.

"I'm not doing that. This fucker has claws and look at that beak! This is an exotic bird, Clarice. Exotic. Do something!"

The bird wasn't moving.

"I am not killing this bird, Larry. I'm not doing that."

I set the box of treats on the ground so I could think. Aha! The doughnuts. I opened the lid and pulled out a great big, fresh glazed one. It was still warm. Such a shame to waste on a damned bird.

"Do peacocks like doughnuts?"

"Oh, funny, Clarice. Very funny."

"Larry, listen to me. I'm serious. If I can distract the thing with a doughnut, to get it moved over to the other side of the yard, you can hop down and come back this way."

"Okay. Let's do that. Toss it over by the fence."

"Well, he's got to know what I'm offering him."

"Don't get too close! He's dangerous. Be careful."

I muttered cuss words under my breath that would have surprised old Jim and Lem and shocked our mama. I inched my way toward the big, beautiful creature with the glazed treat in my outstretched hand. I moved closer, broke off a piece, and threw it on the ground in front of the bird. His plumes contracted and expanded as he moved toward it. He pecked and poked, then finally gobbled it right up.

Larry was delighted.

"Good. He likes it."

I used the doughnuts to coax the bird toward the other end of the yard until the coast was clear. Larry hopped off the table and ran toward the truck. I threw the rest of the box toward the bird and followed him. We sat in the truck, catching our breath. I looked over at my brother and couldn't help but notice a wet spot on his pants.

"Well, that went plenty smooth."

I gave a nod toward his little accident.

"You've pissed yourself, little brother, and now a wild bird is eating all the doughnuts, and we don't have Lee in this truck."

As we backed out of the driveway, a sleepy looking Lem showed up on the front stoop, grinning like he'd enjoyed the show. I rolled down the window and hollered at the son of a gun.

"We're coming back, Lem. We're coming back!"

We didn't say much on the trip back to my apartment. Our pregnant little sister was about to pop. She ate her meals from the gas station or what I brought by from Slapp's, and the baby's father was spending his money on expensive birds. Knowing Lem, he'd made himself some kind of wild ass trade. I was going to have to take care of this myself.

Chapter Twenty-Four

Violet

After months and months of cutting myself to ribbons, each little stab brought less pleasure. That meant I had to seek pain that was deeper and more satisfying, just like Jules said I would.

Together, we chased that lemon juice edge. A simple cut alone was no longer enough. We looked for ways to enhance the sting. He showed me how to prepare my skin so it would be extra sensitive before each cut. And just like the lemon juice trick, we sought more ways to prolong what we felt after the initial pierce.

Broken glass was a surprising favorite. Those cuts felt almost gritty, like the shard left a trail of daggers to remind me how dangerous and subversive my newfound love for opening my skin had become.

"When was your first time?"

I asked Jules one day, after we'd both cut ourselves behind our knees with Gloria's paring knife.

I wasn't sure he would answer me. Jules could go quiet sometimes, and I was almost afraid to hear his answer. He came from a family with nothing. I'd heard Skip and Gloria's whispering about it one afternoon when they were sure I was out of earshot. Their phrases were loaded with contempt:

"*Piss poor . . . slim pickings . . . bottom feeders . . . takers.*"

Hearing those words made me feel more sorry for Jules than I did before. Sometimes, I forgot he was poor. He was always willing to cut a little deeper than me. His blood seemed darker and thicker than mine. He had something different running through his veins. I was sure of it.

Jules told me a story that should have frightened me, but I found myself drawn to it. He started mingling his pleasure with pain at an early age, when his mother shaved his head in her mad rush to get rid of his latest crop of head bugs.

"I must have been five. I know I was in kindergarten because I missed the Valentine's Day party at school. My valentines were waiting for me in an envelope in my cubby when I got back. It was cold, and Momma didn't want to stink up the house, so she took me out back and had me hold my head over an old bucket. She used a big cup to dump kerosene over my freezing head."

Jules said the tears stung his eyes and he wasn't sure if it was the kerosene that made them burn or the agony he felt as it soaked into the spots where his mother hadn't been careful with the razor. She'd left more than one nick open to the penetrating sting of her home remedy.

"I didn't cry much, though. I decided to stop because I could see Peg and Suze pressing their faces against the window from inside. Their little babydoll heads had been shaved, too, and they were next. It was gonna sting them soon enough, so I made myself laugh as hard as I could. That's all I could do. I laughed and laughed, so they wouldn't worry about what was coming. And then, while I stood in the house and heard them howling and screaming, I cried long and loud to drown out that awful sound."

I should have been satisfied with his horrible story. The old Violet might have cried or offered a hug. But I was hungry for more. Jules was deep in thought and went quiet again. He and I could stay quiet when we were together without feeling any need to say stuff just for the sake of answering the silence.

Those empty spaces meant that something worth hearing would be said soon enough. Jules was as exact and precise with his words as he was with his cuts. But this time, even though it was gutsy and bold and maybe even cruel, I probed further into the fresh wound Jules shared so openly with me.

"But that was someone else hurting you, Jules. What about the first time you cut yourself?"

I looked straight at him. Jules didn't seem to mind. He shot me an approving look, like I was his eager apprentice. I'd done him proud. His approval sent a surge of pleasure right through me.

He wiped his face with the sleeve of his jacket and started picking at the ragged cuticles of his fingernails with his teeth.

Jules was selecting his words, thinking carefully about each one he wanted me to have.

Chapter Twenty-Five

Clarice

I went back for Lee.

With the promise of a fluffy, lavender bedspread and matching sheets, I coaxed my little sister out of Jim's house. Together, we marched past Jim and Lem and that damned bird of his, which had left poop all over the stoop and down the driveway. The shambles we were leaving was no place for a fifteen-year-old girl with a baby on the way.

Larry was waiting for us at the apartment. He'd assembled a crib that sat in the corner of the bedroom I'd given up for Lee. For the time being, I would sleep on the couch.

That night, the three of us ate TV dinners and drank soda. Lee's shirt was stretched tight across her belly, and she was too far along by then to worry about maternity clothes. The warm food and soda must have given the baby a burst of energy. We could see our little sister's midsection move and shape shift as the child she carried tried to get more comfortable in such tight quarters.

Larry was especially fascinated by all the movement.

"Damn, girl, that kid of yours likes Coca-Cola, don't he?"

Lee nodded. She was already dozing off. She was about to become a mother, but she was in sore need of some mothering herself. Poor kid.

"Lee, honey, you should get yourself to bed," I said. "It's been a big day, and you're going to need your rest."

She didn't fight me and let me slip her into an old, roomy tee shirt. I tucked that little mama into her new frilly bed and left the hall light on, just like I did when she was little and still scared of the dark.

Larry and I watched her sleep.

"Well, Sister, you did it."

"*We* did it, Larry. We."

"Was that goddamned bird still there, shitting all over the place?"

"Yep."

I could tell Larry was a little ashamed that he'd cried like a girl and pissed his pants because of that damned thing, but I let it go. Last time I went there, I called ahead to make sure the peacock was put in a pen. A new box of doughnuts made it safely into the house, and after an hour or so, I talked Lee into coming with me. Jim and Lem didn't put up much of a fight. I was thankful for that, and plenty sad, too. They didn't care if she came or went. I think Lem would have made more of a fuss if I'd tried to load his exotic bird into the back of Larry's truck. It made my brother sick, too. He was the only one I could say any of this to who would understand.

"What the fuck is that poor white trash Lem Hauser doing spending his money on a peacock when he's got no pot to piss in and a child on the way? That's what I want to know."

"I have no idea, but Jim Marks is no better. What's he doing letting the likes of Lem move in with him, carrying on with Lee like that? It's a disgrace. I miss her, but I'm glad Mama's not here to see this mess."

"Me too, Clarice. I guess we just wait, now, right?"

"Yeah. I'll be at the diner first thing. Lee will be okay by herself for a few days, and I'll be home at night. It looks like she's about to pop, so we won't have to wait long."

"Then what, Clarice? What will we do once the baby comes?"

I had to think about that one. I hadn't thought that far ahead. We were going to have to wing it and do what we could to keep Lee from bolting back to what she considered freedom.

"I'm not sure, Larry. We'll take it one day at a time, I guess."

Chapter Twenty-Six

Larry Downs

That baby could grow on you. Cute little bugger. Mama would have eaten Jules right up. Then again, if Mama was alive, that baby never would have been born. There's no way she would've let that Lem come sniffing around our Lee. There'd be no fucking peacocks strutting through the yard and no lizards scaling the walls of the garage. But Mama was long gone, leaving me and Clarice to take care of the whole goddamned mess.

I worried about Lee. She was our blood, after all. But that girl was hard to protect. I was afraid to tell Clarice what I was thinking. She might not like it if I sounded like I was giving up on that girl. Maybe that was true. She had a strong will. Never would be tamed. Not really. Our best bet was to set our sights on that baby. He was worth saving.

Once he started filling out, that baby boy grew on me. He was hard to resist. It might have been girly of me, but I just loved his doughy little arms. They brought a smile to my face every time I got to see him, especially when I got a chance to sniff around his sticky little baby neck. Jules smelled so warm and sweet. It made me wish I was the boy's daddy, not just his uncle.

Chapter Twenty-Seven

Clarice

Jules arrived four days later. He was a tiny one, so I was relieved when the hospital said they'd keep him and his scrawny little mama a bit longer so he could put some meat on his bones. His soft little face reminded me of baby Lee. It was hard not to feel sorry for the little booger. Jules didn't know it yet, but he'd have to toughen up.

When it was time to bring them home to my apartment, I waited outside the hospital with Lee and Jules for Larry to pull up in his truck.

We took turns with fussy Jules, who always preferred to be held. Once in a while, when he'd calm down, he'd look us over as if he was wondering who these three fools were taking care of him. My nephew, with his wise baby face, could probably tell he'd drawn the short straw.

I wished our healthy old mama would show up at the front door and take over. Once she got over the shock of it all, she'd have us whipped into shape. I hoped she'd be proud of Larry and me for doing what we thought was right.

Lee was squeamish about breastfeeding, so we opted for bottles. I didn't fight her on it, even though breastfeeding was what we could afford. I washed diapers and bottles, and took turns with her holding that precious baby, all the while working at Slapp's.

Nothing felt good about leaving Lee alone with a helpless baby all day, but we didn't have any options. Before I headed out the door each morning, I'd make sure that the little man had a clean diaper and a full tummy. I'd hold his soft cheek to mine as his head bobbed up and down against my face.

"Okay, Jules Martin, you be a good baby today. No fussing, you hear me? You got that, Little Man?"

As he got older and wiser, I knew he preferred me to his mama. It was our little secret. He would reach for me with his arms outstretched, begging me with those deep brown eyes to pull him to safety, away from Lee's slapdash clutches.

She was scrawny and wobbly, and she used to hold him on her hip in a casual way you might expect from a babysitter or older cousin, but not a mama. She was not careful with him, no matter how much I coached her. She'd let him stew in his soggy diapers longer than I liked. He didn't seem to mind all that much, but I'd usually cave and change him before lazy Lee got around to it.

"Lee, I want you to come here and look at this little boy's bottom. Do you see that red all over? That's diaper rash, and it doesn't feel good. That's what happens if you let him sit around in soggy pants all day. You're his mama, Honey, and it's up to you to make sure he's dry. Jules is counting on you."

For a second, Lee would appear interested, nodding slightly to get me off her back. She barely watched as I smeared cream all over and secured Jules with a tight, dry diaper like he deserved.

There was no saving any money from my tip jar that first year. All my spare change and much of my pay went to rent and buying food. Not a cent came from Jim or that shiftless Lem. Good riddance.

Lee grew up a little, but not nearly enough. Larry came by often, usually with a toy for Jules. As I watched him with our nephew, it seemed like our brother had the makings of a good father. If he could find the right girl, someone sweet, but not too fussy, that might be nice.

Sometimes, we'd stew about the lack of interest or help from the peacock farm, but it was just as well. We didn't want any of their white trash stink luring Lee back to Lem and Jim or dripping its foul odor on the baby. Best to leave that right where it was.

Word got around that Lem had added new critters to the mix. He had himself one kooky, expensive menagerie out there after adding another peacock and a big lizard that roamed free in the garage. That news, once confirmed, set my brother and I off again.

"What the hell is he thinking? How's that shiftless son of a bitch scraping together money for another fucking bird? And a lizard?"

During all that time, we had one saving grace. Gloria Sellers, my friend from the diner, the one who was in the hospital at the same time as Lee, kept dropping by with clothes and food and all kinds of things for Lee and Jules. Gloria had her own baby, named Violet, to love on, but she had money to throw around. She was generous and lovely, and offered those gifts with such a sweet intent that I was thankful. I kept reminding my little sister how lucky she was to have someone doing all that for her.

"I sure hope you're saying thank you for all of this, Lee."

One afternoon, Gloria dropped off shopping bags of brand-new clothes for Jules from Kline's Department Store. Gorgeous overalls and little turtlenecks, undershirts and new bibs and shoes that were cute as a button, and way out of our price range.

Little Jules was dressed to the nines, and so was Lee. Her clothes came wrapped like gifts, one nicer than the next.

At Christmas time, Gloria picked up Lee and Jules and took them down to Kline's to have Jules' picture taken on Santa's lap. Santa didn't have to lift a finger that year. Gloria took care of making sure we had a tree, with presents underneath it, and a stocking for the baby.

"What does Mr. Gloria do for a living?" Larry said.

"He's a banker," I said, "so they've got enough to spend."

"Wonder how long *that's* going to last."

I wondered the same myself. Either that husband of hers was going to get tired of being the gravy train, or Lee was going to mess it up. She was starting to seem even more itchy and scratchy. She was restless, and her fancy bedspread was old hat by then. She started catting around again, and often talked Gloria into watching Jules while I was at the diner and Larry was at school.

I didn't like it.

"Lee, you listen to me. You're taking advantage of Gloria. I don't think I've ever heard you say *thank you*, little lady. Not once. She's gonna get tired of you, and I wouldn't blame her. Not one bit."

I took Gloria aside a time or two to let her know she'd done enough. We didn't expect this to go on and on. It wasn't right. But Gloria just smiled at me or waved me off.

"Clarice Downs. I wouldn't do this if I didn't want to or couldn't, so you hush. It's my pleasure to help Lee and that darling Jules, and you, too. One of these days, Lee won't need me one bit, and that will be that. Until then, just let me help."

I was thankful, but wary. Our little sister was going to blow it. I just knew it was only a matter of when.

I loved that scrawny kid. Lee and I have the same nose and build. We're both skin and bones, with sunken chests that make us look like we're always hungry. We picked up those bony bits from Mama, right along with our pointed beaks.

But we had different papas. Mine was tired most of the time, but he was solid and reliable. With his blood running through us, Larry and I had common sense. Our eyes could take in the facts around us and make sense out of what worked.

Lee's blood ran thinner, though. Her daddy, Jim Starks, had a wily weakness about him. He slid right in with a charming smile that swept

Mama off her feet but dropped her on the floor when nobody else was paying attention.

He and Lee shared a steely recklessness that showed itself in fits and starts, just unpredictable enough to keep you on your toes. Lee had a wildness about her that made the average person skittish. Sometimes, I could coax my little sister off the ledge or bribe her with a trail of treats toward dry land. But there were just as many times that she snuck out the door like a feral cat who would come back when she damned well pleased.

I knew the pretty bedspread and matching lamp would lose their magic before long. Lee loved on baby Jules when it suited her, but she couldn't be counted on to keep him dry and clean, let alone cuddled.

That baby boy preferred me, even Larry, to his flesh and blood mother. She was smart enough to know this and let it sting her. If it hit her in a soft spot, it made her ready to pick a fight with an aggression that shocked us.

Larry and I would have never spoken to adults like that, not without getting our faces slapped, but Lee was a different story.

Chapter Twenty-Eight

Gloria

Skip thought I'd gone too far. For the longest while, he didn't mind that I helped out Lee and Jules. A kind gesture here and there didn't wound his banker instincts too much. But there were secrets hidden in the receipts at the bottom of my purse. I spent as much on Lee and Jules as I did on our Violet.

I liked our buying power. I liked being able to show someone how easy it was for me to treat them and introduce them to the finer things.

Since Skip was brand new to fatherhood and the actual price of children's things, my husband had no real way to know the difference between reasonable and ridiculous.

Right before Vi's first birthday, before we had our combined family over for cake, ice cream, balloons and presents, he started to poke around our finances a little. That was his right. He was earning the money I was plucking off trees and spending so freely. The only nudge he needed was a large pile of presents in the corner of the dining room, wrapped in blue with bright red ribbons.

"Gloria, are these for Vi?"

"Oh, no, Honey. Vi's gifts are upstairs. They're wrapped in pink, silly. The blue and red ones are for Jules."

He nodded, took a sip of his iced tea, and peered out the window. I busied myself tidying up the living room. As my pulse picked up, my face flushed. I felt caught, slightly ashamed and self-conscious. We'd never quarreled about money at all. The air in the room felt like it needed filling.

I croaked a weak explanation for Skip.

"It's nothing much, really."

That was a great big lie. I'd spent more on Jules for his birthday than I did for Violet. Our lucky girl would have presents to open for the rest of her life—from us, from grandparents, aunts, and uncles, but poor little Jules had no such bounty coming his way.

I looked at the birthday pile that I needed to deliver to Lee and her baby, feeling guilty and defensive, but righteous and indignant.

"Honey, that's the sweetest, and I love you for it, really, I do," said Skip. "But it's too much. I'm sure Jules is great, and I know he was born at the same time as Violet, but we don't owe him or his mother anything. We don't. You've done *enough*. One small gift would have been more than enough. I see at least ten packages over there. It's overkill, Gloria. Once you deliver those, that's it for a while."

My cheeks burned. Skip's observation wasn't wrong. It was spot on. I knew it, and I didn't like it one bit.

I stomped off to our bedroom and slammed the door behind me. I didn't appreciate the chiding. I pressed my hot face down on our bed and let the heat engulf me.

Skip's comment had sapped the joy I'd come to experience by heaping myself onto this wretched girl and her innocent child. His tone, the authority with which he delivered his edict, wounded me.

As I walked back to my car after delivering the gifts to Lee and having received no *thank you* from her at all, I decided then and there that enough was enough. Skip was right. The Gloria gravy train was pulling out of the station. I slept on it that night after I'd tucked our own baby in tight.

I woke up the next morning feeling sure I'd made the right decision. Skip was already at the office. He worked awfully hard, trading his time and smarts to keep us living comfortably. We didn't need to apologize for that to anyone with less good fortune. I could break this one-way friendship with a child and her baby with a squeaky-clean conscience.

As I fed Vi, she sounded a little stuffy and her eyes looked glassy. I hadn't been a mother all that long, but I could detect it when my baby was coming down with something. A little fresh air would perk her up. We needed a walk. Just as I zipped up my parka and bundled Vi up to weather the chill, the phone rang. It was Lee.

Shit. My resolve was being put to the test. The fates weren't so sure if I was strong enough to follow through. They knew me well.

"Hello there, Lee. How are you? How's that Jules?"

There was no need for me to be rude. I could still be friendly with my charge card tucked away.

She was breathless and sounded desperate.

There had been an argument with Clarice. She and Jules had to get out of there, and right away. I let that girl pull me right under. I didn't even try to save myself. My plan to walk around the block with Violet was quickly aborted.

I loaded her into the car and headed over to Clarice's apartment to make a valiant rescue. It wouldn't cost us any money, so Skip would have to calm down. I was needed, and I knew it deep inside. With my own sick child strapped in for the ride, I had some saving to do.

Chapter Twenty-Nine

Clarice

Lee took off right after we celebrated Jules' first birthday. She was used to my nagging and coaxing, but we had ourselves a spat. I hurt her feelings, and she hurt mine.

I made Jules a birthday cake and Larry brought a carton of ice cream. Larry, Lee and I wore party hats, and while there was a pile of presents in the corner from Gloria, we decided to open our own simple gifts first. We didn't need anything fancy that day. I got him a stuffed frog and Larry brought a red firetruck. All the fun tuckered our baby out. I wiped the cake off him in the sink and put on a fresh diaper. He was ready for a bottle.

"Lee, Honey, can you warm up a bottle for Jules?"

"No can do. We're fresh out of milk."

Shit. Larry had already left, which meant I'd need to go get some. I swore I'd just bought two cartons. Oh, well. Poor baby needed milk.

"Come get this little man and I'll run to the store."

I handed Jules over to Lee, who shrugged as she took him. I wanted her to hold him a little tighter, to plant a mama kiss on his cheek. He deserved that, at least on his birthday.

"Okay, but hurry up," Lee said. "He's winding up and I never can get him calmed down like you."

The trip across town took longer than I hoped, and the line at the store was long. As I stood there with my two cartons of milk, I was sure that Jules was pitching a fit and Lee was probably not giving him much comfort at all.

I finally made my way back to my apartment. Much to my surprise, Jules had cried himself to sleep on his birthday.

"Lee? Lee, Honey, I'm home!"

"I'm back here."

I walked to the room she shared with Jules.

"Shush now, Clarice."

Lee nodded toward the crib. I tiptoed over, sure I would see our tuckered-out baby snoozing with his butt in the air and his thumb in his mouth, like he always did.

The Good Lord had decided to give us all a birthday break.

Jules was lying on his back, holding a bottle with his pudgy hands, guzzling as fast and frantic as he could. I could see by the tears in his eyes and the slime on the tip of his nose that he'd worked himself up into a lather.

"What's in that bottle, Lee?"

It wasn't milk.

"Oh, calm down, Clarice. I had to give him something. He was screaming so loud I didn't know what to do. What took you so long?"

"Lee, what's in the bottle?"

She was avoiding me. I walked over, tempted to pull the bottle right out of the baby's mouth, but I wouldn't need to. Close up, I could see that the liquid was brown.

"Lee Marks, did you put Coca-Cola in that bottle?"

She shrugged and wouldn't look me in the eye.

"It won't kill him. Calm down. He was thirsty and Coke was all we had. He likes it."

I could feel my face getting hot. Jules' eyes were finally closed. He had the longest lashes. Beautiful. He'd let the bottle, still sloshing with fizzy liquid, fall to his side. I snatched it out of the crib and covered up our baby with a blanket. I turned toward Lee, lounging there on her bed, without a care in the world. I wanted to throttle her. I think Mama would have approved.

"Lee! You don't give a baby a bottle full of soda! Not ever! What's the matter with you, girl? That baby deserves better!"

"You hush yourself, Sister, or you'll wake the kid up. What's the difference if he's got cold soda or milk? He liked it, didn't he? He'll be drinking it soon enough anyway. He's mine, and if I want to let him have soda, I will. He's mine, not yours."

"You won't be giving that baby soda under my roof, Lee. Not under my roof. You got that, little sister?"

She shrugged as I walked out of the room. Before I settled myself on the couch for the night, I put the cartons of milk in the fridge. There were six bottles of Coke lined up right next to the ketchup and mustard. I pulled every one of them out and fished out the bottle opener from the junk drawer. The streetlights out my kitchen window glared yellow for the bugs gathered for their nightly get-togethers. I watched them buzz while I opened all six bottles of soda and poured them out in the sink, fizzing and hissing down the drain.

The next morning, I changed Jules and sat with him on the couch while I fed him a warm bottle of milk. He patted my face as he gulped down the full bottle. Poor baby. Lee finally pulled herself out of bed and walked into the living room.

No apologies.

She snatched her son from my lap. He fussed but was distracted quickly enough by his new firetruck. I tidied up my uniform and grabbed my purse. Before I closed the door, I called out to my sullen little sister.

"Lee, we'll talk about this when I get home tonight. You hear me? I'll bring us supper from the diner."

I brought home two cheeseburger baskets and lemonades that night for supper. The burgers were fresh off the grill, hot and ready for me to extend them as a peace offering.

"Lee? You home? Lee, I brought us burgers and fries."

Usually, a treat would bring my half-sister out of the shadows, but the apartment was quiet. The pile of unopened birthday goodies from Gloria had been cleared from the corner.

"Lee? Lee! Jules? Jules Martin?"

I ran down the hall to the bedroom. Jules' crib was gone. The fancy sheets and bedspread and pillows had been stripped from Lee's bed. The dresser was empty and so was the closet.

Surely, they were out at Jim's again. Damn that little fool. I was worried about Lee. My little sister was a mess. She needed protecting but resisted us every step of the way.

I picked up the phone and dialed Larry. I'd need a lift out to the peacock farm to get that foolish child. I'd drag her by her scrawny neck if I had to. Jim and Lem wouldn't fight me.

As I waited for my brother to answer the phone, I felt a headache taking root at the back of my neck. This wasn't going to be the kind of light brown headache you bring with you to that first cup of morning coffee. This headache was going to be dark brown, thick and slow to dissolve with aspirin. It was an ache of the head that settled behind the eyes and stretched its legs to start kicking at my temples. These dark brown headaches of mine could only be chased away if I laid still on my bed in the dark for hours and hours.

No time for that kind of nonsense.

Larry finally answered the phone. He sounded groggy, like he'd been catching a few quiet winks himself.

"Hello?"

"Little brother, it's me."

"What's up?"

"She's gone, and so is Jules."

"What do you mean they're gone?"

"I mean their bodies are not in this apartment and all their things are gone. That's what I mean. She's out there with Jim and Lem. I'm sure of that. If she wants to stay there, I guess that's her business, but we're not leaving that baby boy with those good-for-nothings and their nasty birds and lizards."

"Ah, shit, Clarice. Shit. I'll get in the truck and come get you. I'll be there in ten minutes."

"Great, Brother. I'll be ready."

"Hey, Sis?"

"What?"

"Just need you to know that I'm bringing my gun with me, and this time, I'm going to use it. We're not fighting with doughnuts this time. You got that?"

I got it. And I was in no mood to come bearing gifts.

Chapter Thirty

Larry

"Clarice, let's make sure we agree on one thing before we knock on that door tonight."

"Larry, I already told you, you can shoot the damned birds if it makes you happy."

Clarice was tired. Her face looked slack and drawn, just like our mama's before she died. The streetlights must have been playing tricks on me. Clarice was not much older than me, so it was too early for her to start looking like that.

"No, I'm serious. Look at me."

She lifted her head and turned to me. I felt sorry for her. She was a strong one most of the time, but not then.

"You got you a sore head, Sister?"

Poor thing was fighting one of those nasty headaches of hers. She needed to lie still in the dark but she was out chasing down our foolish girl and a baby boy who needed something better. Seeing her like that made me angry. My big sister was always taking care of other folks, but never herself.

"Clarice, I'm serious, so listen to me. You're not gonna like this, but I just have to say it. Don't pitch a fit on me. Just listen, Honey. We might not be able to get Lee in this truck and back to the apartment. You know that, right?"

She nodded weakly. Her eyes were filling up with tears, but that chin of hers was jutting out strong and tough. She knew what I was about to say.

"We might not be able to save Lee. She might be too long gone for us to help much. We'll invite her, but that's not the fight you and me are here to fight. You got that? We're settling for Jules. He comes first, not that wild mother of his. You got me?"

I was talking to my big sister like I was the one born first, like I had the most sense, like I would take care of things, and hatch a plan. We drove down the driveway and parked in front of the garage. The stoop light was off, and the house was dark. Jim's truck was gone.

"You stay put, Sister."

I hopped out my side of the truck and fished my flashlight and gun out of the lock box. I made my way around back, praying the whole time that Lem had traded in his exotic birds for something useful, like diapers and milk, or if we were lucky, he'd run off with the circus and taken Jim with him.

Sure enough, there were two peacocks in a pen, their black feathers gleaming back at me. There was no room for them to spread those threatening feathers. They looked less high and mighty, trapped there like that. It made me feel foolish for letting myself get so worked up the last time that I cried like a baby and pissed my pants.

There was nobody in the house. I walked back to the truck where Clarice was waiting.

"They're not here, are they?"

"Nope. Where the hell do you think they are?"

Clarice looked determined.

"I know right where they are, Brother. Let's go."

I backed the truck out of the driveway and let Clarice point us in the right direction. We headed across town, far away from Shakey's Half, past Slapp's, Kline's Department Store, and South Christian Church, where Mama wore a light blue dress with a flower tucked just behind her ear to marry Daddy.

We rolled through a part of town I'd only seen as a kid when our parents packed us up in the car at Christmas to see all the lights on a Saturday night. That was an easier time when there was no Jim, no Lee, no Lem, and no Jules.

This part of town was clean as a whistle, with smooth streets, wreaths on doors for the Christmas holiday, and manicured, tidy lawns. The windows revealed just enough light and shadows for us to know we didn't belong. The closest we'd get to the sweet scenes inside those places would be if we had the nerve to walk up onto the porch and press our noses to the glass. Window shopping was all we'd ever do in that kind of neighborhood.

"Okay, it's just a few houses over from here," said Clarice.

She was hopping mad.

Not me. I was relieved that our Lee hadn't run off with Jules back to Jim and Lem's dirty place. Clarice was always one or two steps ahead of me. She had brains, that one. She could have done something different with herself, something better than waiting tables.

"Pull over here, Larry."

I wasn't about to cross her. She was in a mood.

"You stay put. I'm taking care of this one."

I watched my sister stomp across the lawn of that pretty house. It looked like a nice place. It would have intimidated me, but not Clarice. She marched across that porch with a straight back and something to say. She rapped forcefully on the door and waited less than a second or two before she pounded on the door with her fist. She meant business.

"Lee Marks, you come out on this porch right now! I know you're here! You come on out, you little fool!"

The door opened nice and wide. The woman standing there was not Lee. It was that Sellers woman, the one who was all up in our business, bringing over expensive clothes and toys and money all the time. It was too much. There had to be a catch. The do-gooding of that woman made me think that she was feeling awful guilty about something. There was no way that kind of generosity just sprung out of nowhere. Nope. And it wouldn't last.

I couldn't see Clarice's face, but I could tell by the way her head bobbed that what was coming out her mouth wasn't sweet tea. The look on the Sellers woman's face was all I needed to see. We weren't going to be invited inside. They sparred for the longest time. Clarice's hand was planted on her hip as she leaned in closer. Then, the door closed, and there she was, just standing there with her arms folded tight.

"Clarice, what's going on? You think we ought to just go home?"

She shook her head and shushed me.

The door creaked open, and there was Lee. Clarice lunged for her.

"Lee Marks, you get your scrawny ass on this porch!"

Lee was a tough cookie. She must have thrown her nasty sass back at Clarice, because the next thing I knew, Clarice's hands were on Lee's scrawny shoulders, and she was shaking that kid as hard as she could.

The Sellers woman moved in between them and tried to hold Clarice at bay with her hand. That wasn't the smartest thing I'd ever seen someone do. It was time for me to get my hide out of that truck. This was a cat fight if I'd ever seen one.

The Sellers woman was trying to make peace.

"Clarice, why don't you go on home now and calm down? Okay? You are both quite upset and nothing good is going to come of all this scratching and screaming."

I piped up.

"She's right, Clarice."

"Larry, we're not leaving this porch without that baby. I don't give one damn about this sister of ours, but I'll tell you one thing. I will have that baby in my arms tonight. You hear me?"

The door closed again. We waited for the next move from the other side. The door creaked open one last time, but it wasn't Lee. She'd retreated behind her new friend, who held Jules in her arms.

As soon as he saw me and Clarice, the baby reached for us and started to whimper. He was dressed to the nines in an expensive pair of overalls and brand-new baby shoes. That kind of get-up wasn't Lee's doing. That was for sure.

Clarice handed Jules to me, and I walked with him to the truck. Ten minutes later, Clarice came back with a grocery bag of clean diapers and bottles, and Jules' new birthday firetruck.

That made me smile. I loved playing with him and those trucks. I couldn't wait to get down on the floor with him in Clarice's apartment and show that little man how to push his new truck across the rug.

I stayed with Clarice and Jules that night. We didn't have a crib, but we did have milk. Jules sucked quietly on his bottle while Clarice held him tight against her flat chest.

She had the makings of a good mama. Maybe someday.

We both knew this was a half-ass solution that only felt good in the moment. The two of us needed to get to work in the morning, which meant leaving Jules with someone who had sense while we tried to solve our Lee problem.

All three of us fell asleep on that old couch and let the night roll in.

Chapter Thirty-One

Clarice

I'm not proud of what happened that night on Gloria Sellers' front porch, but I'm not sorry, either.

Gloria was nice enough. Too nice, if you ask me. At first, we'd bonded over the strawberry malts I made her at Slapp's. She seemed lonely. Why would a woman like that sit around a greasy diner, making chit chat with a scrappy waitress?

She wore leather sandals and carried a matching purse that must have come from Kline's, both solid and expensive. Those maternity dresses she wore must have also come from Kline's. She could afford them all with her banker husband's charge card.

I bought Mama one thing from Kline's for a birthday years before: a pair of tan leather gloves. She had tears in her eyes when she opened the tightly wrapped package. Mama was so careful with those gloves, like they were the finest thing she'd ever been given. The truth is, they might have been.

Gloria had her own baby to love. I'm not sure why she set her high-and-mighty sights on Lee and baby Jules like she did. At first, it was sweet, and we sure needed the help. But it soon became too much of a good thing. There wasn't enough room in my apartment for all the loot she delivered for Lee and Jules. Lee wasn't grateful enough to suit me. I coached her to say *thank you* and to recognize that it could all come to a screeching halt one day.

"Don't get used to this, Little Sister. Gloria's nice and all, but she won't keep this up. There's no way, and she shouldn't. She doesn't owe you anything."

My advice was a waste of effort. Lee could be bought by the highest bidder. Gloria didn't realize that there was no need to shop at Kline's, not for this girl.

The exchange I had with Gloria that night was unsettling. She'd never seen me mad like that, but she crossed a boundary I just could not accept.

"Gloria! How dare you even think about taking in that kid and her baby like this? She's got family, you know. She doesn't need you, and we don't need your nose in our business. It's not your damned place."

Gloria answered softly that she believed Lee had nowhere else to go, that I'd yelled at her, and scared her. That was bullshit. She didn't know Lee like we did.

"Gloria, that is *not* what's happening here. You took a call from a spoiled, wild brat, because that's what she is, and then you took it upon your little savior self to come into my home, pack up all their things and bring her and Jules to your house, without talking to me first. I suggest you dig a little deeper before you push yourself into places you don't belong."

Gloria's half-smile turned sheepish when she learned what the fight was about, how her precious Lee had put Jules to bed holding a bottle full of Coca-Cola.

My half-sister had left that part out.

After Gloria shut the door in my face, I heard her questioning Lee. I couldn't make out everything, but I heard disappointment in Gloria's tone and Lee's sputtering response.

She'd been caught in a big lie, and those two fools on the other side of the door knew it. No wonder Lee retreated to the back of the house when the door opened up again.

Gloria tried to apologize.

"Now Clarice, these things happen between sisters. I've got a sister myself, and we've had our spats."

I shook my head.

"This is no spat, Gloria. This is a spoiled child with no living mother and a good-for-nothing father. She's been allowed to run amuck and get away with bucking the rules for too long, but that's really none of your business. You think because you buy things for her and Jules that she's got anything to offer you in return? Find friends your own age, from your own side of town. Lee's not your little project, and Jules isn't, either."

I'd pegged her. I think Gloria was ashamed of herself. Her face was hot. She hadn't considered that her generosity might make me and Larry suspicious.

At that moment, I didn't give two shits about what Gloria did with Lee. All I wanted to do was go home with Jules. I mentioned calling the police, and just as I thought, Gloria did not want that.

Chapter Thirty-Two

Margaret Burns

You don't forget time spent in Shakey's Half. Nobody plans to land there on the border of Poulson, tucked into the woods, about a dusty mile southwest of Tilly Road. If you're lucky or have your head up your ass, you might never know it's there.

There are only a couple ways to land in a place like that. Most are born into it through a sad but fertile womb, entering the world as if they belonged there, but no one really does. Their arrival is noticed, but just barely, and every new child is expected to blend in, take what meager life is offered and never look for more.

Others stumble into places like Shakey's Half after they've had some kind of freefall. The landing isn't soft, and once they look around, they never like what they see or smell. They are sure a mistake has been made, and they are correct.

Who is to blame? Were they pushed? Careless? Sloppy? Did they simply not believe that a place like this could be real?

Once these poor folks get their bearings, their next task is to claw their way out, but it's not as easy as you think. People on the other side don't know you're there. You are not missed. Most don't care and won't give you a second thought, even when you make it back to higher ground. You've brought something with you.

The stench is the first thing most people notice. It's what you take away from the place, too. Taking deep breaths while you're there isn't advised. You'd best keep your breathing nice and shallow. It keeps the stink out of your lungs. There's not much you can do about your skin.

It's going to sink right in. The smell is hard to wash off. The stink will find you and cling to you. It will find every inch of you.

Scalps don't go unscathed, either. No amount of brushing and combing will keep the itch from creeping up your neck. That itch, it will find you.

Chapter Thirty-Three

Clarice

Over the next few years, Lee bounced between my apartment and Gloria's house. She landed wherever it suited her. Gloria, the fool, still gave Lee whatever she wanted, but Larry and I didn't let Lee take Jules with her to Gloria's or anywhere else. We drew the line there. Still, Lee was hard to keep track of, and the only reason I let her pop in and out like she did was so Jules could see his mama from time-to-time.

Lee was getting around, you might say, even landing a night or two back at Jim's place. We didn't figure that out until another bomb dropped. Naturally, Gloria knew more than we did. She dropped by the diner one morning, which surprised me. We weren't exactly friendly, but she was a customer at my counter, so I had to wait on her.

"Gloria, what can I get you?"

"Hello, Clarice. How are you?"

"All good. What do you need?"

I wasn't interested in making nice-nice, and if she wanted one of my strawberry malts, I would charge her extra for the full treatment.

"I'll have a coffee, and maybe a piece of apple pie."

"Coming right up."

Best to keep things strictly business. I poured her coffee, sliced her pie and placed both in front of her.

"Thanks, Clarice. I'm wondering if you have time to . . ."

She didn't exactly say it, but I knew she wanted something, and whatever it was involved Lee.

"I'm working, Gloria. What do you want?"

She gave me that look, the one that said she was wiser, wealthier and better than anyone in that diner, including me. We were supposed to be thankful that she associated with us, grateful that she was doing us a great big favor.

"Clarice, what I have to tell you is serious, so we might as well be nice to each other. Okay? I love Lee, and so do you, so I'm coming here in peace."

Did she really love Lee? What about this girl was so lovable? I shared a mama with this child, and most days, I found her harder and harder to love.

"What is it, Gloria? Just tell me."

The next ten minutes made my guts weak.

Gloria's words sounded soft and loving. When she reached for my hand, I let her take it. Crying in Slapp's Diner was not an option. The boss wouldn't like that, and our customers would get uncomfortable. Nobody wants a weepy waitress with a runny nose bringing them a burger basket with fries or warming up their coffee.

I wanted Mama. I wanted to turn off the griddle and go home to play with precious Jules.

Gloria spoke softly.

"Clarice, are you okay?"

We had a problem, and I knew I needed this woman's help, even though I hated her for knowing the news before I did. She seemed sweet and concerned on the surface, but smug.

Lee was pregnant. Goddamn.

A little girl named Peg was born before we knew it. That didn't stop the floodgates with our girl, Lee. Suze, then Patty and then Lolly were next. One baby girl after another landed into Lee's brood.

We called this batch of children "the girls," to distinguish them from their older brother, Jules. Serious Jules. That little man never had time to be a boy. He was needed to help his foolish mama. Jules and his girls would have been a lot for anyone. But Lee and Lem were not up to the task. They scrapped and scratched, grubbing for whatever came their way next.

Jim went missing in action. Larry and I considered this a win. We couldn't conjure up enough curiosity to wonder where he'd gone.

That house had gone to hell.

When Mama died, it was still respectable, but that was long ago. After Daddy died, she still held the mortgage, but she never willed it to us before she was gone. It was no longer convenient squatting grounds. Even Lem seemed to understand that Lee and their brood would need somewhere to land, and he had just the place for them.

Chapter Thirty-Four

Gloria

Lee and her brood haunted me. Jules was a doll, and those girls were precious. Not one of them could help it if their mama was nothing but trash.

Trash. That was Skip's word. He used it first. I'd thought it, but never let it come out of my mouth. For the longest time, I shamed my husband into helping Lee.

"Skip! Skip Sellers. You take that back!"

He'd just made another snarky comment about Lee. By this time, she was in Shakey's Half. Lem Hauser had scrounged up a place for them to stay. She had the hardest time understanding that bringing one baby after another to the equation was going to dilute her resources.

Helping out when it was just her and little Jules was one thing. The second baby complicated things. I had more explaining to do.

Peg was a baby doll, every bit as cute as Violet. I could keep Jules in new clothes, and Vi, of course, but Peg would have to make do with Vi's hand-me-downs. It was common sense. I would have made the same calculation if I'd had another girl myself. There was no shame in second-hand clothes, not for kids.

Turns out Lee didn't agree. What she'd grown accustomed to for Jules was exactly what her second and third babies should also have. She'd sniffed at the castoffs before, but took them, nonetheless.

I figured that Clarice had set her straight. Lee couldn't afford to be choosy. She'd come over one afternoon to pick up things I'd set aside for her. Some things Violet had only worn once. Most came from Kline's. I'd washed everything, too, and even tucked in a fresh stack of cloth diapers and new bibs. There was a new book for Jules and an envelope with cash in it for groceries.

Skip was glad to see that I'd downgraded our greedy little friend to hand-me-downs but thought the envelope of cash was overkill.

"Gloria, we've been over this. Lee has a family to help. Hell, the father of those kids is coming up for air. Let him do what he needs to do, Gloria. He'll step up and so will Lee if they have to. You must let them do this."

"But Skip, we can afford to help. It doesn't hurt us."

I *had* dialed back. I'd met him half-way, hadn't I?

"Just one last envelope, Skip, I promise. They just need to get on their feet."

Skip slammed his hand on the table. That was unlike him, and it startled me.

"Gloria! Stop! They've had all kinds of time to get on their feet. Let someone else buy them more time. What they need, Gloria, is to get off their asses. They need to stop having children they can't provide for. We've done enough. I mean it."

As my husband's chest heaved, my lip quivered.

"Okay, okay, Skip. This will be it. I promise."

"Perfect. If you need a bad guy, count me in, Honey. Tell your little friend that I said you must stop. Tell them your cranky old husband says the party's over."

I felt stung. Skip was right. I pulled the envelope out of the basket and tucked it back into my purse.

Lee arrived. The babies must have been with Lem, which made me shudder. The only other place they might have been was with Clarice. It was hard to keep track of where things stood with the two of them. Some days they were on speaking terms, sometimes not. I'd stopped trying to keep track. I didn't wait for Lee's quiet knock.

Violet *is* Blue

"Hello there, Lee."

"Hey, Gloria."

Lee looked tired. I could only imagine. Our Vi kept me on my toes. I couldn't imagine how I'd manage with more than one. This tired thing had three little ones, plus Jules. Even if they were perfect angels, like our Vi, so many children would run anyone ragged.

Skip and I had determined not long after we had our girl out of diapers that one child was enough for us.

"We'll have no problem sending her to college, Gloria."

That's all Skip had to say once we broke the news gently to his large Catholic family.

By now, the chit chat Lee and I once shared had dwindled to almost nothing. I'd ask about the girls. I'd only seen them a handful of times. Jules and Violet were still solid ground for small talk.

"How's that Jules?"

"Oh, he's something, that one. He's something."

By then, Jules and Vi had passed their third birthdays and weren't far from their fourth. Vi already knew that she wanted a wagon for her next birthday. I'd have to buy one for Jules, too.

We smiled and giggled about those two. I resisted the urge to fill the awkward silence with idle words that would get me into trouble. The last time Lee had come over to pick up something, I'd casually mentioned that she ought to bring Jules by sometime. I hadn't meant it, but Lee, still a child, accustomed to only receiving and never giving, thought I'd extended an invitation. The next day, she knocked on the door and there was Jules, standing next to her.

He was wearing something fancy from Kline's, a darling sailor suit that was really meant for a more formal occasion. It still had the price tag on it, and his grubby little boy feet were bare. She left him with me for the whole day. I didn't mind. Not really. I took that darling boy inside and gave him a bath. When she picked him up, he was wearing brand new shoes and socks.

For what turned out to be one of our last visits on the porch, Lee picked through the box of things for the girls. She seemed disappointed.

"There's sweet stuff in there, Lee. I think Vi only wore them once or twice. You got yourself a pile of things that are practically brand new for those girls."

She didn't seem convinced. Still, I was eager to please her.

"You know I tucked a book in there for Mister Jules. He still likes fish, doesn't he?"

She nodded.

"Lee? Is something the matter? Are you okay?"

"You forgot something, Gloria."

She looked straight at me. I was afraid this was coming. I knew exactly what she meant but played dumb.

"I don't think so, Lee. I think we should be all set."

She stood up. It felt like a challenge.

"The envelope, Gloria. Where's the envelope?"

I sighed. There was no avoiding this particular conversation. Lee didn't operate in subtleties. The lack of an envelope filled with cash was not going to go unaddressed. Lee Marks couldn't let its absence quietly speak for itself.

"Lee, I can't do that anymore. I just can't."

"What do you mean? Why not?"

"It just doesn't work for us anymore, Lee. We've given you and Jules a lot, more than you ever would have had without us. This can't go on forever, Honey."

Ending my sentence with honey didn't hide the bitter taste of the message. Lee looked straight through me. There were no traces of shame or embarrassment on her gaunt face. She did not experience those kinds of emotions. I'd been around her enough to know that this young thing wasn't wired to respond in ways you might expect. She didn't even cry. The quiet between us was heavy. I resisted my usual urge to fill the void with chatter.

"Are you telling me, Gloria, that you've run out of money? Is that what you're saying?"

She was a gutsy thing, that one. It shocked me. I swallowed. Heat filled my face. What did I have to be embarrassed about? Why was I the uncomfortable one right there on my own porch?

"Lee, I'm more than happy to give you these clothes. And I don't regret, not for a second, all that I've given you since Vi and Jules were babies. I'm happy to have done all of that. But enough is enough. You have Lem, and your brother and sister. You have people to help. It's time for me to bow out."

She rolled her eyes at me and sneered.

"Lem? I don't think so. He's gone, Gloria."

"Well, let's give Clarice a call. I'm sure she can help."

"Clarice? What are you talking about? Clarice hasn't been by."

"What about Larry? Are you mad at him, too?"

Lee nodded and folded her arms.

At that point, I was no longer thinking about her envelope. As far as I knew, Lee's circle was small. She couldn't afford the spats she had with all of us. Her bench was not deep.

"Lee, who is watching the babies? And Jules? Who is with them?"

She shrugged but seemed to realize she was exposed.

"Lee, please tell me that you haven't left your children alone in that shack. Please tell me you didn't do that."

Jules was just a little boy, not even four years old. Peg was barely two, still in diapers. Suze was one and Patty was a newborn. Her little neck was still wobbly. I was sure of it.

Vi was safe and sound, napping upstairs.

"Lee, did you leave those babies alone?"

I wanted to shake that girl until her teeth rattled. Skip was watching the game. I let him know I was giving Lee a lift home and that I'd be back soon.

"Get that box of clothes, Lee. I'll take you home."

"I don't want the clothes."

"Too damned bad. Your girls need them. Get your ass in that car. You'd better hope that nothing has happened to those babies. You don't leave your children like that, Lee. You know better than that."

I sounded like her mother. This kid needed one. She sure did.

We rode in silence out to Shakey's Half. I'd never been. It was only a few miles from home, but a distant land, something altogether foreign to me.

Chapter Thirty-Five

Clarice

I'd just gotten home from the diner. My dogs were barking, and I couldn't wait to run myself a hot bath, crack open a beer and sink into the night.

I slipped off my uniform and stood in my slip while the tub filled up. A knock at the door startled me. I guessed it was Larry, so I didn't even bother with a robe. I opened the door, ready to let him know he couldn't stay long. Big sister was beat.

It wasn't Larry. It was Gloria, and she had Jules with her.

"Clarice, I'm sorry. I should have called, I know, but we've got ourselves a problem."

Shit. My relaxing evening was going right down the drain.

"Come on in, Gloria."

I hugged Jules. I'd not seen him in a bit.

I ran into the bathroom, turned off the running water and slipped on my robe. Shit.

Gloria spilled the whole story. I wanted to shake Lee, and Gloria, too, for expecting anything different.

"Where is Lee?"

She was waiting in the car with the baby girls. They were all hungry and worked up. Jules was hungry, too, so I made him a peanut butter sandwich and sat him on the couch.

Thank God that Jules and the girls were okay, and that Gloria had the sense to bring them to me.

"Lee doesn't want to come in, Clarice, but I'm not leaving her in that place. It's awful. It's no place for children, Gloria."

She didn't need to tell me. I knew all about Shakey's Half.

"Well, that's what the father of these children can provide, Gloria. You think we haven't fought that? You think I haven't seen the inside of that dump? You think we don't toss and turn every night thinking about those babies being there?"

Gloria looked at her expensive watch.

"Lee and the children can't stay with me, Clarice. I can't do any more for her. She's not teachable. She's not even thankful. She's mad at me now, too."

Aha. So, the patient, perfect Gloria had also lost a bit of her shine. Finally. I had to admit I enjoyed seeing her like that.

"Let me guess, Gloria. You told her no, didn't you?"

She nodded.

I heard all about the hand-me-downs and the cash standoff. I learned that reckless Lee had left those kids alone. My stomach sank.

"She doesn't want to come up here, but she can't come home with me. Not this time, Clarice."

Of course she couldn't. I envied Gloria. She was going home to a husband. She could take a hot bath if she wanted. She could have a beer, but I pegged her for a wine girl. Oh, yeah. She was a wine girl.

"You stay here with Jules for a minute."

I stomped down the stairs in my robe, barefoot. Fifteen minutes later, Lee and the girls were in the apartment. The little ones wouldn't remember any of this, but I feared Jules might.

"Gloria, I'm going to ask you for one more thing. Just one more favor, and we'll never need anything else from you. You're not helping Lee. You're helping me and these kids. My little sister is a foolish child, a stupid girl. We know this."

We needed diapers, milk, graham crackers and soap. Gloria nodded and reached into her purse. She handed me the envelope of cash she was no longer willing to give directly to my wild sister.

"I don't need that, Gloria. Thank you, but I've got it. Can you stay here with them while I run to the store?"

Gloria looked uncomfortable. Maybe that wasn't such a good idea. Lee had stomped off to the bedroom to pout, but she'd lash out at her latest enemy if given the chance. I was sure that this wine drinker hadn't seen Lee in her full glory. It was something to see.

"Tell you what, I'll stay here, and you go get what we need. Here, let's make a list."

Gloria looked relieved. I handed her cash from my wallet, but she stopped me.

"No, Clarice, let me do this. Let me do this one last time."

She was shaking and tearful but determined. I started to argue with her, then stopped short. We needed to get the show on the road.

I nodded and thanked her before she walked out the door.

Jules had finished his sandwich and was thirsty. Peg was trying to pick up Patty, who had worked herself up into a good, justifiable cry.

Chapter Thirty-Six

Skip

Vi was already tucked into bed by the time Gloria made it home, tearful and tired. I knew it would come to this. That girl, Lee, would show herself. Good riddance. I was relieved. I ran a hot tub for my wife. I knew just how she liked it. I helped her slip out of her dress and watched her sink into the steaming water.

"I'll be back."

I closed the door and returned with a big glass of white wine. Still weepy, Gloria took it and thanked me. We sat in the dark a while before Gloria spilled every detail, which was more than I wanted to know about that night and the three years before that. We were deep into this, and the banker in me couldn't help adding up the numbers.

"I'm sorry, Skip. I'm really sorry."

I needed a minute.

"Did you hear me?"

Gloria was eager for me to take the initiative and wave off this slow-motion, expensive mistake.

"Gloria, we're fine, but you must listen to me next time. That girl is bad news, Honey. She's trash."

She protested.

"What about Jules? What about those little girls? What about them?"

"Honey, you have nothing to be ashamed of, not one thing at all. Someone else will come along and help them. I don't want you to worry one more minute. You hear me, Gloria? Not another minute."

Our sleep was uneasy that night. My wife was usually chilly, but I could feel the heat on her soft skin. She didn't need my arms around her. She needed room to thrash and kick and dream one last time about Jules, his little sisters, and their trashy, lost cause of a mother.

The next morning, we brought Vi into bed with us. Her dimpled hands tickled the stubble on my face.

"You're scratchy, Daddy."

She was right.

Gloria looked refreshed.

"Daddy does look scratchy, Vi. Why doesn't he stay up here and shave while we make breakfast?"

I could smell hot coffee brewing, and bacon. Perfect. I heard a knock at the front door. It was too early for company.

"I'll get it, Skip."

Order was restored, and I loved it. No more secrets between us, no more throwing good money after bad. I dressed for another day at the bank. As I headed down the stairs, I heard Gloria on the porch. She was angry. There could be only one person making her sound like that.

"Go home, Lee. Get yourself back to Jules and those girls. You're their mother, Lee!"

I could not make out the girl's response.

"Absolutely not, Lee. The answer is no. I used that money last night to make sure Clarice wasn't left in a bind with your babies. They've got what they need for now. You get off my porch, girl, and don't you come back. Go on, now."

Gloria slammed the front door and locked it. I heard more rustling as she opened the door again and marched out to the top of the steps.

"Hey, Lee? I forgot to tell you something."

The girl must have turned back to hear what Gloria had to offer.

"You're welcome. You hear me, Lee? I never did hear a *thank you* come out of that sassy mouth of yours, but you're welcome anyway, you piece of trash!"

I suspect that the words my wife hurled down the street for all the neighbors to hear startled that Marks girl. Gloria sounded tough and confident, like she was calling a spade a spade.

Lee Marks and the neighbors couldn't detect it, but I heard my wife's voice waver. She still wasn't completely sure about sending that girl packing. Gloria's heart wasn't thumping for Lee anymore, but those kids and the memory of her one visit to Shakey's Half would take turns haunting her.

Chapter Thirty-Seven

Violet

I envy Gloria and Aunt Ruth. Something old and ugly continues to rumble between them, but whatever it is has been papered over with a steady flow of birthday and holiday cards that are so pretty you can't help but turn them over to see how much they cost.

I wasn't ready to tell either one of them what happened. If I had asked Aunt Ruthie for anything other than a pad during my summer weekend at their house, she might have thought I was an impetuous child, weaving a tall tale.

My story would have included a heroine and a monster. I imagine my aunt would have soothed me and told me that monsters aren't real. If I insisted that they were, she might have humored me. As she tucked me in that night, she might have given me permission to leave the night light on. But if I came downstairs in my bare feet for breakfast, still talking about the same monster, she might have lost her patience.

Even good Aunt Ruthie had her limits. If I pressed on about the monster, she would have helped me pack my suitcase and driven me straight home herself. She was a boy mother, not a girl mother. There were different things that tested a parent's patience, and I needed the kind of attention my mother could give, not Aunt Ruth.

My monster would have frightened her, too. She probably would have to reassure herself that I was just a child with an active imagination, or a spoiled brat in need of a good spanking. She wouldn't have the heart to tell her sister what a terrible lying child I was, that my pants were on fire. Best to simply send me packing.

After I left with my mother, I imagine Aunt Ruth went straight to the kitchen to clean up and focus on her chores instead of wondering what I might have been trying to tell her about the monster in her house. She'd shoo him out the door to go do what boys do, and by the time all the breakfast dishes were cleaned, rinsed, dried and put away, she had already forgotten what a challenge I must be for my mother.

Gloria wouldn't want my story, either. She liked buying birthday cards sprinkled with glitter. For the longest time, my mother made sure to read my books before I did, removing any that mentioned sex or violence out of circulation. No sense in frightening her darling girl.

If I had told her what happened with my cousin, she would have assumed I'd been reading books that weren't on the approved list or had somehow slipped into an adult movie with one of my naughtier, less supervised girlfriends. No cousin of ours could ever do something like that.

But it wouldn't take Gloria long to focus her suspicions on the unsuitable Jules. That meant he would no longer be welcome, not even on our porch. My grubby friend would be greeted with a tight-lipped smile and a polite suggestion that he run along home. My friend, my partner in cutting crime, would be banished.

Jules, not Jamie, would be officially blamed for Mr. Bones. I'd be forced to sit across the Thanksgiving table from the smiling monster whose fangs could only be seen by me.

Nothing would come of coming clean.

I didn't need justice. I needed Mr. Bones and Jules. The tattoo would protect me, and my boy would believe me.

I knew he would come back, ready to hear my story and share a pocketknife or a piece of glass he'd found in the dirt on the way back to Shakey's Half.

Violet *is* Blue

Proud Jules would have to get over my story, even though it had more bite than his. The girl with the shiny, clean hair who took a bubble bath every night now had the upper hand.

Chapter Thirty-Eight

Jules

Damn that Violet. Most boys would want to see or even touch what was just below that tattoo of hers. Maybe someday she'd let me. But I wasn't getting past that ugly Mr. Bones without hearing the nasty story she was itching to tell.

We'd have to stay outside on her mother's clean, white stoop, drinking lemonade out of fancy glasses while Violet spilled her story. I'd sit back and take it in, looking less than impressed. No hugging or squeezing her hand. The only respectable thing to offer might be a slice, maybe two.

If the story was really good, I'd have to grant Vi some status. She might deserve a crown and could be my cutting queen.

We could stay on her porch for the longest time. Her mother wouldn't send me home. I could bring Little Kitty Cat with me, too. She could have lemonade from a tiny, fancy cup, just her size. Violet would wash my sister's hair with expensive shampoo, the kind that smells like Vi. I'll run a clean comb through it.

We wouldn't share our stories or our cuts with Kitty. We'd just pet her and let her meow and purr. Nothing sharp for my baby sister. And we would never speak of Mr. Bones.

One of these days, when we're all grown up and Kitty's sleeping, Vi and me will be tired of our old stories. We'll be over our cuts, and Mr. Bones will let down his guard. This wasn't likely to happen, and I knew that. I had too much Shakey's Half stink on me to last long on Vi's porch. I'd never get inside or past Mr. Bones, but a boy like me could dream.

I could want a cookie or a slice of birthday cake, too. I'd prefer chocolate milk, not white. I could want my little sisters to have long hair and wear clean, pretty dresses. I might like me a bubble bath, too, and clean socks that match. A boy like me might like to have my hair tussled by the coach or someone's dad.

I didn't know why Mr. Bones appeared on Vi's flat, white belly, but I knew how he got there. That was Lem's doing. That son of a bitch would do anything for a buck. I'd seen his sloppy handiwork before on Momma's arms and his. I could tell by Mr. Bones' crooked mouth and the way his uneven head cocked just east toward Vi's belly button that Lem was drunk and staggering when he did it. His tools were rough and jagged, and not clean. His kind of customer wasn't fussy. They bought whatever he was selling.

He visited our house when it suited him and Momma, but he stayed in the shadows, lurking on the edges of Shakey's Half. Truth be told, he wasn't even welcome there. He'd drop by from time to time, to drop off an envelope of cash for Momma. She'd nod and shoo him away.

"Not even a *thank you* for old Lem? Don't Lee have manners? Where you stash those manners, Lee?"

Momma would give him a cockeyed smile while she counted the cash. If she had enough to buy a bag of groceries, a pack of cigarettes and enough coins to send me and the girls up to the laundry mat to wash and rinse the sheets, he might be rewarded. If not, she'd shoo him back out to the shadows to scratch up something else that would be of use to her. That's how Momma and Lem did the bulk of their business.

Mr. Bones would never have made his way onto Vi if we hadn't run into Lem one afternoon at the edge of Shakey's Half. We never should have been there in the first place. We should have stayed on her clean porch, brooding, and cutting up. But Vi insisted that I take her to see where the poor kids live. She was a girl used to getting her way.

"Jules, it can't be all that bad. You live in a small house at the edge of town. So what?"

Her challenge angered me. She had no idea. My head had just been freshly shaved, and I'd missed school. She'd missed me and was taking it out on me in this weird way of hers. I guess she'd come to need me as much as I needed her.

"I've been a little busy, Vi. You wouldn't understand. I know it. You just wouldn't."

"Oh, stop feeling sorry for yourself, Jules. It can't be all that bad. Just wash your damn hair every now and then. You can't blame your mama forever. I thought you were washing your hair after gym class."

I wanted to slap my friend. She was just a pretender. She didn't know a thing. I wanted to make her eyes water. She was just going to have to see it for herself. I wanted to show her and watch her squirm. Violet needed to see the rust at the edges of our front door and the weeds growing up where flowers might grow, the peeling paint and our broken front window taped over with a piece of grimy cardboard.

I wanted to watch her precious nose curl as soon as the stench hit her lungs. I wanted her to dodge hungry cats and skinny dogs looking for scraps. Then she could beg me to walk her home, but I wouldn't do it until she said she was sorry. She'd need to mean it, too.

After that, I wouldn't be her token poor friend anymore. Her porch was nothing special, but it was a heavenly far cry from the rotting stoop that met my front door.

"You'll be sorry, Vi. You are so wrong, you know, and too stupid to even know it."

I laughed at her, hoping she felt my hurt. I hoped it matched mine. She was a stupid, spoiled girl, that Violet Sellers. I couldn't wait to see her jaw drop.

"We'll see about that, Jules."

The next afternoon, on the way home from school, we turned left instead of right. Vi tried to act casual, like there was nothing strange about heading down the gravel path past the rusty bench where the bus stopped to let Shakey's Half kids walk the rest of the way home. She was a stupid girl that day.

We turned the corner toward the first tin house at the edge of Shakey's, and there was Lem, looking shifty, but headed toward our house. It was high time he showed his face. There'd been no drop of cash in a couple weeks, and Momma's mood was grim. He gave me a big smile, acting like he was my daddy, putting on a show for the strange, clean girl I had with me.

"Well, what do we have here?"

He showed his yellow teeth with a wide smile I'd never seen.

"Jules, Jules, Jules. This must be the girl that Lee's been telling me about. Yep! She told old Lem all about your friend here, you gutsy little bastard. Look at you, living large. What are you doing bringing her over here? Is Lee having you two over for tea?"

Lem laughed his nasty, silly laugh, the one I hated more than I hated his smile. Vi froze and then smiled back at him and watched me.

"Well, aren't you going to introduce me to your lady friend, Son?"

I shook my head, but Vi, that stupid girl, moved forward and put out her clean hand toward Lem's to shake it.

"I'm Violet Sellers."

He nodded. His smile was creepy and toothless.

Vi was mine. She was not meant to be shared.

One day, she would discard me. She would grow more beautiful and cleaner. Vi would only recall that I had ushered her to the poor side of Poulson, where disgusting men waited for their next hustle.

I could forgive Lem for fathering me, and Peg, Suze, Patty, Lolly and Kitty. I could give him a pass for dropping by with his wads of cash and spending a night here and there with Momma. But I would not give Lem Hauser a hall pass for Mr. Bones. That was a bridge too far.

It made me think about aiming one of my sharp tools away from my own skin and toward his head. I wondered what color his blood might be. Most nights, I imagined it thick and black. I guessed that his muscles, if cooked like meat over a spit, would be chewy and hard to swallow. Enjoying a roast of Lem's stringy shank would surely require tenderizing, a pounding I longed to give.

Our father had never raised a hand to me or my girls. He never hurt us like that. Instead, he mocked us and dropped by to poke at us the same way he poked at the burn barrel out back.

I was sorry that day for letting Vi bully me into bringing her to Shakey's Half. I didn't owe her a damned thing. All I wanted was for her to catch a whiff, to see the stray cats and the boarded-up windows. That would have been enough of a shock.

It should have impressed her to know just how perfect she had it compared to me and my sisters. But Violet was spoiled, and she was just pretending to be angry and tough. She was trying it on for size like an old Halloween costume she couldn't quite zip up in the back. The scariest costumes never fit my fancy girl right because underneath all her bravado, she was a glittery princess.

Chapter Thirty-Nine

Gloria

My sister Ruthie used to believe everything I told her.

Once I had her convinced that she was adopted. It was a lie that had legs because freckled, carrot-topped Ruth didn't look like any of us. She was a gullible seven to my mature eleven. After I told her we picked her up from the orphanage, she sobbed until her face was puffy and red and snot ran from her nose onto her upper lip. Still, I wasn't moved enough to tell her I was just funning her. Our mother couldn't believe I would do such an awful thing to her sweet, freckled baby, and she made sure I'd think twice before I decided to do something that cruel again.

"You just don't know when to quit, do you, Gloria?"

I guess I didn't.

She motioned for me to assume the position across the back of the sofa, so Pop could restore order with rapid-fire cracks to my butt while my little sister watched. It hurt, but not nearly enough to stop me from torturing Ruthie whenever I could. Just looking at her made me mad. She was not attractive, but she managed to elicit comments of adoration wherever she went. Ruthie was "Carrot Top" and "Campbell Soup Kid." Pop called her "Red," which made me want to pinch her on the softest part of her arm. How could someone so damned homely get the kind of devotion she enjoyed? The injustice of it all brought out the pinch and nip in me. Most of my savage moves went undetected. My sister quietly endured, but there were just as many times I was caught red-handed. Mother and Pop were ready to pounce and dole out justice. Even that certainty did nothing to slow me down.

Once, when Ruthie was only five, I talked her into sticking a kidney bean up her right nostril. We were in the back seat of the car, waiting for Pop to load the trunk. She was charged with holding a big bowl of our mother's bean salad on her lap. We were on our way to a picnic with Auntie Maude, Uncle Fox, and our cousins. Like usual, Pop was making a big fuss about what a good job Ruthie was doing, holding those beans and Ruthie beamed as he praised her.

"Now Red, you know this is an important job, don't you? We don't give this job to just any girl. Do you think you can keep those beans in the bowl?"

She nodded as he gave her a wink and ruffled her messy mop of red curls. She just tickled him. Mother slipped into her seat, checking her lipstick as Pop started up the car. We were off. Pop looked at us through the rearview mirror.

"How are those beans, Red? You keeping an eye on them?"

She nodded vigorously, which made him chuckle. Soon, he and Mother shifted into their usual chatter. While they blathered on about getting the oil changed, paying the mortgage and making carrot cake that was moist as it could be, I gave Ruthie a poke.

"You better check those beans, Sister."

She gingerly lifted up the tin foil to peek.

"Be careful. Those suckers are tricky. They'll hop right out."

She closed the foil down quickly.

"Did you know that beans are magic?"

For the next five minutes, I had my little sister believing that beans could really do magical things. They could feel it when we bit them but didn't scream because they didn't have mouths. Beans only understood English and hated being smothered in red sauce with rice. Before too long, I had Ruthie pick a kidney bean from the bowl to prove that they could wiggle from the back of the nose and come out the ear.

"Ruthie, I'm telling you, it will come right out your ear. Do it, Ruthie. Try it."

She crammed the bean as far up into her nose as she could before panic set in. She started crying and Mother and Pop assumed I was behind every tear my sister shed. Pop stopped the car so he could take off his belt and whack me on the side of the road. We were late for the picnic, so I figured it would be quick.

"Jesus Christ! What have you done now, Gloria Jean?"

Gloria Jean was up to her old tricks. Mother yanked my sister into the front seat while Pop glared back at me. Ruthie was howling and blubbering like a little brat.

"Bean in my nose!"

Mother buried her forefinger up to the knuckle inside Ruthie's nose, searching for the wayward bean. Pop held her feet as Mother performed the ad hoc procedure. Ruthie's little black and white saddle shoes flailed in the air, and in her frantic attempt to escape Mother's sharp, manicured nails, she kicked Pop right in the jaw.

"Holy shit!"

He turned red, then white.

Thirty minutes later, we were at Dr. Fisk's front door. He'd just sat down with his family to what smelled like roast pork and gravy when we were ushered into his parlor, where he used a long metal device to remove the bean from Ruthie's nose. Then he stitched up Pop's lip.

Mother drove home while Ruthie cried and hollered the whole way because we missed the picnic. She'd caught wind that Aunt Maude would be bringing poppyseed cake with lemon icing, and we were missing out on it.

I took advantage of the moment.

"You stupid little girl! Next time, don't shove a bean up your nose!"

Ruthie wailed even louder.

"Gloria told me to do it. She *told* me to."

"I know, Red," said Pop. "I know."

He eyed me from the passenger seat. He was holding an ice pack to his face with one hand and couldn't reach back to smack me. He liked to do the driving, and the fact that Mother had taken his place behind the wheel wasn't helping his mood. A price would be paid.

"Jesus Christ! Gloria! A goddamned bean! Up her little nose! What were you thinking?"

When we got home, Mother took Ruthie upstairs for a nap.

"That's alright, Ruthie. While you're getting a good rest, Mama will rustle up a cake, just like Aunt Maude made."

Pop escorted me into the living room. He never tolerated whining or crying or "blubbering," as he called it. In fact, he could usually be counted on to offer one response to anything louder than a whimper.

"I'll give you something to cry about."

Then, he'd point a finger at the red-eyed, sniffling offender.

We knew that "something to cry about" meant that we'd just bumped into the outer edge of his patience and that we would soon find ourselves in worse shape if we didn't dry up, and quick.

Pop was a trigger spanker. He could get up from his chair, have you turned over and deliver the first crack in what seemed like one swift, fluid movement. There wasn't any time to wince or catch your breath before his hand landed again, then again. About a full minute of that kind of hands-on attention and we found that Pop was right. We did have something new to cry about.

Mother usually just swatted at us, hoping to land a little smack as we streaked past her. Her cracks were half-ass. Not like Pop. Nope. He believed in swift justice, delivered with precision, force and no regrets. We knew that once he delivered, he would walk away without giving it a second thought.

Pop wasn't a brute, but he was sure of himself.

The truth is, we needed direction, especially me. I was a stinker. A bee in a bucket, Mother liked to say.

I especially relished buzzing all around Ruth's red head. Her very existence irritated me. I don't know why. I can't explain the cruelty I reserved only for her. The dark emotion I reserved for my red-headed, little sister toad was a special, sibling variety of hate that left a bitter taste in my mouth.

What should have been whispers exchanged between us under the covers at night, full of secrets and love, were one-way, spit-filled hisses delivered from a distance, and only by me. I still have no answers for why I behaved like that.

Ruthie never retaliated like she could or should have. She absorbed my aggressive advances and quietly cruel moves year after year, while others saw to it that I was corrected.

As we grew up, the vitriol I delivered seemed less potent.

I was sure that enough time had passed, that all had been forgotten, and then my forgiving little sister produced the instrument that would torment me. My comeuppance had been waiting all along. A debt had come due and been paid in full before I even knew what hit me. And when it came, I knew that karma was indeed a patient, nasty bitch.

Chapter Forty

Skip

I didn't exactly rob the cradle, but let's just say that by the time Gloria was starting high school, I was already out of college and had been working for two years. It didn't matter. I brought experience to our marriage. I knew the ropes. I could support her, and we both wanted a family.

My wife was young but ready to settle down. I could see it. She seemed eager to catch up to her younger sister, Ruthie, who beat her down the aisle and to motherhood. It bothered Gloria, but I shrugged it off. She and her sister had an odd connection. They made nice on the surface, exchanging gifts and cards at the appropriate times, but their hellos and goodbyes were stiff and forced.

I hate to say this, but I think Gloria was the problem. It sure wasn't Ruthie, who was as friendly and natural as could be, despite her looks. My blue-eyed blonde had all the makings of a beauty queen, but she held back. Still, I loved her, and boy, did she love me.

When Vi came along, we were ready. My folks were thrilled she was a girl. I was one of five boys. We were all married, and all my brothers had boys, so when Violet June arrived, my mother wept.

It was nice to contribute something different, new and pink to the larger Sellers clan. All four of my brothers and their wives settled in the city, but not me. Gloria was a small-town girl, and if I wanted her, I'd need to move to Poulson. It took some getting used to. The nights were still, and everyone seemed to think they knew your business.

I could afford a wonderful place for us there. We could start big, and we did. Gloria beamed when we got the keys to our castle. It was white with a porch that went on for miles. We bought a swing before the new stove was delivered, even before we'd met the neighbors.

It felt good to be able to say yes to a girl who seemed to have heard more than her fair share of no's. Her father was grumpy with Gloria but he seemed to have sweetness to spare for the redhead. The unfairness of it made me say yes, yes, yes to my wife. Nothing she wanted was ever out of line, and it wasn't long before I said something to her that I thought she needed to hear.

"Honey, listen to me. You don't need my permission for every little thing. I trust you. It's all good, Sugar, okay?"

Gloria nodded and carefully made our house into a home I was proud to share with friends and family, a place that felt good to come into each night. I was proud to bring our daughter into this nest that we had feathered so lovingly.

Vi was a lovey. Our baby looked just like her mama. She was just what we needed. Violet June brought out even more lovelies in Gloria. She was sweet and nurturing, and the only woman I wanted bathing, feeding, and raising our child.

The sweetness of what we had wasn't enough for Gloria, though. She insisted on sharing our bounty, which was an attractive position. What kind of good Catholic boy would I be if I didn't nod vigorously at the way my wife noticed someone in need and then moved beyond noticing to acting?

It was a new and lovely side of my wife, something I hadn't initially detected when all I could think about was how to get her somewhere alone so I could remove the burden of her clothing, one piece at a time.

"What will I find, Mrs. Sellers, if I left this office today and came home for lunch?"

I hoped she could imagine the smile on my face while I waited for her answer. I knew what Gloria's face looked like and the way she cocked her head to one side while she teased me with talk of how her hair was pulled back into a high and tight ponytail that had taken her all morning to get just right.

"I could fix that for you, but it will cost you."

My wife played along. We had this dance choreographed and each of us knew our parts.

"Don't expect money, Mr. Sellers. My husband keeps me on a budget. I'm afraid I don't have any change to spare. Not today."

Within minutes I was in the car, driving home, hoping she was wearing one of those flowing skirts that zipped up the side. I'd walk in the front door, knowing she'd make me come find her. Once I did, she'd look up as if she were surprised to see me.

"Well, Skip. What are you doing home in the middle of the day like this? Don't you have work to do?"

"Oh, I have work to do. I am terribly busy. But you see, I have a wife who refuses to wear her hair the way I like it."

She'd flash a sly smile.

"Oh? Does she know how you like it? Have you told her?"

I'd move in and pull the rubber band from her hair, releasing that vexing ponytail, while whispering in her ear.

"Oh, I've told her exactly how I like it."

By then, no matter what room in the house she'd been hiding, we'd drop to the floor so I could get her hair just right.

Those parts of Gloria I knew well, and I never tired of them. Her generosity took me by surprise, but it was a pleasant one. It would make her a good mother, and thinking about this turned me on in ways that were deep and substantial.

When it comes time to scan the horizon for a mate, some say that men subconsciously look for someone like their mother. It's hard for me to imagine my own mother tangled in a heap on the floor with my father in the middle of the afternoon, but my mom must have had that in her. She had five strapping, lusty boys to prove it. Other parts of my mother were easier to think about for comparison. She took good care of us, but she was always thinking about others. Her daily to-do list was loaded with all things hearth and home, but she was just as concerned with cupboards that belonged to others. We always donated food, clothes, old toys, books and money. She always had a knack for finding someone to save, a hole to be filled, questions that needed answers. If our needs were being met, my father didn't usually mind.

My folks didn't argue much, but when they did, their spats were always about Mom's excessive generosity. Those squabbles were memorable. My brothers and I knew it was best to stay outside while Mom and Dad squared off. They needed every inch of the house for one of their fights. Divorce was never on the table, but these knock-down, drag-out fights must have been blessed by the Pope.

Putting a weekly offering in the plate at church was never the issue. It was expected. It was just as important to make certain that someone was around to bear witness to the act of placing the gift in that plate. No arguments there.

Dad didn't mind giving away canned goods, but he drew the line at boxes of pudding mix or cherry pie filling, or God forbid, cocoa. He blew a gasket when he noticed that Mom had tucked a box of graham crackers and a bag of marshmallows into the box that was waiting at the back door for one of us boys to haul it out to the station wagon for the next food pantry drop.

He stood indignantly in the hallway with the large box of graham crackers in one hand, and the marshmallows in the other.

"Thelma, this is a bridge too far!"

Our feisty mother was having none of it. She'd fly out of the kitchen with her hands on her hips, ready for battle.

"Jim Sellers! Shame on you! What is the problem with sharing a box of graham crackers and a bag of marshmallows?"

Mom was tiny, but mighty. She stepped right up to my large father and waited for his blustering answer.

"That's the point, Thelma. We're not *sharing* these items. Whoever gets this box of crackers isn't taking one or two out and then handing the box back to us. We're *giving* them, Thelma. And they aren't needs, Thelma. Marshmallows are *not* a need. They are a *want*. I'm more than happy to help with needs, Mrs. Sellers. The Good Lord expects that of us. Needs, we can do, but not wants! In fact, let's see what other kinds of nonsense we've got here to reward these good-for-nothings!"

He was on fire, righteous as he stooped over to look for proof that our mother had gone wild again with her reckless, overzealous giving.

"Aha! I thought so! I can't believe I missed this! Well, well, well, Mrs. Sellers. What do we have here? I guess we've got all kinds of money to throw around, don't we? We're just here to spread joy all over the place now, aren't we?"

He was holding up a can of cocoa mix in one fist and an especially offensive can of condensed milk in the other. An unnamed poor family on the other side of the tracks almost got a pan of hot chocolate with marshmallows on a cold Saturday night if it hadn't been for my father's eagle eye. For shame!

Dad was a smart man, a good man, but sometimes he stepped right in it. There was shit on his shoe and Mom was always there to tell him how bad it smelled. She could be counted on to chase him out to the front porch to get it cleaned up before he tracked that mess into her clean house.

"James William Sellers! Are you suggesting, as you stand there in your brand-new pants and with your belly full of hot pancakes, bacon, and freshly squeezed orange juice, that a poor family we'll never see can't have themselves a treat? A pot of the same kind of hot chocolate I make for our family after the boys have played out in the snow?"

Dad doubled down.

"Yes, Thelma, that's *exactly* what I'm saying. Hot chocolate is something that is earned. Our family enjoys hot chocolate because I work hard to pay for it. We deserve to have it. Any family that comes to the food pantry has not earned a thing, Thelma. I'll give them corn. I'll give them spinach. Hell, I'll give them canned meat! I'm not saying they should starve, for Christ's sake. I'm saying, they don't get treats! Not on *my* dime!"

By this time, our mother had walked back to the kitchen. Dad had followed, determined to win. We didn't have to move from the front porch to hear the next round. The whole neighborhood could hear my folks carry on.

"Is it the sweets, Jim, that bother you most? It seems like the sweets are the sticking point for you. Please, tell me more."

Dad blathered on about hard work, about getting off your ass, about helping those who help themselves. He'd throw scripture in there, too, usually selecting hardline verses from the Old Testament. The Bible would be slammed down on the table.

Big mistake. Our mother was a wicked Protestant. She knew her good book. She'd actually cracked it open and read it long before she'd married Dad and converted to Catholicism to keep Grandpa and Grandma Sellers from having heart palpitations.

Bringing up Scripture was a tactical error on my father's part. He could mutter over his rosary beads with the best of them and eat fish on Fridays without question, but he was no match for Thelma Sellers.

Mom had a way of making Dad feel like he'd decisively won a round. I remember the cocoa argument. Together, they marched back to the controversial food pantry box and she fished out a few other items that might tip the scales of justice: a box of oats that could make their way into a batch of delicious cookies instead of served hot and mushy for breakfast, a can of biscuits that might be fried and rolled in sugar and cinnamon, a dangerous bag of rice that could get mixed up with a box of raisins for a pudding if it got into the wrong hands.

Dad seemed satisfied. The battle was over, or so it seemed. Our father should have known better. Two days and nights went by. We boys were at the kitchen table, scarfing up pancakes. Dad took his place at the head of the table.

"Pass the syrup, will you, Skip?"

There was no syrup on the table.

"Honey, did you forget the syrup?"

My mother was standing at the kitchen sink, cleaning the griddle. She gave no answer.

"Thelma, are we out of syrup?"

She turned to him and then to us and smiled.

"Yes, boys. I'm sorry, we're fresh out of syrup this morning. You'll have to make do with jam or honey."

Jam and honey weren't ideal, but we could manage. My father grumbled, but he slapped jam on his cakes and washed them down with hot coffee.

Maple syrup never made it to Mom's grocery list. About a week went by, and we were out of jam, too. We ate dry pancakes for the rest of the week. Next, there was no cream for Dad's coffee. We were out of catsup and were forced to eat our tomato soup with no crackers.

Dad was onto Mom's game. He scrawled a note for her that he left on the kitchen table.

We need syrup, catsup, crackers, jam, honey, and cream for coffee.

Thelma must have been waiting for this. By the time Dad got home from work, she'd made notes to his notes.

Syrup nope. (Want, not need). Catsup not necessary. Crackers nice to have but not required. Jam nope. Honey too sweet. Cream for coffee better for you black.

When Dad pounded his fist on the table we made ourselves scarce. Mom came up from the basement with a basket of laundry in her arms.

"What's all the fuss about?"

"Don't get smart with me, Thelma. You've made your point."

Mom smiled.

The next morning, we had syrup for our pancakes and Dad's coffee was milky the way he liked it.

The next food pantry box contained syrup, a jar of honey, a bottle of jam, two pounds of sugar, two cans of condensed milk and a tin of cocoa. Dad had surrendered, forced to quietly concede how closely *wants* danced next to *needs*.

As a kid, I always agreed with Mom. Dad always seemed greedy and unreasonable. I was on Team Thelma, but once I sat at the head of my own table and was the one bringing home the bacon, I started to see old Jim's point. He worked his fingers to the bone for our family, so we had all we needed and much of what we wanted. He was territorial about his good fortune, and within his rights.

How much giving was enough? How much was too much? Didn't my father and I have some say regarding our families' largesse?

Chapter Forty-One

Gloria

Violet's tattoo was horrifying. If we played our cards right, nobody would see it. We were confident that only four souls knew anything about her new sinister artwork: Papa Bear, Mama Bear, Baby Bear, and a mysterious tattoo artist who would eventually be found if it was the last thing my husband did.

I was equally troubled by Vi's emerging association with Jules Marks. That was harder to hide. It was a complicated entanglement I hoped would go away as suddenly as it appeared. If I stayed calm and didn't let Violet sense my fear, Jules just might evaporate into thin air.

There were many unsavory kids Violet might have chosen to vex me with, such as that pack of girls who dropped out of Girl Scouts and took to smoking cigarettes behind the grocery store on Friday nights. She could also be hanging with a group of middle-class, dirty-minded boys, which would have been preferable to Jules Marks.

Violet's distress had its own set of eyes. It could see me in the dark. It could read my mind and my secrets and knew where my shameful bits lived. It shaped itself around me like an intricate Origami creature, folded carefully to trap me with artful angles, forcing me into corners I feared the most.

Her distress guided my troubled child to pick a poor kid from Shakey's Half instead of finding solace and comfort with me. That sad truth humbled me in the morning, pecked at my ankles throughout the day, and most nights, it dangled sleep just outside of my reach.

The nights were the hardest. When Violet was in school and Skip was at work, the daily drip of household chores and errands was enough to quiet my mind. But the nights lingered like an unwelcome guest. Long after Vi locked herself in her bedroom and Skip rolled over to his side of the bed, the nights and I shared endless space and time.

I watched the clock on my nightstand do its best to mock me with slow, determined precision. These nights would not be rushed. They had paid for their ticket and would stay in their seats until their sunrise curtain call.

The moon's gentle glow in the window should have soothed me, but I wondered how something so silvery and constant could carry on calmly, knowing full well that my world was filled with worries.

I wondered if Violet could see the same moonlight and if she felt as insulted by its beauty as I did. Perhaps once she closed and locked her door, she allowed her ill-fitting tough girl posture to relax. I wondered if she secretly wished I might come knocking, like I had so many nights before, to comfort and love on her. I wondered if she missed me.

Unlike the constant moon, I had retreated. If I thought too hard on that, I'd cry softly to myself, moon be damned. Quiet shudders would sneak up on me, and I swallowed those, too.

There were not too many places to hang my latest worries out to dry: Violet's awful new attitude, her tattoo, Skip's flaring temper, and Jules Marks. He was like a weed that needed to be pulled out by the roots to stay gone. But I would have to pluck carefully and treat him like a hothouse flower.

Jules was the oldest son of Lee Marks. I had helped her, and even championed her when few others would, and I now regretted that.

She was only fifteen and having her first baby. I was much older, but having my first baby, too. We shared a room in the hospital, but we were worlds apart.

Jules arrived before Violet, and by the time she arrived, Lee was sitting up, enjoying breakfast.

My side of the room was celebrating with a giant bouquet of pink roses, but there were no flowers on Lee's side. Even though my lower half throbbed, and my breasts ached, I felt ashamed of the contrast. My roommate didn't even have a robe or slippers.

Lee's scrawny body looked unscathed from the birth while my paunch looked like the doctor had forgotten to remove the baby from my womb. I was quite sure my scrawny young neighbor would go home in her cut-off jeans and a tee-shirt, while I would be forced to wear the same maternity dress I wore when we arrived at the hospital.

"Hello there," I said.

I was waiting for the nurse to bring Violet from the nursery. Skip would arrive soon, eager to hold our new little girl.

Lee looked up from her plate.

"Oh, hi."

She was pleasant enough and seemed nonplussed by my finery and her lack of it. In fact, she didn't even seem to notice. She was still a child. I could see this by the way she licked the butter and sticky syrup from her fingers. The napkin on her tray had not been touched at all, much less draped properly over her lap.

"I'm Gloria. What's your name?"

"I'm Lee."

"Well, congratulations, Lee. How is your baby?"

"He's a tiny little thing. Only five pounds. Doc says we have to stay a little longer to fatten him up before we go home."

"Oh, a little boy. How lovely for you. That is small, but you're tiny yourself. He'll be fine, I'm sure. What is your little boy's name?"

"Jules Martin Marks."

"Congratulations!"

When the nurse rolled Violet in, we cooed over her and peered into her tiny face, wondering whose mouth, eyes and nose she had.

"You aren't disappointed that she's not a boy?" I said. "Even just a little bit?"

Skip shook his head and shushed me.

"Gloria Jean, this girl is just what we need."

I could tell by the way he touched her soft, little pink cheek that he meant it.

Our nurse came in to retrieve Violet.

"Mr. Sellers, you'll have to come back later, I'm afraid. This new mama here needs rest, and so does your baby."

Skip kissed me on the forehead and gave me a squeeze.

"I'll be back, Honey. You sleep, Mrs. Sellers."

It's never easy to rest in a hospital. Nurses come in and out, visitors, too. Flowers are always being delivered, and vitals are taken at regular intervals. New life is wheeled in and out for feedings and to create rich moments with proud new parents.

I awoke to see that Lee and her baby had a visitor. I'd assumed that Jules' father would not be darkening the door. A young woman stood by the bed, clucking and fussing.

"Lee, Honey, you need to support his little neck. Oh, my, he's a hungry little thing, isn't he?"

As the woman pushed the curtain open, I recognized her right away. It was the waitress from Slapp's Diner. She was a real nice gal, always friendly when I stopped in for a strawberry malt while I was pregnant. She recognized me, too.

"Well, hello there!"

She was still wearing her uniform, and I could smell a whiff of French fry grease and hamburgers.

"Clarice, imagine running into you here! See where all those malts landed? That's your fault, you know."

She always gave me an extra scoop of ice cream.

"Oh, stop it. You look lovely. And let me guess, you must have yourself a girl."

I laughed.

"What gave it away? The pink flowers or my pink robe?"

We exchanged chit chat while Lee tried to hold her baby properly. He looked uncomfortable. His squeaks and grunts sounded as if he knew full well that he was in the hands of an amateur.

Clarice pounced.

"Here, Honey. Let me help you. Okay? You've got to keep this baby bundled up nice and tight, so he feels safe. Now be gentle with his head. See that soft spot on top? We've got to be careful with that."

I wasn't so sure that Jules' mama understood her assignment. The baby fussed and squirmed, working up to a good cry that would make any new mother nervous.

"Here, Honey. Give him to me."

Clarice gingerly took over.

"There we go. Just have to keep him soothed and safe."

Lee shrugged and yawned.

"You take him. I don't want to hold him right now."

"Honey, are you sure? This baby is going to get confused. We don't want him thinking Aunt Clarice is his mama."

She rolled her eyes at me when she was sure Lee wasn't looking.

Aha. They were sisters.

"She's my half-sister. Our mama passed awhile back, and Lee needed somebody, so here I am. She's staying with me for a while until we get things sorted out."

I nodded but could see she had to be beat, standing there rocking a newborn baby back and forth as his mama slept soundly. I felt ashamed of myself, sitting there like a queen in my fussy finery, waiting for my baby to be brought to me.

"Oh, my, Clarice. You have your hands full. Do you have help?"

"Not really. The baby's father is a piece of shit. Sorry. Pardon my language, but it's the truth. We don't want him around. Lee's daddy let this happen, so we can't count on him, either. That's for sure. My brother, Larry, is helping, but we both work, and I don't think this girl here is ready to take care of a baby. She's just a kid."

Clarice smiled at the bundle in her arms.

"He's a cute little guy, though. I don't know. We'll just have to see how it goes. I guess Lee is not the first teenage girl to have a baby, and she won't be the last. We'll figure it out."

The nurse popped in and took Jules. Clarice pulled on a sweater, grabbed her purse and gave me a wave.

"Clarice, you better get yourself home and put those feet up."

"You got that right, Honey. Diner opens at six, which means coffee needs to start brewing by 5:30. Bring your baby by sometime when you're feeling up to it. I'll make you an extra thick shake."

I leaned back to relax and waited for the nurse to bring back my pink bundle. I couldn't wait to see her face again, and wondered if she wanted to see mine, too. Alone with my thoughts, I pieced together a prayer of thanks and relief.

Chapter Forty-Two

Violet

Jules came back. I knew he would. He couldn't resist, and while I waited for him, I made sure I had the details ready, so the story would really give him a fright. It would have to be good. My friend from Shakey's Half was hard to impress.

"Violet! Jules is here!"

Gloria sounded annoyed that she had to yell, but more annoyed that Jules was at our door again. There he was, with his hands in his pockets, waiting for me like a dirty puppy. The side of his face was puffy and looked sore.

"Hey."

"Hey, back."

I pushed the door open and moved toward the steps, knowing he'd follow me, trying to look casual.

"Thanks for sticking around like you did."

He looked ashamed. Good.

"I needed to get home. It wasn't a good idea to have your pants down like that."

He nodded toward my hips and Mr. Bones.

Ha ha. Good one. Jules was responsible like that. Still, no apology. I pushed.

"I think you're scared. That's what I think."

He shrugged. That was all Mr. Proud Jules had for me.

"I don't know, Jules. I'm still deciding if you deserve to hear it. I'm not sure you can take it."

"I can take it."

He moved closer to me, close enough that I could smell his sweat. It was a telltale stench that pegged him as a boy from Shakey's Half.

"If you run off like that again, like last time, we're done."

"I won't, Vi. I'll stay."

I'd never admit it to him, but when I saw my friend standing on the other side of the door, asking for me like he was, the sight of him made me want to cry with relief. If my mother hadn't been standing there to witness it, I would have let myself fall into him and put my arms around his neck and just held on tight.

Jules waited for me to weave my true, tall tale. It was the first time I'd said it out loud, although I'd practiced in my head over and over. To spit the words out into the air felt good, but dangerous. I was giving the story long legs, which could get away from me if I wasn't careful.

I started with my visit to Aunt Ruth's. I gave Jules the where, when, how and what. Why was missing. Jules knew the heroine. He was smart. Then, I introduced him to the villain. He was older and bigger than both of us. He smelled better than Jules. I described the basement, the expansive pool table, the dartboard, red shag carpet, the rain and the wedding taking place at the church.

Jules nodded, as if he'd seen a basement like that and had been to a wedding. This irritated me a bit because I knew there was no way he'd experienced either. My house was the nicest he'd ever been to, and he'd never been allowed inside. A wedding? Not a chance.

Jules Marks was full of it.

I described how I was ticklish and open to a tickle fight with my handsome cousin, who started off playful. I told Jules the moment when the fun stopped, that precise second when play time was over. My arms twisted, the bite, the hand tight over my mouth, his fingers tangled in the hair at the back of my neck, the sharp yank that meant business.

I watched Jules' face as I shared each detail, hoping he'd grant me a sign of horror or an indication he believed me. Nothing yet. I moved to the next scene, the one full of thrusts and bumps and scratches and grunts, and the sticky blood that trickled and pooled beneath me.

I would be proud to have made it through without crying but I saw my friend's eyes fill with surprising tears that dripped down his cheeks. He was quiet. His response would make or break what we had, and he knew it. He'd have to hand me the hurting crown. I deserved to wear it and for him to kiss my hand.

We let the quiet sit for a minute.

"You have to tell your mom and dad, Vi. You have to."

"I never will. I won't."

Jules was thinking, coming up with a tool or sharp trick we could pull out to manage what I'd just spilled between us. Notebook paper? A piece of glass? A sharp stick from Skip's burn pile? He sniffled, sucking up the tears and the drip from his nose.

"If you don't tell, I will."

We let his threat hang between us. Jules moved closer.

"I mean it, Vi."

He did, too, and I hated him for it. I was sorry I was a show-off and revealed Mr. Bones to this weakling. I should have gone and let him be the cutting king who was tougher and more tortured than me. Why had I tried to one up my so-called friend? I wanted to order him off my porch, but I didn't. He might never come back, and I needed him.

"He'll do it again, Vi."

He put his hand too gently on my knee.

"Mr. Bones won't scare him off. Not one bit. He'll tear right through you again, and I won't have it. No way."

Tears streaked down my face. I angrily brushed them away. I looked ugly but didn't care. Jules didn't care. I could see that. He had that same look of determination when he was ready to make a deep, impressive cut. But now, his face had a soft angle I had never noticed. He leaned toward me and rested his hands on my shoulders. His teeth were brown and crooked, and his breath was bad, but his lips were soft and sweet as he planted a gentle, protective kiss on my upper lip. He didn't seem to mind the moisture that dripped from my nose.

"I won't let another girl of mine be hurting like that. I'm not taking it anymore. I'm taking care of you, Vi, and then my girls."

"My parents won't believe me."

"They will. If they don't, I'll back you up."

"Jules, you're not exactly Gloria's favorite person."

"I know that. She thinks I'm nasty. I got rotten teeth and an itchy head. She knows about my momma. She knows I got nothing to lose. Let her kick me off this porch. At least it will be in her mind, Vi. She's seen Mr. Bones, right? A nice girl like you doesn't do something ugly like that for nothing. Right? She knows that."

Maybe Jules was right. Maybe Gloria wouldn't be so surprised. Maybe she felt a little something on that day we came home from the Pullmans. Maybe she and Skip would believe me and then come to my rescue. They'd thank Mr. Bones. They might even decide to thank Jules for talking sense into me.

"They love you, Violet. You got people. Look at this house. Your yard. Your clothes. You shouldn't be cutting yourself or putting a nasty tattoo down there. They'll do something."

This was a new Jules. I liked him. Maybe I loved him just a little. We didn't say anything for a long time.

"They won't be happy that you've seen Mr. Bones."

He nodded.

"Yeah, they won't like that one bit. I'll take the blame if you want, Vi. I'll tell them I wanted to see it."

"Well, you did, didn't you?"

Jules blushed. I loved it.

"I don't know. I wish he wasn't there."

"Me, too."

"If you take the blame and say you wanted to see it then they won't let you come back. That'll be it."

"You got that right, Vi. I know that."

"Would you want that, Jules Marks? No more sitting here? No more cutting up? No nothing?"

I wanted to make sure that this stinky, cut-up boy of mine knew what we would be giving up.

He nodded.

"I wouldn't like it, but I'll do it to keep you safe."

"You would?"

"Yep."

This Shakey's Half trash was awfully sure of himself. We both knew what was happening. Me being me and us being us, I needed to one-up my friend. It was just what we did.

"I'll make you a deal."

"What kind?"

"You can tell them about me, but promise you'll also tell them about you and Kitty and your sisters and the kerosene. You gotta."

I expected that Jules would object, but he didn't. He'd obviously been giving this some thought.

"Maybe. But if they can't do something, and I mean really, really do something, then it'll be worse for me and for all of us at home. I need to think about that one. Nice people don't care about us. We don't matter to anybody. But you do, Vi."

He wasn't wrong.

"Fair's fair. If I'm taking a risk, you got to. And what happened to your face?"

"Never mind about that. Let's talk to them about you first."

He pointed at Mr. Bones so directly it made me blush.

"We'll take care of me and my girls, too. Don't worry. Now, are you gonna do this, or am I?"

I looked up at my boy from Shakey's Half and nodded.

Jules stood up and walked to my front door, leaving me on the steps. He looked taller. I could hear his knock and my mother's footsteps. She was at the door, staring at him through the screen. I kept my back to them and tried to concentrate on the cars going by.

My gut felt hollow about Mr. Bones and my throat clogged up with tears of shame. They might not believe me or maybe they would. I was afraid either way. Mostly, I felt a sense of relief more satisfying than any cut I could make.

"Yes, Jules," said Gloria. "How can I help you?"

His voice was confident and clear.

"If you don't mind, Mrs. Sellers, I'd like to step inside."

Chapter Forty-Three

Gloria

Giving birth to Violet was harder than I imagined, but I did it. I was thankful for the successful birth, but my gratitude tilted more toward something less attractive I knew about myself. I suspected that God knew, too, long before I prayed to Him.

Violet was breathing with strong lungs. Fabulous. She came with ten fingers and ten toes. Wonderful. For these things, I was grateful. But more than anything, my heart felt lighter as soon as I could confirm that my baby didn't look like my sister Ruth.

Despite the tall tale I'd tortured her with when we were kids, we hadn't picked her up from an orphanage. Little Ruthie's red hair and that splotchy skin of hers hadn't cropped up in the bloodline on my father's side of the family for three generations, but it surfaced with her. When it did, the whole family marveled at how that wild splash of jarring color had finally made its way back to the surface.

A great, great grandmother on that side, Polly Francis, was known for the same coloring. They called her Red, too. The whole time we waited for Violet's arrival, I knew that it was entirely possible that my own child might have drawn the red straw. It would have served me right, as nasty as I'd been. But our fickle gene pool passed us by. My little Vi was a brown-haired, brown-eyed girl.

I kissed my baby on her forehead and checked one more time for telltale signs of a claret disaster. We were safe.

Lee slept soundly through the night.

I shifted, trying to get comfortable, moving my hips gingerly from side to side to respect my tenderness and to keep blood from soaking through to my brand-new nightgown.

The curtain that divided me and Lee, along with the shallow thanksgiving I'd made official with my prayer, made me restless and self-conscious, ready to make amends of some kind.

Poor little Lee, sleeping deeply without a care in the world for just a little longer, would wake up soon. Baby Jules would be pressed into her unsure arms. He would suck milk from a bottle for more days and nights until he tipped the scales to the doctor's satisfaction, and then those two children would be wheeled out the front door of the hospital.

Their homecoming would be different than the cossetted one that awaited me and my baby. Clarice and her brother would do their best to piece together something for Jules and his mama, but it would not be enough. They were scraping by, too, like you'd expect with a school janitor and a waitress.

I felt guilty. The world was a capricious place.

In that moment, I decided to befriend Lee and her baby so I could share my bounty with them. It would help them both, and Clarice, too. Now that I was a mother, I needed reforming, and pronto.

Now, I did befriend Lee and little Jules for longer than I should have and even longer than I liked. It had a clear and sweet beginning, but there was no graceful way to exit stage left.

Over time, it became clear to Lee and to me that those early mother and baby days we shared by happenstance were sweet, but nothing more than that. She was a poor girl who came from a long, pathetic lineage of takers, and at the time, you could say I came from an equally long, even more pathetic line of givers.

Our kind are the worst. We give not because it comes naturally, but because we are making amends of some kind. I was the older of the two and had much to offer that poor little mama. But I learned something from that wiry waif, Lee Marks. She had a thing or two to teach me about the cruel nature of takers.

Takers are skilled at looking like abandoned kittens when you first meet them, but once they discover you'll put out a bowl of milk every morning, they reveal their true lion selves. They start demanding fresh meat, and they don't care where you get it, as long as you show up with the finest cuts. And the first morning you show up without meat or milk, that kitten-turned-beast will open up her mouth to reveal the sharpest fangs you could imagine. I don't care how Christian, or ready to make amends for old sins you are, you'll regret the day you stopped to pat that pitiful, helpless kitten in the first place. You will.

By the time Lee popped out two more babies, Peg and Suze, I was onto her game. I was not appreciated as I had hoped to be. Those sweet children were precious, but their mother was a taker. It took me awhile to admit that I'd had enough.

On the day I ordered her off my front porch, Lee didn't seem all that surprised. She didn't look back or stop to say thank you for all I had done for her. No time for that. Time was a wasting. She needed to find her next sucker.

Chapter Forty-Four

Sally

My mother pointed out that my move from Poulson Elementary School to the high school had the potential to yield a prize I'd yet to achieve: a husband.

As a kindergarten teacher, I was surrounded by other women, but the high school had more men. They weren't big earners, but there was a passel of full-blooded males teaching social studies, biology, and shop, one or two in the math department, and a full selection of former athletes with pot bellies and whistles around their necks who all turned their heads at the word *coach*.

In the beginning, mother had her sights set higher for me. There was certainly nothing shameful about being the wife of a principal or superintendent. But one year blended into the next and she set her sights lower: a teacher or coach might have to do. Time was ticking, and her daughter was on her way to becoming a bona fide spinster. My mother needn't have worried. I had myself a man. He was my little secret.

I am perfectly capable of fastening the clasp on my necklace all by myself, but it's been well worth the wait to let him do it for me. To feel his rough, calloused hands gently push my hair to one side of my neck and let his thick fingers fumble at the tiny mechanics of my jewelry is delicious. Sometimes, the outermost tips of the skin on his fingers will brush against the invisible hairs on my neck, the ones that never see the light, and when that happens, the meat falls right off my bones.

Some women are completely turned off by men with dirty hands, but not me.

In fact, it was Larry Downs' filthy hands that I first noticed when we met. Larry's mitts were dirty, despite his occupation. My parents would have been appalled that their own daughter, a respectable home economics teacher, would even consider associating with the school janitor. One would think that the constant plunging of his hands into steaming, hot buckets of soapy water and the exposure to all the other cleaning agents would make his hands soft and pink, but not so.

My man also filled in as the school mechanic and spent as much time hunched over the engines of the school buses and the boiler as he did, cleaning the cafeteria floor.

The greasy, filmy crud wedged underneath his nails was there to stay. Even the cracks and crevices in the skin of his hands seemed stained with varying shades of brown and black that could put a good fortune teller out of business.

Because I teach cooking and sewing, my hands are on display a good part of the time. I stand over students and help them cut and slice and thread needles.

My hands are small and white. I maintain them with the kind of perfection that can only be achieved by a single woman who lives with one cat. When I'm feeling lonely, I close my eyes and try to imagine Larry sitting at a table in my classroom. I show him how to place his filthy, calloused hands over the cutting board, like he's my dirty little student. I nod with approval as he learns to pare an apple or remove the seeds from a lemon.

Before Larry and I began loving each other, I could tell that he was embarrassed by his paws. He'd stuff them in his pockets or hold them behind his back while we talked about the weather.

Before that afternoon when I first saw his bare belly and chest, I assumed that the rest of his body must also be stained and dingy looking. I was wrong. The surfaces of his stomach and chest and back were white and clean without a blemish in sight.

As I pulled him toward me, one thought helped me get over the top. Larry Downs had just pawed at my white, lace bra, finally reaching the sensitive flesh of my even whiter breasts. The contrast of his rough hands on my soft skin—his dark on my light—made me quiver and weep and laugh with a relief that only a woman living alone with a cat could understand.

Chapter Forty-Five

Larry

Growing up, I never knew how to handle something sweet.

At first, most kids are wild. They gobble up treats like there's no tomorrow or sick guts to reckon with later. You get a little older and you're able to remember the good parts of a goodie, and then you start thinking about it ahead of time. You might not have much for brains, but you can control yourself, at least a little bit. While you're thinking about it, just the memory of that treat's taste on your tongue gives you a lift in your waiting belly. It's no different than hanging stockings on Christmas Eve or sneaking a sip of your mama's cold Coke when she's not looking.

Then something happens. The treat tastes the same, but you're harder to impress. You've lived long enough to know that treats come and go, and that there's a price to pay for having them in the first place. You might get yourself a thick belly or be asked to share the treat with your sister. You might be old enough to know that treats cost money that is hard for your family to come by. You might know that the treat would be even better warmed up or served with a glass of cold milk, but be ashamed of yourself for your greedy thinking, for knowing that good things can be even better.

Knowing these things takes away from the sweetness of it all. Santa is just a man dressed up in a costume he takes out of the box after Thanksgiving and packs away after Christmas. The Easter Bunny is brown, not white. The tooth fairy doesn't always have change to spare.

If I could, I'd go back to those wanting and waiting days, the times when you knew something sweet was coming your way and nobody could know how deep your insides were smiling, just thinking about it.

That's how I started to feel watching Sally out of the corner of my eye. She'd been Jules' kindergarten teacher, then moved over to the high school to take over the home economics class. I knew she was a treat beyond my reach the first few times I saw her.

"I think the word you're looking for, Downs, is *buxom*," said Rod.

My buddy drove the school bus in the mornings and afternoons but wasted his time in the shop bugging the shit out of me in between his driving duties. Every once in a while, I'd toss him a wet towel so he could make himself useful.

We laughed, but I felt ashamed that I'd been so loose and free with my observations about Sally. It wasn't like me. I fell asleep that night dreaming about bringing her home with me and asking her to teach me how to crochet b-u-x-o-m on one of her sweaters.

I began looking for excuses to do some work on her side of the building so I could catch a glimpse of her walking to the office to make copies, ducking into the teacher's lounge for a smoke, or walking to the parking lot when school was over. Once I knew which lunch shift she took in the cafeteria, I made it my business to be there, sweeping up invisible crumbs.

Anticipating these Sally sightings kept me energized all day and into the night. The thought of her pretty face, held up by a long, white neck that needed kissing, made me feel like a little boy thinking about a cinnamon roll, but I was also a grown man who needed something more substantial.

For many weeks, Monday mornings meant I had five days to catch promising glimpses of my girl. When Fridays arrived, it meant I had only one day to indulge before the weekend became unbearably long.

I grew to resent all of the time I had to spend inside of the school garage—changing oil, checking tire pressure, rotating tires or cleaning windows because those chores kept me from seeing Sally, even from a great distance.

One Friday, there was so much garage work to do that I didn't get to indulge in my usual lunchtime glimpse. I was ready to call it a day. The Saturday crew would be there in the morning for a full-building mop and tile wax, and I'd be there alongside them.

I'd already stayed way past the school bell and was thinking about dropping by the diner to pick up dinner and say hello to Clarice. A cheeseburger basket with onion rings, rinsed down with a couple of cold beers, sounded good enough.

I turned off the lights and locked the door behind me. The air had finally gone crisp, just like it should for football season. Some nights, I'd run up to watch a game and have a hot dog with my buddies, but I wasn't in the mood for that nonsense, so I hopped in my truck.

As I turned the corner, I saw a single car in the lot. The hood was up, and someone was huddled over the engine, poking and prodding. I thought about driving by, but my mama taught me better. I pulled over just in time to see Sally Lend's beautiful face pop up from the hood. She was even prettier up close.

"Hey there. Can I take a look?"

She nodded and put her hands in her pockets as she pushed out a sweet *thank you* from her soft, smiling mouth.

"No problem."

It really was no problem. Sally just needed me to jump her battery, which I was more than willing to do. She watched as I made all the necessary connections. Within a few minutes, the job was done, and I closed the hood of her car.

"I'm Larry, by the way. Larry Downs. I work here in the shop and all around the school. You've probably seen me around."

I reached out with my dirty hand but pulled it back quickly and stuffed it in my pocket.

"I don't think I have seen you, Larry, but I'm sure thankful that you stopped to help me. I'm Sally Lend. I teach home economics."

I didn't tell Sally that I knew her name and what she taught, that I knew where her classroom was, and what time she arrived at school each morning. I didn't let her know that I knew when she took her lunch shift or that I loved it when she wore those red slacks or that my heart was broken just a little that she hadn't noticed me.

"Well, Sally, it's nice to meet you. Glad to help."

She smiled back and stood there in the chill, looking me over. The teacher knew a janitor when she saw one, especially when she caught a glimpse of my dirty hands.

"I'll have to be on the lookout for you come Monday. I'll be sure to give you a wave. Thanks again, Larry."

I watched Sally slide behind her steering wheel and start the car. She was no girl. She had wise eyes and real class. She wore a watch and knew what time it was. Sally Lend was beyond my grasp. I knew this. But those moments I spent under her hood, with her gazing at me the way she did, gave my mind new things to think about as my heart kept thumping all weekend long.

Chapter Forty-Six

Clarice

My brother was no longer a boy. His broad shoulders and strong arms said so, along with the stubble on his face, the size of his boots, the spare change that jingled in his pockets and the big wad of keys that hung from his work pants. They all reminded me that the little brother I remembered was long gone.

Important people counted on him for his ability to fix things. He approached each new problem with his sleeves rolled up and mud on his boots. Sure, there was mopping and scrubbing to do at school. He still did that in a pinch. But he'd moved up. Now, he ordered tools and supplies and was the go-to brains for the water main break that closed the school down for three days. Since he oversaw inventory at the end of the school year, Larry knew exactly how many desks and trash cans were in that building. He could address the principal and the president of the school board with confidence when old school buses were ready to be retired.

"I wouldn't put my kids on one of those buses, Sir."

That's what Larry told them, and they believed him. When the new school year began, two brand new yellow school buses were parked behind the school. My brother did that. Our mama would have been proud of this man. Daddy, too, from what I could remember.

But there were other things to notice. Larry dressed a little nicer. His hands were cleaner, but he still kept them tucked in his pockets. He stopped by Slapp's all the time to just say hi or to grab a bite but always insisted on paying me and made a habit of leaving me a generous tip.

"Honey, you don't need to do that."

I'd say it every time.

"And why not? Don't you take my order and bring it to me? Aren't you the one who keeps my coffee cup filled? Don't you bring me a piece of pie? Aren't you about to tell me to have a nice day, and come back soon?"

His teasing made me shy. I put the tip in my pocket and gave him a tap on his wrist.

"You have yourself a nice day, Lawrence Downs. And you come back soon."

Chapter Forty-Seven

Larry

Sally's softness got to me.

There was nothing harsh or clipped about this teacher I'd come to love. We settled into something warm and sweet. We kept our distance from each other at school, revealing nothing but a polite wave or nod across the hallway. I had my toilets to tend to and floors to mop. She had a complex classroom to be maintained and tests to be given. We saved something to share with each other on weeknights and weekends.

It would never last. Sally had a reputation to think about. There were more suitable men to step in to her life where I never belonged. I was convinced of this, so one night, I tried to break it off.

We'd finished our take-out from Slapp's. We'd been together long enough that I knew what Sally liked on her cheeseburger: pickles and mustard, no tomato.

She crushed the bag and threw it in the trash, then started making moves to feed Bootsie. This dance was practiced and soothing, the same one each time she filled that dish to the brim. That cat didn't know how good he had it. She placed his dish on the counter so softly and carefully that you couldn't hear the point of contact.

Sally could be trusted with her grandmother's fine china. She'd bend slightly at the waist to open the cabinet where the cans of cat food were stacked neatly. Sometimes, she'd take a while to decide which flavor of vittles that lucky bastard might be in the mood for. I didn't mind one bit, watching her glossy hair swing while she considered her cat's options.

Her lips twisted into a slight grimace as she popped open the can and peeled it back. The strong smell was offensive, but not enough to move me from my seat at the kitchen table, waiting there for the best part. She'd scoop the food into the dish and then start talking tempting kitty talk as she crouched down to the floor.

"What a good boy you are. What a hungry, starving boy."

Bootsie had a big behind on him. He liked his kibble.

I let myself watch this one last time before I stood up and cleared my throat.

"Well, I guess I'd better get on home, Sally."

She turned and looked at me, surprised.

"What do you mean? It's only seven o'clock on a Friday night."

Her pretty head was cocked to one side. She was confused. For weeks and weeks, our routine, easy and wonderful as it was, had not changed. It was understood that I would stay the night. That decision was easily made. We'd watch TV together on the couch and start to snooze, finally deciding to retreat to her soft, warm bed.

At the start, those early-to-bed sessions were frantic, exciting and breathless. Neither of us were sure it was going to last, so we'd best gobble each other right up. Later, as we settled in, I came to know that my Sally liked morning romps even better and Fridays were less rushed. Knowing full well that we could have it all—dinner, a movie and dessert anytime we wanted—took the pressure off. We were a thing, even if we were the only ones who knew it.

"Oh, I don't know, Sally. I gotta go."

I couldn't make eye contact with her. Teacher noticed.

"Look at me, Larry."

She was standing there, still in her teacher's clothes that I loved helping her out of.

"What is this? Are you trying to leave?"

"It's not that, Sal. It's just that, well, what are we doing here? What is this we're doing?"

"Are you trying to break up with me? Why on Earth would you do something like that?"

I felt like a student in trouble. I stood before my teacher in my grimy janitor clothes. I'd not even taken the time to change into something clean for this special woman. We never went anywhere but her house. Only Bootsie the cat knew about how involved we'd become. Bootsie and Clarice, of course.

My big sister knew I was someone's fella. And Miss Burns, Sally's old neighbor. She knew. She gave me a nod and hello each time I stood at Sally's front door. She smiled a wicked, wise smile at me when I left early in the mornings, too. Our secret was safe with her.

"Don't you want someone who can take you out, Sal? Don't you wish you didn't have to hole up inside your house with me? Don't you want to walk down the street holding someone's hand? I'm not sure you want me for that. You might be looking for another kind of man when it comes to that."

Bootsie had already gobbled up his meal and was all ready for his after-dinner rub. He meowed loudly to remind the room that his needs had not yet been met. The cat would have to wait. A human needed Sally's petting and assurances.

"Well, yes, Mr. Downs. Now that you mention it, I *do* want those things. I want a movie with popcorn. I want to walk with you in the park. I want you to take me to Slapp's and introduce me to your sister. I want you to be my date at the faculty picnic."

There were tears in her eyes as she walked toward me.

"I want all of those things, Sir."

"With me, Sally? Are you sure you couldn't do better than me? Don't settle. You're too pretty, too sweet to waste yourself on someone like me."

Sally shushed me by putting her lips on mine and melting right into me. We stood there and kissed like we had the first night we let things fly. She came up for air.

"I want all these things with you, Larry, with *you*, but not tonight. Not tonight."

Her skirt dropped to the floor, and she unbuttoned her blouse. She gave me her hand, leading me past the living room and the television, past her bathroom with pink tiles and the shower curtain that had cats on it. We shut the door to her bedroom, leaving her fat cat to fret for a while in the hallway.

Bootsie could wait.

We had a new understanding between us. Sally was not ashamed to be with me. We would go public with our love. People would get used to seeing her standing next to me. We would share meals and walks and someday, a last name and a home.

Sally Downs.

I liked the way that sounded. It was a new thing both of us could stop wanting and just start *having*.

The newness of knowing this was worth a private celebration that neither of us would ever forget. It was quiet and thunderous, safe, and wild, and wonderful in all its promise.

Chapter Forty-Eight

Margaret Burns

Watching little Sally and her gentleman janitor come and go was more entertaining than watching game shows on television.

They were sweet, those kids. Looking out my kitchen window, it was easy to see what they'd worked out. The janitor thickened up across his chest. After a while, he stopped knocking at the door and waiting for little Sally to greet him. Things were getting cozy over there. He walked right in the front door. There was not a problem if she wasn't home. He had himself a key, which was big news. This was a development that needed reporting and discussion. I knew just the ears waiting for what I had to offer.

Clarice Downs, the janitor's big sister, poured me a cup of coffee while my slice of pie was warming up in the oven. I liked to walk over to Slapp's on Wednesdays with my paper and take my spot in the back booth so I could see what was for sale, who was moving, who'd gotten a ticket, who was married and who was buried. The paper was the source of truth for the price of a pound of hamburger and a pint of strawberries, if they were in season.

Clarice came toward me with my hot pie. She was a worker, that one. And kind.

"What we got in the headlines this week, Margaret?"

"Oh, my. I haven't cracked that open just yet. But I do have a tidbit you won't find in this old rag. I sure do."

The kind waitress had to know more.

"Do tell, you naughty thing. What's the scoop, Miss Margaret?"

I told her all about that handsome brother of hers. He was a frequent visitor next door. Very frequent. I couldn't be sure, but I just bet he was eating breakfast over there most mornings. Things across the way were heating up. It looked to me like Sally's man had himself a key to the place. It sure looked like that from my kitchen window.

Clarice nodded and smiled.

"Oh, Margaret, that's old news!"

Clarice clucked her tongue as she poured more coffee into my cup.

"That's *real* old news. Those two are long past being sweet on each other. They're long past that and have been for some time now."

Rats. I thought I had something. I needed to pay more attention.

"Do you think there might be a wedding coming round the bend? That would sure be lovely, wouldn't it?"

"I bet you're onto something, now, Miss Margaret. That wouldn't surprise me one bit. My little brother's smitten with her. He sure is. There's no doubt about that. He's got it bad."

I liked this news.

These two lovebird neighbors felt like they belonged to me in an arm's length kind of way. I was more vested in how their story unfolded than anything the soap operas had to offer. These people were real. What they had was believable, and they were worth watching.

Chapter Forty-Nine

Larry

Sally and I settled in. I had nice, clean shirts hanging in her closet and I let her cut my hair.

We made the rounds. Word was out that a janitor and a high school home economics teacher weren't such an odd combination after all.

Clarice approved.

"She's a sweet one, Larry, real sweet. When are you going to make an honest woman of her?"

That was for me to know and for my sister to find out. I'm sure Sally was wondering, too. We'd been together for several years and she still hadn't introduced me to her folks. They knew about me. I was no longer her sweet secret, but I was a great big question.

Before I popped the question, we needed to deal with the subject of Thanksgiving. We usually parted ways on these holidays. Sal would head over to her folks' place, and I'd hole up with Clarice to eat turkey and pumpkin pie on paper plates.

Sally's family liked apple pie. The night before Thanksgiving, I sat in her kitchen and watched her make a crust from scratch. The whole place smelled like apple, sugar and cinnamon. She was making two pies, one for the big day and the other for us to share later.

I drank coffee and watched her work.

"Sal, you don't have to make two pies if you don't want to. Just make a big one, and we'll take that to your folks."

I was working for an invitation to her family's Thanksgiving and she picked right up on it. She didn't miss a beat, that one. When she turned to me, I was pouting.

"But I want to make us a pie, Honey. I like making things for us to share, just the two of us."

Sally never was a good liar.

"That's not what's going on here, Sal. You don't like making two pies. There's something else happening and I know what it is."

"What are you talking about?"

She put both pies in the oven and shut the door.

"You don't want your folks to meet me. That's it. Plain and simple. You'll sit with me at a football game. You'll take a bite of my hotdog. You'll take me to the teacher picnic where the principal has to hand me a lemonade whether he wants to or not. Those things are just fine, but you don't want me to come face-to-face with your family."

I was onto something.

"You know, Sal, I took you right over to meet *my* family. Clarice is all I've got. Taking you to her was as good as taking you to meet my mama. I didn't think twice about it. I'm proud of you."

She was quiet. I'd hit a nerve.

"Why don't you just come right out and say it, Sal? You're ashamed of me, aren't you? You're afraid I'll say or do something to embarrass you. Do they even know about me, Sal? Do they know that I know every inch of you? Do they know how good I am at waxing floors and fixing anything that needs fixing?"

Sally looked me over like I was just another one of her students who needed attention. Did I need a tissue or a hall pass?

"Larry, that's not it. You aren't even close. Stop making me feel bad about my family. You aren't the problem, Babe. Believe me, you're not the problem."

What was the problem? I was ready to put the tiniest diamond I could find on her finger and make room for her underneath my name. Didn't she want her family to know where she was landing?

"Do we have to get into this now? Tonight? Can we talk about it later, Larry?"

I shook my head. Later wasn't soon enough to suit me.

"I am not, not, not ashamed of you, Larry Downs. I never could be. I'm not worried at all about how you would conduct yourself in front of my parents. I'm proud of you, too."

"Then what's the problem, Sal? Why are we still making two pies? Why can't I spend Thanksgiving with my girlfriend? And Christmas? What about Christmas?"

"It's them, Larry. It's them, okay? I am nervous about introducing you to my mom and dad, but it's not about anything you would do, or say. It's not. It's them. They will be rude, okay? Just rude. My mother, especially. It's just easier this way. She'll hurt your feelings. She'll cut you to the quick, and I won't stand for that. I'm protecting you."

"Hey, now. I'm a big boy. Do you think my feelings haven't been hurt before? Do you think I'm going to wilt? Do you think anything your folks have to say is going to scare me off? There's not a chance of that, Sally, not a chance in hell."

As we waited in that sweet-smelling kitchen of hers for the pies to finish baking, Sally confirmed what I had suspected. My occupation was a big problem for her folks. They lived two towns over and were more comfortable in a country club setting. They bought wine by the bottle, not by the glass, sharing it with the doctors, lawyers and bankers who wondered if they would get invited to the Lend girl's wedding. That had been a long time coming. Sally was no longer a girl, and she wasn't the type to be all that interested in a country club wedding.

I tried to imagine bringing my clan to an affair like that. I could get myself cleaned up. Clarice could do that, too. But it was funny to think about Lee hauling her pack of dusty kids into the room. Lem was a moving target. Depending on where things stood between them, he could be her plus one or not. I cringed just thinking about it.

Sally's people used cloth napkins. Someone else mowed their lawn and trimmed their shrubs. Her father's shirts were always perfectly pressed, and he wore cuff links. He dressed up to read the paper. They had their groceries delivered. There was a line item in their budget for fresh flowers. They didn't wear shoes in the house.

Explaining to their set that their only daughter had snagged herself a janitor was going to be tricky. Scare tactics would be the only way out. They'd have to dust off their sneers. They might need to take their preconceived notions for a drive around the block to get them warmed up before Sally and I showed up with our apple pie.

It could be funny, at least for me. But I could understand her dread. I'd been embarrassed by my own people, too.

Daddy was quiet, and Mama, too. But they were simple people. Dad wore white socks with his black shoes and drank beer from a can. Mama shopped for her own groceries, loaded them in the car and into the house, week after week. She put plastic flowers on her own mother's grave.

Sally and I came from different places. We were worlds apart, and somehow landed in her tiny kitchen together, where I washed and dried, and she put away. The universe had allowed that to happen, and I was grateful for it.

We let the pie cool just a bit, then cut ourselves two big slices. It hit the spot that night. We'd have pie again the next day at her parents' house. It wouldn't taste as good as the warm treat we'd just shared, but we both knew what we had was hard to beat.

Chapter Fifty

Sally

There were times when I was sure I should break it off with Larry, even without thinking of what my mother would say. I'm educated. He isn't. I come from an upper-middle-class family. He doesn't. I'm clean and neat and meticulous. Larry isn't. I like cats. Larry doesn't like cats at all. But by the time I get to the cat argument, I think about how Larry picked Bootsie off my bed one afternoon and tossed him out into the hallway and shut the door so we could fall together on the bed without a feline to witness what we were about to do.

And then I'm reminded that Larry Downs the janitor and Sally Lend the home economics teacher are both warm in the morning under the blankets. I remember how we both enjoy drifting off into blissful sleep after sex. I remember how we both sort of smile and laugh when we're on the verge. I remember how he held me the entire night after my Grandmother Williams died and how I wanted him there. I remember how touched I was that he gave me an old snapshot of himself as a little boy. I responded by giving him a picture of me when I was about the same age.

And finally, I remember that we're just people, the two of us. We both started out as babies who grew into children who liked imagining what it would be like to be grownups. We both have pumping hearts and nerve endings that tingle. We both use our hands all day long. And we've both noticed that the differences between his hands and mine aren't all that easily detected as we sit together in the dark and laugh quietly at our unlikely, preposterous love.

Chapter Fifty-One

Larry

I loved Sally even more after that Thanksgiving.

Two hours into the visit, I marveled at who she was. I could see the cracks she'd found to work her way toward the sunlight. She had her mother's face, but it wasn't wound so tight. Sally's skin wasn't taxed. She didn't have to work so hard to maintain her smile.

Her father's handshake was limp. He was saving his enthusiasm for a different Mr. Right. That was fine. I expected it.

Our meal was served on china that had to be hand-washed. We had one fork just for salad and another for the rest of the food. The dinner conversation was as dry as the turkey. Her parents lacked curiosity, and frankly, social skills, which surprised me. They limited their comments to the weather and when holiday break would start for Sally. They hardly looked at me. They could not bring themselves to inquire about my work or my family and were not concerned if I needed another scoop of potatoes or gravy.

Sally's folks did not ask me if I'd ever tried their daughter's apple pie. Had they asked, I would have told them how familiar I was with their daughter's pie, her stew, her chicken noodle soup and her lethal thumbprint cookies.

Janitors didn't need seconds or homemade pie. We drank our coffee and ate pie in silence.

When it was almost over, Sally's father cleared his throat and placed his napkin on his plate.

"Sally, if you don't mind, your mother and I would like to have a private conversation with you. Larry, excuse us, but would you mind giving us a moment?"

He was asking me to leave the room. Flustered, I stood up and looked at Sally. Did she want me to leave?

"Larry, you don't have to go. If you want to stay, stay. If you step out, don't worry. This won't take long. I can promise you that."

"It's okay, Sal, really. I don't mind stepping outside."

I pushed my chair in and walked out to find my shoes by the front door. I slipped them on, opened the door and waited in the chill. My coat was tucked into a closet somewhere.

There was no screaming. What was happening inside that nice home was a tense, quiet storm. I wondered if I should march right back in there with my shoes on and protect my Sally. I looked at my watch. If five more minutes went by, I would do that. I had nothing to lose with these people.

The door creaked open, and Sally stepped outside. My coat was in her hand. She was wearing her long, red wool coat, my favorite. Her smile was broad and natural.

"Well, Honey, they love me, don't they?"

I enjoyed returning her smile. She laughed.

"Oh, they do. They sure do."

I took Sally by the waist and pulled her close. My lips needed to touch her forehead.

"I'm sorry, Sal. Really, I'm sorry. You were right. I have to give it to you. You knew what you were doing. You knew."

How did those vile people produce such a lovely human? Her humanity and sweetness bubbled up from somewhere deep beneath her upbringing. Decency was not genetic or tied to vocation. A teacher and a janitor could choose one another.

We drove home quiet, but happy. I wanted to tell this woman all my secrets. I kept my eyes on the road but did allow myself to look over at her now and then. She was staring out her window. The space between us and the unwelcoming place we'd just been rolled on past us. I knew that the trip was longer and more significant for Sally.

We were almost home. I looked over one more time to check on her. I was worried. This time, she was looking at me. Was she having buyer's remorse? Her smile told me that wasn't the case.

"I love you, Sal."

"Love you, too."

We waved at Miss Burns, who waved right back and watched us go inside. Sally let me help her take off her red coat.

"I've always liked you in this coat."

"Thank you. My father bought it for me at Kline's. It came with matching leather gloves and a scarf."

"Fancy. Did you lose the gloves?"

Sally nodded and sighed.

"Well, Christmas is right around the corner, Miss Lend. So, if you behave yourself, maybe Santa will bring you a new pair."

This made my girl smile.

Bootsie had grievances. We hadn't greeted him appropriately.

"Tell you what, Honey. Why don't you let me feed that damned cat and you can heat up what's left of that second pie?"

We ate by candlelight that night. I watched Sally's face for signs that she might be ready to talk, but nothing came. There was time to rehash our day later. She needed to let the break she'd just made sink in. I understood this. We had all the time in the world and guts full of pie. My girl's heart had been battered but was still beating strong for me. She had chosen me. My own heart was bursting.

Chapter Fifty-Two

Jules

I couldn't let Vi or her mother see me scared. As I knocked on the door, I was nervous about asking to come inside. The answer would likely be a polite no. Mrs. Sellers might come out on the porch to visit with me or suggest we take care of our business with the screen door between us. You never know what nice people might do.

I'd come to Violet's house that day knowing she had more to tell. I owed it to her to listen. I missed her. I hoped she missed me, too.

Mr. Bones startled me. Nice girls don't have tattoos on their arms, or their legs, or anywhere, and they sure don't let them peek out the top of their underpants. Nice girls don't even know where or how to get a tattoo. Girls like Vi had money for the movies, magazines and sodas, not permanent designs burned into their skin.

When I walked away from her that day after she showed me Mr. Bones, I knew exactly how he got there. By the time I reached the top of the road that led to Shakey's Half, I was light-headed and shocked. I never should have let Vi bully me into taking her to my part of town. That was no place for a girl like her, or any girl, for that matter. I let her break me down.

All I wanted to do in Shakey's Half was show her that she didn't have it so bad, that her head wasn't stinging and smelling like gasoline. I wanted her to see the dirt, stray cats and a starving dog or two. I wanted Violet to catch the full stench of the unwashed by standing downwind from a pack of us.

I didn't count on running into Lem. That was too much for Violet. His hands had touched hers. I didn't like that. I didn't like the way his lip curled upward when he heard her name. I didn't like that he knew who she was or that Momma had been talking about us.

I moved with purpose that afternoon. My feet felt heavy on the stoop. I swung our front door open with force because I wanted Momma and the girls to know I was there. I slammed it shut to be sure they heard me. I felt like a man.

The big girls were in the corner by the open window, perfecting cat's cradle and other string games with a ball of mustard-colored yarn nobody would ever pick to make a sweater or even a hat. It must have been free, scrounged from the trash by Lem on one of his shifty rounds.

My sisters turned around to look at me for just a minute, then went back to their work. Even Kitty was in on the fun they were making out of someone's castoffs.

Momma was in the kitchen, smoking a cigarette and making toasted cheese sandwiches in the oven.

"Jules Marks, don't you slam that door like that. We don't need another thing around here to fix, do we? Where have you been?"

She knew where I'd been. She liked it that I had Violet as a friend. She always wanted to know anything I could tell her about my visits. It was the most interest she'd taken in me that I could remember. I didn't give her an answer.

"What's the matter with you? What's all the huffing and puffing about? Huh?"

She seemed amused, not concerned. My mother found the anger I brought into the room funny. She was ready to have fun with me.

"Well, Jules, I didn't think you had it in you, so I have to know what this is all about. Did you get yourself into a fight with that little girlfriend of yours? I bet that's what happened. That's it, isn't it?"

She took a long draw from her cigarette and smiled at me. It wasn't the smile a mother gives to her son. It was a smile that confirmed for me what I'd known all along. The adult in the room was just a reckless child herself. She was right. I *did* have more sense in my head than her. I had more sense than Lem, too. The truth was, even our little Kitty brought more to the table than those two fools.

"Where's Lem? Has he been by yet today?"

It was an odd question. Lem and Momma didn't work like that. None of us ever knew where he was. He popped up when it suited him. He brought scraps, and if the mood was right, he shared a laugh with Momma. The two of them made black magic between them.

Chapter Fifty-Three

Violet

No self-respecting skull lets itself be seen without cross bones under its chin. That would be akin to a man showing up at church wearing no tie. It just wasn't done in polite circles.

Mr. Bones almost didn't get this important accessory when Lem Hauser and Jules' mama helped burn him into being.

I nearly fainted when his dirty hot tool first touched my white belly. With stinking Lem hunched over me, smiling and exchanging amused looks with his assistant, I nearly wretched a few times. The full-cooked smell of my own skin didn't work up from my belly to my nose until the skull was completely crafted. Once it hit, I lurched up from the cot and turned to one side to dry heave.

"I'm good," I said. "I think this is good enough. Stop. I'm finished. I want to go home."

Lem cleared his throat and turned his head to spit out a blob of brown tobacco.

"Vi, may I call you Vi? You paid me for a skull and cross bones, so you better let me finish the job."

He motioned for me to lie back down.

Tearful, I did as I was told. He could hurt me. I'd asked for this. Lee held my arms to my sides so the artist could get back to work. I cried through it all as Lem kept his gaze on me.

Once his work was done, I sat up and took a look around the tent. It was dirty and piled up with all kinds of rusty junk.

I did not belong there.

"Thanks for your business, Vi."

Lem leered as I made my way through the tent's flappy door.

"Yes, thank you, Violet," said Lee. "I hope you are pleased with your purchase. You be sure to tell your mama *hello*."

Chapter Fifty-Four

Jules

It was okay for Vi to bring me to her neighborhood, where all the goodness could rub off on both of us. But bringing someone clean and fresh and sweet-smelling like Violet to our neck of the woods was kinda dangerous. The scrappy, ragged patch of the world I shared with my sisters had barbs and deep holes, which were tailor made for trapping the innocent.

I stared at my mother.

"I *said* where's Lem?"

Momma put her cigarette out in the sink. Maybe she heard my voice change. Maybe she saw that I had in me the makings of a man, someone who could do more things of consequence for her. Maybe she could see, now that I was already a head taller than her, that I was on the verge of being able to hurt her if I wanted to.

"He's out back."

I made sure to slam the door hard on my way out. If I wanted to break it, I would. I'd be the one fixing it anyway.

I walked around the corner of our tin can house and soon saw Lem poking a stick into a burning barrel. It was burnt orange with rust and riddled with holes. We needed a new one for a long time, but Lem was waiting until it crumbled into pieces before he went to the trouble of scrounging something up for us.

I stood still to gather up my nerves, watching the man who was my father take up space and time with his foolishness.

He'd been wearing the same pair of nubby corduroy pants for as long as I could remember, even in the heat of summer. He liked flannel shirts and had taken to wearing a pair of used cowboy boots he'd dug out of someone's trash. He had no socks, and I was sure he never wore any underwear.

I wondered where this father of mine washed his clothes, if he ever did. I'd never seen them thrown in with our clothes at the laundromat. He took to wearing whatever ballcap he could find that someone had left behind. On that day, he was a Chicago Cubs fan, standing there long and lean, thinking about his next move.

As I moved in closer, he turned and flashed his wild smile at me.

"Well, look what the cat dragged in! What's up, my man? What's Jules Marks up to this fine day?"

He winked. He didn't have a care in the world, and I shouldn't have any either. I hated him.

I nodded and moved in closer. We stood together, staring into the burn barrel, still and quiet.

"You got something to say to me, you'd better say it, boy."

His hunting knife was tucked neatly into his belt. He kept a pack of Camels in his shirt pocket and a can of chew tucked into the back pocket of his pants. Most mornings, the girls didn't have milk for their cereal, but Lem's tobacco needs were always met. Always.

"Spit it out, boy."

I cleared my throat, hoping like hell that what I was about to croak would sound tough.

A breach had been crossed, and he needed to know it.

"You stay away from Violet. You hear me? Do you hear? You stay away from her!"

Lem smiled.

"Well, will you look at that, Jules? Old Lem didn't think you had it in you, Son. I thought you were as soft as that pack of girls in there."

"I mean it. I've seen the tattoo. You did that, you piece of shit. You stay away from her, you hear me?"

I was screaming, letting spittle fly and land where it would. Just like Momma, Lem seemed amused. He wasn't bothered in the least by my wrath.

He gave the wad of chew that was tucked into the side of his cheek a suck and spit. It was disgusting.

"Jules, Jules, Jules. Whoooweee, my boy. You're a fast one, aren't you? I didn't think you had it in you, you soft son-of-a-bitch. Well, I'll be damned. Look at you. Just barely in high school and already seeing that part of a girl up close! I gotta give it to you, Jules. I got to. Wait till I tell your momma."

I hated him. I hated every last thing about him.

"Now, Jules, I hate to tell you, but I got there first, you know. I saw that before you ever did. I saw that before your little gal let me work on her. I saw that clean and white as a brand-new sheet, my boy."

He laughed some more, nearly choking on the dark tobacco juice sloshing around in his mouth. The childish, but powerful nature of his laugh stung. He wasn't taking me seriously.

I lunged for him. I caught him off guard, and we both tumbled to the ground. I could feel the dust on my teeth and the smell of his wet tobacco breath. My body was on top of him. I started swinging as hard as I could. His ballcap had fallen to the ground, so I could see his greasy black hair, slicked down with pure meanness. I landed some good punches and kept swinging until he stopped me and pushed me off him. The push was hard enough to knock down the burn barrel.

I scrambled to my feet and ran back at him, but he'd already made it to his feet. He saw me coming. Momma and the girls were at the back window watching us scrap. Lem threw a hard punch at my jaw and pushed me to the back wall of the trailer we called home.

That took the wind out of me. I stood there for a minute and let it sink in that Momma wasn't coming out to separate us, despite the shrieks coming from the girls. The air between us bristled. Hungry dogs barked in the distance. My face throbbed.

I ran toward the front of the house. Lem followed me, stopping at the corner to catch his breath.

"Hey, Jules, you come back any time and wrestle with old Lem. Anytime, Sir."

Angry tears started to pool behind my eyes. I didn't want them to drip down my face until I'd put more distance between us. They started falling anyway.

"Jules Marks, are you crying, boy? Where's the big man I just saw back there? He didn't stay too long, now, did he?"

Lem howled with laughter.

I headed back to town. I hoped to find Aunt Clarice who could take me in for the night.

"Hey, Jules! Before you go, you might want to talk to that momma of yours. Your little girlfriend's tattoo wasn't all my doing. No, Sir. She was right there with me. Whoooweee!"

Lem's cruel cackling could be heard all the way to the top of the gravel road. My girls were there in that mess, but I'd be back to get them. I would.

I splashed my face with cool water from the drinking fountain at the city park and caught my breath. It was time for me to hear why Violet let that nasty Lem and Momma burn something so ugly onto her beautiful skin. By the time I made it to Vi's, I knew I wouldn't be back at Shakey's Half until I could pack up those girls and leave forever.

Chapter Fifty-Five

Sally

I had a new dress for the first day of school. Larry approved.

"Look at you, Miss Lend. Just look at you. I'm not sure I can let you take off looking like that."

I looked fine. The dress was nothing special, just yellow cotton with a wide belt. A sunflower choker around my neck gave the whole thing zip. It was good enough to face the day.

I wouldn't see Jules until fifth hour. The first day of school usually zoomed right on by, but not this one. This day was slow. The lunch that Larry handed me on my way out the door didn't look good when I opened it. I took one bite of a peanut butter cookie, then tucked the rest back into my bag.

Third hour dragged on, then fourth. The bell finally rang, and the halls were filled with footsteps, loud shouts and flirty shrieks from a bunch of teenagers who wanted attention. Most were happy to be back in the same space together. Some were cutting up; some were shrinking into themselves, some were lost, and some were way more sure of themselves than they should have been.

I watched from behind my desk as the next patch of kids filed into my room. They came in clumps: one girl, two boys, two girls, three boys. On and on, they took their places. The troublemakers couldn't resist messing with each other.

As if he knew I was on the lookout for him, in walked Jules Marks. He'd made it just in time before the bell rang. This grown-up Jules could tell time and write his name. He could read.

His hair was wet and slicked back with a comb. He'd just come from gym class and taken his first shower at school. I was happy for him. I imagined that it was worth being naked in front of all the other boys just to have that water fall all over him. I wondered if anyone told him he'd need to bring a towel.

Jules had a freshness about him. I was glad he moved from shop class to my home-ec room and that he would finish the rest of the school day smelling neutral.

He was taller, too, which, of course was to be expected after so many years. He was still skinny and long-legged. When his hair was wet, it looked dark. When it dried, you could see the dirty blonde. His face was less round. His button nose had become just a little less pug. But his dark brown eyes were unchanged—deep and endless, framed with the longest lashes I'd ever seen on a boy or a girl. Still remarkable.

His beautiful eyes widened a bit as he took in his new surroundings. They popped bigger and brighter once they landed on me at the front of the room. I saw a smile of recognition as he remembered me.

I wondered what he saw. I probably looked smaller, and my waist was a little thicker. Perhaps this wiser, older version of Jules could now accept an older, wiser version of me with less awe.

In the years that had passed since I'd last seen him, other people had imprinted themselves on him with acts of kindness and cruelty. Other adults had spoken to him and expected a response. They had called him by his name, introduced new things to him, tried to save him, disappointed him and noticed him.

Other teachers had been charged with telling him to gather his things because he had to go home to take care of that head of his. Surely such a duty moved them like it had me.

Watching him take in the message that he was not acceptable, that he would need to leave and not come back until his head and neck had been inspected, stopped them in their tracks, or at least I hoped it did.

Fifth hour flew by. I could feel his eyes on me as I passed out a new lesson for the day. He watched me help someone thread a needle.

The bell startled me. Class was over. I stood at the door as the kids filed out one by one to merge into the traffic of the crowded hallway.

Jules was the last one out. He smiled at me.

"Hello there, Miss Lend. Do you remember me?"

Chapter Fifty-Six

Gloria

I could pick Jules Marks out of a crowd. His face had not changed. That dimple and those brown eyes gave him away.

Since he started coming back around, I worked hard to minimize contact. It still hurt to think of that boy and to imagine what his sisters looked like. Occasionally, I'd see one of them, or even Lee, from afar, and quickly avert my gaze or duck behind something.

I still felt shame for abandoning them all like I did. But there he was, just on the other side of my screen door, asking to come in. If the kid needed to use the bathroom, I was going to let him.

"Come on in, Jules. The bathroom is down the hall and to the right."

He stepped inside but didn't move much past the threshold. He was planted there and wasn't moving until he said what he was there to say. He looked out of place.

"Mrs. Sellers, I don't need to use the bathroom, but I would like to talk to you for a minute, if you don't mind."

He licked his dry lips as I led him into the dining room. The light in that room streamed through the open window and cast a patch of late afternoon sunlight onto his face. I could see a purple bruise. It was dark, freshly acquired and looked like it might get darker. Instinctively, I reached to touch it. He flinched.

"Jules, what happened to your face?"

He shook his head and stepped back.

"That's not what I'm here to talk about."

"Okay, okay."

I made a mental note to not let him leave without an ice pack.

"What do you want to talk about?"

He swallowed, then blurted out what he'd been holding back.

"It's Vi. I know about Vi's tattoo. I know all about it. I'm sorry I've seen it, but there's nothing we can do about that now. But I know how she got it, and I know who did it, and I know why she asked for it. I know all of this. I know everything about Mr. Bones."

Jules was talking so fast there was no stopping him. He seemed relieved to have pushed all of it out into the air, where someone else could decide where it belonged, which was anywhere but inside this scroungy, brave boy's head.

Lice be damned, I drew him to me. Jules didn't resist. He let his head land on my chest. I kissed the top of his head, and we stood there. I could see Vi standing at the door. Ugly tears ran down her face.

She looked small. She *was* small.

"Vi, Honey, come in here. Come, Baby."

She ran toward us and landed in a wet wreck on my other side. Jules put his hand on her back to pull her in closer. That whole thing broke me to bits.

Jules fed it all to me in waves, while Violet stood by to confirm. She had shared the story with her friend and could do no more.

Dirty, lovely, bruised-up Jules did the talking for her and he did an admirable job.

Our Vi had been distant from us for so long, but she'd not been alone. She'd found safe harbor in this boy from Shakey's Half.

Skip came home expecting supper as usual, but I hadn't prepared anything. We settled on tomato soup and grilled cheese. Vi went up for a bubble bath, leaving us alone with Jules. He ate two more sandwiches and another bowl of soup.

"Son, we've got to talk about this tattoo," said Skip. "I want you to tell me every last thing you know."

Jules seemed comfortable with my husband's hand on his shoulder. He needed assurance, just one more time, that he wasn't in trouble. He wanted promises that his sisters would escape Shakey's Half.

"I promise you that, Jules. Look at me, Son. I promise that."

Skip was relieved to finally assign a name to the person responsible for Mr. Bones. Hearing Jules was hard. Thinking about our girl seeking that out and enduring it was even harder.

I could tell that Skip was ready to get in the car and head to the police station. He wanted to show up at Shakey's Half and watch them round up Lem Hauser and Lee Marks in a squad car that very night. But Skip didn't know what happened before the tattoo. He didn't know that it was worse. It was much, much worse.

Chapter Fifty-Seven

Jules

My jaw ached from Lem's knuckles. I'll never forget the smile on his face as he watched my cheek crush from the force of his fist. It wasn't the hit that hurt the most. What hurt worse was his smile.

Lem had never hit me before. That was the first time, and as I held an ice pack to my face, I swore it would be the last.

Vi's mother let me take a shower. The water was hotter than at school. I washed my body with a bar of white soap that smelled like my friend. Then, I dried off with a fluffy, white towel. Mrs. Sellers had thrown my clothes in her washer and handed me an old robe.

I slipped into clean sheets. Their coolness felt strange as they met my clean neck. Falling asleep was hard. I couldn't stop thinking about what had happened over the past few days. Mr. Bones, my fight with Lem, coming to Vi's porch to hear the rest of her story about her nasty cousin and knowing as soon as the story left her lips that we had no choice but to tell somebody.

The window in the guest room was open and I felt a breeze whisper across my sore face. In that moment, I was safe. For that night at least, I was comfortable and sure of the next minute, and the minute after that. Just across town, not far away at all, my girls were in another world. Their sheets were tangled and dirty. Outside air never made it inside the trailer to calm the nerves or cut the smell in half.

I needed three bowls of hot soup to fill my guts. I could have eaten more. Peg, Suze, Lolly and even Patty would have loved one bowl for each of them. We would have to coach Kitty to finish hers, but it would have been a start.

We could eat soup and let our hair grow long. We could take deep, clean breaths. We could claim space for ourselves that wasn't ugly and dry or dusty and tired. We could be watered and fed, washed and held, protected and loved. These were things we could claim as our own.

My jaw still smarted. The sheriff was right. I had myself a shiner. Lem's knuckles could have landed on me more if he had wanted. I'm glad he thought one punch was enough.

I stayed out of scraps like that. You wouldn't catch Jules Marks fighting in the school parking lot over a pack of cigarettes or just to fill the time before the bell rang.

I couldn't think of too many things worth fighting for, but I was glad I threw the first punch my first time in the ring. I'm glad each one landed on the same part of Lem's face.

The next day, my punching hand smarted, and the day after that. It might be a while before I could hold a pencil or cut a cucumber the way Miss Lend wanted, let alone my own skin.

In the midst of that lingering pain, something stuck with me even worse. What came out of Lem's mouth as I scrambled out of Shakey's Half hit me hard. It made me shudder and stung like no punch ever could. They pierced right through me, and the truth they brought hurt more than a second punch from Lem's fist ever could, more than any sharp tool or needle, or even one of Vi's fancy seam rippers.

My father was trash and so was my mother. Me and my girls, all six of us, came from the bottom of the burn barrel.

Chapter Fifty-Eight

Skip

I cannot tell a lie. I thoroughly enjoyed watching Lem Hauser and Lee Marks walk into the police station with their hands bound behind their backs. I sat on a bench in the hallway to watch the parade. Gloria was worried I'd make a scene.

"Skip, are you sure you need to be down there?"

"Yes, Gloria. I am sure. I will be there. You can count on that."

There was a grittiness about those two. Lee was still scrawny but looked like she'd settled into being shifty. She was no longer a hungry girl. She was now a hardened woman. Feral. I'd never laid eyes on Lem. I'd heard stories. It was hard to tell just how old this boogeyman was. He needed to be taken out back so someone could hose him off and scrub his ass with a wire brush. The fool needed to stop hiding behind his crazy.

Neither one of them made eye contact with me as they passed me in the hallway, but they saw me. I *wanted* them to see me. They would see me, all right.

Chapter Fifty-Nine

Sally

Jules was a unique enough name that Larry and I had to be talking about the same kid. He was no Bob or Jim. Andrew didn't suit him. Neither did Todd or Tim. He was a Jules. How he landed that name mystified me, but it suited him.

I thought I knew every corner of the man in my life. I knew how he liked his coffee and that he always put on his left boot before the right. He had a birthmark on the back of his right knee. He liked to watch baseball and asked me to pass the pepper and salt, in that order. Larry Downs didn't want salt and pepper. He wanted pepper and salt. He liked vinegar on his fries, not catsup. I never did understand that one, but the way he kissed me on my forehead in the mornings made it worth having a bottle of malt vinegar next to the pepper and the salt. He could be talked into watching an old movie with me. He let me put a drop of vanilla extract into the mug of hot cocoa he shared with me after we drove through town to look at all the houses lit up for Christmas.

In all the years we had shared together up to that point, I had no idea we shared something concerning Jules. Larry did not know that Jules Marks also haunted my dreams. Getting away from that sweet, sad little boy was what drove me toward the home economics room at the end of the hall that got swept and mopped by the love of my life.

Jules brought me to that wonderful uncle of his. Now, we owed that kid something big and just as wonderful.

Chapter Sixty

Larry

I loved the easy Saturdays and Sundays I shared with Sally. We stayed in bed longer than we should have. We drank coffee on her little patio out back if the weather was right, waving to old Miss Burns and giving Sally's fat cat more attention than he deserved. He seemed to know it was the weekend, too.

My beautiful Miss Lend finally got comfortable handing me a Honey-To-Do list.

"Oh, Honey," she'd say, her head cocked to one side. I still loved how she did that. I needed to get around to marrying this one someday.

"Are you sure? You do nothing all day long but fix things. Why don't you just take it easy for once?"

Nope. Didn't this girl know how much I liked putting things right? I was made to untangle knots and clean out drains. I liked giving lazy cars the kick in the ass they deserved, to sweet talk breaker boxes and to love on Sally. I was meant for *all* these things.

On that Saturday, she didn't have anything for me to do. The whole place was in tip-top shape.

Could I pop over to Miss Burns' place, though?

Her tub wouldn't drain, and her icebox was making a funny noise. I never minded helping the neighbor. She looked a little witchy on the outside, but inside, she was as soft as butter and wanting company. We started each repair session with a cup of hot coffee and a roll. I liked the way this old gal let time and schedules wait on the porch until she was ready to answer any demands from her day.

Miss Burns and I chatted about all kinds of nothing while I worked on her tub. I'd fixed that drain before. All it needed was someone to fish out the long strings of white hair. That woman had a head of hair that went all the way down her back. She kept it in a neat braid.

"Miss Burns, can I ask you a question?"

"Well, yes, of course."

"Now don't get yourself all worked up, but I'm wondering about this tub. How can you get in and out of this all by yourself? It's slippery. It's downright dangerous. You're going to fall one of these days. I can see it coming, Miss Burns."

"You might be right. I've been getting in and out of that tub every night without a scratch for years, but I am getting wobbly. I know it, but I'm not willing to give up my baths."

I shook my head.

"Oh, no Ma'am. I wouldn't ask you to. Once I get this drain cleaned out, would you let me run to the hardware store and get us a pack of those sticky strips that will give you traction? And a handlebar here on the wall to keep you steady?"

She liked that idea.

"If it isn't too much trouble."

"We've got ourselves a deal, Miss Burns. Let's tackle that noisy fridge of yours and then I'll come back with what we need for the tub. You'll be bathing safely by tonight."

As I followed my old friend into her kitchen, we heard a knock on the door. It was Sally and Clarice. Something was wrong.

"Miss Burns, I'll be back with what we need for your tub, and we'll work on your fridge next."

"You go on, now. Don't you mind about that."

She waved me out the door to tend to a new problem.

Clarice was usually at the diner on Saturdays. Her only day off was Sunday. My sister stood there in Miss Burns' tiny patch of a yard, still in her work clothes. I noticed that she'd finally taken my advice and got herself a pair of sensible shoes.

Over the years, Clarice had slowly taken to wearing more makeup, especially around the eyes. On that morning, her eyes were a mess. Tears were smeared with blue eye shadow and black mascara that was supposed to be waterproof.

Sally's hand was on her back, and she had a wad of tissues in the other. It made me love my soft-hearted girl even more.

"Honey, catch your breath and talk to me. Talk to me, Clarice."

She was shuddering.

The last time I saw her like that we were getting one last look at Mama before the casket was closed.

"Girl, look at me. Whatever it is, we can fix it. You know that."

We walked back to Sally's place and sat at her kitchen table.

The police had come to the diner, asking for Clarice. She needed to come with them to the station. Shit. Lem had been arrested. Lee, too. All five of the girls had been loaded into the back of a second squad car that followed the one carrying Lem and Lee out of Shakey's Half. The girls. Shit. Someone needed to get them.

Shit. Shit. Shit.

The girls were a tough little pack. Peg, Suze, Lolly, Patty and Kitty Cat. That little face could make a grown man cry.

Lem was nothing but trash, and Lee was no better.

Clarice and I had been to Shakey's Half more times than we could count—bringing all kinds of food, cough syrup, aspirin, clean clothes and blankets—whatever we could throw into the trailer for those kids.

They were scrawny and wide-eyed. We'd lost sleep over it. We'd reported our sister to the authorities more times than I could count. Clarice had that tallied up somewhere.

Sad. That's how every police officer and social worker described the situation. Sad, but no laws were being broken. Having head lice and unwashed bodies wasn't a crime. It was pitiful, but not criminal.

They could get Lee on food stamps and make sure that the town of Poulson's ministerial alliance knew that the Marks children needed a turkey, and all the fixings dropped off on their stoop for Thanksgiving. They also made sure that Santa Claus didn't forget them on Christmas. They could do that for us.

We left every conversation like this angrier than the time before. We worried about those girls and Jules, too.

Jules. Where was Jules?

Clarice calmed down enough to explain.

"Jules is fine. He's staying at the Sellers' house for now."

Fucking perfect. '

We sure didn't need that family all up in our business. They'd done enough. That was for sure.

Clarice told us more. Each detail made sense but made me sick. A tattoo? On Violet Sellers' belly? For thirty-five dollars? A skull and crossbones? Lem did *that*? With Lee's help? Miss Burns might need to wait a night or two for her next bath. We had ourselves a tangle.

It was time for me to do what I was made to do. With Clarice on standby, and my sweet, sweet Sally, we could make this right.

Chapter Sixty-One

Violet

It felt good to let my mother hold me in my bed that night after she let Jules come inside and stay in the guest room.

She held me like she did when I was little. Her mouth was planted right behind my ear and her warm breath tickled me into a deep sleep.

Jules, Gloria and I went to bed that night sharing something beyond Mr. Bones. The dark truth of what had happened with James was still heavy in the air. I had shared my portion with Jules, and he was wise enough to see that we couldn't hold onto such a load for long. I was in danger. He insisted that we cut someone else in, which was a relief.

We told Gloria about what happened with Jamie. Watching her face as she listened humbled me. It reminded me that she *did* love me. She watched our faces, too, looking for traces of a tall tale. That would be easier to deal with than the truth. She glanced up at the grandfather clock. Time was ticking, and Skip would be home soon.

"Violet, Honey, I don't think your dad can take all this news. Not all of it at once. I need to think about this more, Vi. I just do."

She was pleading with us. We agreed that Skip would only find out about the tattoo that night. That would be enough. Skip needed to be spoon fed the full story, to take it all in with baby bites or he would explode right there in front of Jules.

Skip was ready to go the next morning. I'm not sure he even slept. For him, the tattoo was the only problem to be solved. He was ready to pounce, and that reminded me that my father loved me, too.

The sheriff arrived. The gun in his holster hung black and heavy on his hip. His pants had crisp creases, and a pair of silver handcuffs swung from the other hip. This was official business. He turned down the cup of coffee my mother offered him and talked in low, manly tones with my father in the living room.

Jules was back in his own clothes. They were still ratty, but now they were clean. His bruised face looked sore and the purple patch on his jaw looked like it had spread to his cheek and his eye, which was puffy and half-shut.

My Jules, small as he was, stood next to my dad and the sheriff. They both wanted to talk to him first. He sure did look scared. Dad pulled Jules in by the shoulder. I could see the gold wedding ring on my father's hand as he gave my friend a gentle squeeze. He wasn't alone. He was doing the right thing. He wasn't in trouble. Jules' scrawny frame sagged with relief.

"Jules, this is Sheriff Bates. I've known him a long time. He's here to help us. Bates, this is Jules Marks."

They shook hands. The sheriff lifted Jules' chin to take a better look at his face.

"You got yourself a shiner, Son. Looks like you took quite a hit, now, didn't you?"

Jules nodded as the two men assessed the damage.

The sheriff cleared his throat and shifted his weight.

"I don't think you need stitches, but you'd better keep that iced up. Did you get yourself into a fight?"

"Yes, Sir. Yes, I did."

"You got you some brothers to scrap with? Friends?"

"No, Sir. I've got little sisters. And Vi. I've got Vi."

Jules had me. He had me. He sure did.

"Well, let's talk about what happened. As long as you tell me the truth, you're going to be okay. Do you believe me?"

"Yes, Sir. I believe you. I do."

Jules' voice was getting stronger. He sounded serious and sure of himself as he told them about the fight with Lem and the tattoo and Lem's parting words.

The sheriff knew all about Lem.

"Jules, did you get yourself a good swing or two at old Lem?"

Jules nodded.

"That's my boy."

I was next. The sheriff would need to see Mr. Bones. He excused Jules and called me in. He called my mother in, too. I felt shy and stupid as they gazed at my belly.

"I think we've seen what we need to see here," said the sheriff.

He wanted to know about how it got there in the first place, so I told him. My father's face changed colors with each new detail I added. I'd been to Shakey's Half by myself, without Jules. He was in afterschool detention that week for all his tardies and to make up assignments he'd missed during another head lice episode.

To say any more would have drifted into territory we'd promised my mother to hold onto for a while.

That morning, I didn't tell the sheriff or my father about how I even decided Mr. Bones was needed.

I was ready to do something drastic that day. We'd spent a Sunday afternoon at Aunt Ruth's to celebrate my cousin's birthday. I didn't want to go, but my mother insisted.

"Violet June. You're going. It won't hurt you to have a little cake and ice cream for your cousin's birthday. Your grandparents will be there, too. Now get dressed. We're leaving in half an hour."

All of us stood around my aunt and uncle's table and sang Happy Birthday to Jamie. He blew out the candles. I watched my mother and aunt fuss around the cake, slicing it up and scooping ice cream onto party plates. The first plate went to the birthday boy, of course.

"What did you wish for, Jamie?"

The question came from my grandmother. She thought that Jamie was something else, a real pistol.

"Granny. You know I can't tell. If I tell you, it won't come true!"

Everybody had a good chuckle. He was so funny, my cousin. Full of fun and always teasing us. We watched him open presents and thank everyone with his pretty mouth. He knew just what to say.

My grandmother, Gloria and Aunt Ruthie fussed some more as they picked up wrapping paper and ribbons and clucked about how quickly time had passed. Why just yesterday, he was a little dumpling and look at him now, all grown up and almost out of high school.

I walked into the living room to get away from them. I could hear my cousin's footsteps behind me.

"Vi, hey Vi."

His voice made me sick. I didn't have to answer him. I didn't owe him that at all. I didn't owe him anything except the worst trouble I could imagine.

"Well, aren't you a rude one, Cousin? Don't you want to know what I wished for? Come on, Vi. Don't you want to play Chinese checkers? I bet you're ready for me to teach you how to play chess. I bet you're ready for that."

I don't remember the ride home. When I got up the stairs to my room, I tossed my sewing kit on the bed. The needles and pins weren't sharp enough. The scissors meant for snipping had nothing to offer me, either. A razor blade from under the bathroom sink was the best I could do that night. The next day after school, I left Jules behind to take his consequences like a man and headed for Shakey's Half.

At the top of the road stood Lem, just who I was looking for. He gave me a wave and big, yellow-toothed grin. He was happy to see me. Any friend of Jules was a friend of his.

"If you're looking for Jules, little miss, your friend's not here. I'm not sure where that scoundrel is."

"He's doing detention all week for being tardy too much. And he's got makeup work to do for all those days he missed."

Lem nodded as if he knew those kinds of details about Jules.

"Well, what are you doing here, then? Aren't you lonely without your little boyfriend?"

"He's not my boyfriend. We're friends, that's all. We're friends."

"Okay, okay. What can I do for you, Miss Sellers?"

"I'm here to do business with you. I've got money to pay you."

I patted my pocket. I had birthday money saved up and hoped I had enough to deliver.

Lem chuckled.

I could see why Jules hated him.

"Just what is it you're hoping to buy?"

"A tattoo. I want a tattoo like the one on your arm. That's what I want. How much will one of those cost me?"

I'd shocked him.

"Well, that's not something old Lem can do for you. No, no, that won't go over. That banker daddy of yours will have my hide. Yes, Sir. He'd have that, for sure."

"My dad doesn't have to know. Okay? He'll never see it. I've got that figured out."

Old Lem was interested. He had to know more. I told him what I wanted, and where.

"How much are you willing to shell out for something special like that? That could cost you."

I showed him what I had—thirty-five dollars. Three tens and five singles, all crisp and straight from the bank.

"You stay put. I need to speak with my assistant. Let me see if we have an opening for you."

Lem took off down the gravel road. I watched him turn the corner with his beat-up boots. Fifteen minutes later, he was back. We had us a deal. He and his assistant could fit me in. All I needed to do was show up the next afternoon. I needed to meet them at Lem's tent that was in the woods behind the school.

Chapter Sixty-Two

Gloria

The night I spent spooning our damaged daughter, thinking about nasty Lee and Lem crouched over our child to scar her like they did should have kept me wide awake, but it didn't. Instead, I tumbled into a deep dark swirl of a dream. I wish I'd been left to only toss and turn because sleep did not bring the relief I needed so badly.

I'd only seen Lem up close a time or two. He was large, lanky and odd-looking and he seemed to only get odder as the years went by. My nightmare's interpretation of him reminded me what he was capable of, as if Violet's tattoo wasn't confirmation enough.

Nightmare Lem had no soul. His piercing eyes leered with pleasure as he went about the business of making mothers tremble. His sidekick was Lee. No longer an ignorant, willful little girl, this dream-conjured version was something far worse, an ignorant and willful full-grown woman who could remember unwrapping my gifts from Kline's only as long as there were more.

When the last package was torn open and the ribbons and tissue paper were discarded, the void left unfilled brought out her fangs. She became a hungry lioness saddled with even hungrier cubs to feed. It made her ferocious and unforgiving. It forced her to move along in search of the next feed, but she'd be back to give me one last scratch.

In my dream, Jules was helping Lee and Lem. With his head freshly shaved, he walked Violet out to the woods where she was going to be placed upon their altar. They shaved her head, too, and Lee gathered the locks that fell to the ground to be sold or made into something later. Lee and Lem went about their burning work on Vi, but my dream scene did more damage. Dreamy Jules with his serious face and soft brown eyes held Violet's arms at her side as they burned a new message onto her quivering belly. The mysterious missive was at the heart of it, and they wouldn't let me see it. Lee laughed as she blindfolded me so I could not see my girl's new marking. Jules left the tent as Lem and Lee cackled at Violet's cries and howled even more fiendishly at mine.

When I woke up for a second, I knew that Jules would never be part of that story. He came from Lee and Lem, but he wasn't like them. He would never hold Violet down like that. But then I slipped back into the dream's final, shocking conclusion.

To get a standing ovation for my performance, I would need to look surprised when Violet's skull and crossbones was revealed. My blindfold came off and the curtain rose. Lee and Lem moved out from the spotlight and then James walked with me to see the finished design. He did not seem to remember that we were family as he leered at me and pulled me closer to see a new carving that was larger than Mr. Bones.

Love, James.

As I woke for real, Violet's sheets were wet with my sweat. I looked around the room for signs of morning. Vi had not moved once during the night. My arm underneath her was heavy and tingling. I let the truth settle back into me.

Violet's tattoo was the least of our problems.

Chapter Sixty-Three

Skip

As I watched Vi and the Marks kid hug so hard before he left with his uncle, I felt humbled. Seeing Jules cleaned up and sitting at our kitchen table, scarfing down his food like any other boy his age, made me ashamed that I had supported banishing the kid to our front porch like he was some kind of stray cat.

Gloria, Violet and I had some thinking to do. There were problems to solve that would require careful consideration and we had to start by rehashing old tangles. There was plenty of blame to distribute.

"Where's Vi?"

Gloria was sitting in her favorite chair in the living room with her legs tucked underneath her. It wasn't like her to leave dishes in the sink, but on that day, something had been turned upside down.

"She's upstairs, taking a nap, I think. Our girl needs rest."

I nodded and walked toward my wife. When she didn't have any makeup on, she still looked like a child.

"What are you thinking about, Skip?"

"Just wondering the same about you. Jules is quite a young man, isn't he?"

She nodded.

"Yes, he's a good kid. I'm ashamed that we didn't welcome him into our house sooner. I feel terrible about it."

Gloria's reaction was appropriate. We should have felt bad about ourselves, but there was more to it, a whole lot more.

"Honey, the kid gets sent home from school a few times a year with head lice. Don't beat yourself up about that. It's common sense."

Gloria shook her head at me.

"Skip, this isn't about lice. This is way deeper and uglier than that, and we both know it. We didn't let that kid inside our home because we didn't want to open up a can of worms with his mother. Having him around made us uncomfortable. We didn't want Lee sniffing around, manipulating more from us."

"Gloria, listen to me. Jules is a nice kid. He really is. I feel damned sorry for him, and that whole pack of kids Lee brought into this world. But we can't forget that Vi wouldn't have that tattoo if it weren't for Jules. There's no way that our nice girl would have ever even met a degenerate like Lem Hauser, or frankly, Lee Marks, if she hadn't been buddies with a kid from that part of town. Plain and simple."

Gloria set down her tea.

"Skip, are you suggesting that we should have forbidden Violet's friendship with Jules? Really? That we shouldn't have even let him on our porch?"

What exactly *was* I suggesting? It wasn't about Jules or the porch. Gloria knew right where I was headed, and I didn't need to say a word about it to raise her hackles.

"I know what you're thinking. Why don't you just say it, Skip? Why? It's what you want, isn't it? Come on, banker man. Say what's on your mind."

"Are you sure you want that, Gloria? Are you sure?"

She stood up and stomped into the kitchen. I followed.

"Okay, I'll say it. I'll just say it. None of this would have happened, none of it, if you hadn't insisted on helping Lee Marks in the first place. You never should have done that, not for as long as you did, Gloria. It wasn't necessary, and frankly, it was *odd*. We didn't owe that trashy girl a thing. Not one damned thing, but you kept throwing more and more at her. It took you three years to finally catch on. Three years!

Jesus, I can't even think about the money we spent before you finally cut the cord. I should have cut that shit off the day we brought Violet home from the hospital. That's what I should have done!"

"Do you hear yourself? Don't you think I've already blamed myself for this? I went overboard, and I had my reasons. But what I gave Lee and those kids back then was hardly luxury, Skip. Diapers? Money for groceries? A few presents to put under the tree? Fuck you, Skip."

I couldn't let that one fly. Not a chance.

"Gloria, you've got to be kidding me. You bought clothes for those kids from Kline's, for Christ's sake. Kline's Department Store! Gift-wrapped with a bow and everything! I can assure you that Lee Marks never wore anything from Kline's in her poor white trash life. Never. She never even set foot in a place like that. I guarantee you. Don't try to make it sound like this was all bread and milk. I don't know what the hell it was, but it wasn't bare bones."

"Are you saying that Jules and his sisters, kids that live in places like Shakey's Half, don't deserve something better? Why should they have to wear rags and live like beggars? And what's wrong with someone like me just wanting to help?"

This was exhausting. No matter what I said, I was the one who looked like an ass.

"Honey, there's nothing wrong with helping a little, donating here and there. That's commendable. We *should* help people less fortunate when we can, but what you did was altogether different, and you know it. You got involved with a hole that was never going to be filled, not by you or anybody else! There are consequences when we refuse to see something for what it really is, Gloria. So, the next time you happen to see that skull and crossbones on Violet, please remember that!"

Now, she was crying. Telling the cold hard truth didn't feel as good as I thought it would. '

Lem and Lee were locked up. Jules and the rest of that poor pack of kids were getting what they needed from someone else, from the appropriate next in line—their goddamned family.

My wife was crying. We still had debts to settle between us, and that would not come easily.

Chapter Sixty-Four

Gloria

Skip seemed satisfied. Lee and Lem would never make bail. They would be at the jailhouse for a spell. Justice was being meted out. Skip would make sure of that.

Our work was not done because we had a bigger problem on our hands. Violet's tattoo was there to stay. It wasn't going anywhere. It made Lem and Lee seem like nothing more than flies that needed to be shooed away. Shoo fly, don't bother me.

Skip had the hardest time imagining someone smoothing out Vi's white belly to start burning a design like that. The gritty reality of the deed was far worse than anything we could dream up.

Lem's dirty fingernails and his oily hair and the way he sloshed tobacco back and forth in his cheeks was the stuff of nightmares. Vi had been closer to that than I'd ever been. She went looking for him and what he could do for her. That was bad enough, and it was hard to get over.

What could be worse? Lee being there, too, standing over my girl while Lem did his work. That hurt me. Lem was giving his woman a treat. Revenge. Lee was careless and wild enough to find it funny. I'd done nice things for her, but I'd stopped it all with no warning.

Lee had to know how bad that tattoo would hurt me, and I'm sure she liked watching my girl feel the pain as she got it done. She also liked that Lem had crisp bills in his pocket. She liked the fact that while all this was going on inside Lem's shitty tent, I was home, humming to myself, chopping up a salad and turning on the oven to warm up dinner. For that devil, Lee, that must have been the best part.

When Skip and the sheriff were talking on the porch before they headed out to pick up Lem and Lee, they thought they were clear out of earshot, but I heard them loud and clear.

"We'll get this handled, Skip. Hauser's been on my shit list for a long time, but I never had much on him. This ought to do it. Yep, this ought to put him out to pasture for a while. I assume you'll be pressing charges against both of them?"

"Yes. Absolutely. We'll press every charge there is."

"Can't say that I blame you, Skip. Nope. Not one bit. Forgive me for saying so, but you still got yourself a problem now, don't you?"

Skip must have nodded.

"I'm sure sorry about that. Not sure what I would do if I was in your shoes. You'll have to get to the bottom of it. I'm just not sure what would make a girl have something like that done to her. Nope. I've seen all kinds of things, but this is a first."

Chapter Sixty-Five

Margaret Burns

I watched from my window. My lovely neighbor, Mr. Downs, never needed to know, but I'd have myself a bath whether he made it back to fix it or not. I never missed a bath.

The janitor, the teacher and the waitress walked out the front door. By the way they held their heads and walked single file, I was sure that they had a plan. They left in his old truck and Sally's car. I watched and waited all day long, well past lunch and on into dusk. I was about to give up and draw myself a bath when I saw a sight I never predicted.

Larry unlocked the front door and turned on a light. Along came Sally with a long-legged girl with her thumb in her mouth, holding her hand for dear life. Two taller girls, just as scrawny and gangly, followed close behind. Two even bigger girls came next.

It was the quietest bunch of children I'd seen in a long time. They had a familiar, hollowed-out look about them. I knew that shell-shocked look—gritty, chewed-up-and-spit-out.

Larry left again in his truck. What was he after now?

Clarice pulled up in Sally's little car. She looked a whole lot better than I'd seen her earlier that morning at the diner. She had her hands full of to-go bags from Slapp's. She went inside and came back out with one of the older girls. The two of them rummaged around in the backseat and came out with more bags of food. They hustled it in and closed the front door.

I went ahead and took my bath. It was getting dark, and the show was over, at least until morning.

Chapter Sixty-Six

Larry

The last time I was on that porch, Clarice was handing me Baby Jules to take back to the truck. I still had the same truck, but Jules would have to walk himself out the door this time.

Every time I saw that kid, he was taller. He was damned near taller than me. I loved that kid. I'd give him rides here and there. He'd let me take him home. If I saw him walking down the sidewalk, I'd slow down and roll down my window.

"Jules. Hey, Jules. Want a lift?"

He'd flash a shy smile, that scrawny little son of a gun, before he hopped in and slammed the door behind him. He knew he could trust me. We rode around town and kept the windows down. Thank God for that. Jules was ripe. Damn that Lee. Damn her.

I always had a hard time not handing the kid something on his way out of my truck. A strawberry milkshake we'd picked up from Clarice, a candy bar or a handful of coins.

It was never enough. I knew it. Each thing I pressed into his dirty hand was paltry and pitiful in its smallness. Each offering relieved my guilt while I watched that boy walk away toward his own hard world.

I knocked on the Sellers' front door. Skip came out and shook my hand. I followed him inside to their kitchen. There was Jules, eating a sandwich and guzzling down a glass of milk. The left side of his face was more black than blue.

He stood up and ran toward me. I pulled that boy right in.

Jules didn't have anything to gather before we left, just the clothes he was wearing. He finished his food while I talked quietly with Skip and Gloria. I planned to be there for Lem's hearing and Lee's too.

"Larry, that young man has courage. He's a brave one. He's been a good friend to our Violet. We are grateful to him. Gloria and I, we sure are thankful to Jules."

I was still piecing together all that had happened. Later, as I learned more, I was proud of Jules, too. He gave Vi a long hug. It made me glad that someone in the world wanted to hold my nephew close.

Once we got inside the truck, we just sat there, thinking about our next move.

"Where are the girls, Larry?"

"They're fine, all five of them, Jules. I promise."

I told him all about the morning, about his mother and Lem being arrested, and the girls following behind in the back seat of a second car. I told him about the police finding Clarice at the diner and about her finding me and my girlfriend, Sally.

"You got a girlfriend?"

"Yes, Jules. I have a girlfriend. Don't act so surprised."

Jules smiled. His face was a mess, but I liked that smile. Gloria and Sally had helped get all five girls showered. Kitty needed to be looked over by a doctor, who met us at his office. She had a nasty ear infection and a urinary tract infection, too. He gave us antibiotics and made Clarice promise to bring her back in a week.

"Where are they now?"

"They're at Sally's. Everyone's there. Should we head over, too?"

Jules shook his head. He wanted to go one more place.

"Are you sure, Jules? You don't have to go back there, you know. Uncle Larry and Aunt Clarice, and Sally, we're going to do everything we can to keep you out of there, and the girls, too."

Jules believed me. I could tell that he did. But he still wanted to go back to Shakey's Half. I could not deny this young man one more thing. I turned the truck around so he could get whatever it was he needed by taking one more look inside hell.

Chapter Sixty-Seven

Sally

Those girls were hungry and thirsty. As soon as we cleaned up one meal, Clarice and I were planning the next one.

Thank God for Clarice. I didn't have enough juice glasses or plates at my house to meet our expanded needs. Each time she came through the door with another sack of groceries, she also had a box of something from the diner we could use—silverware, glasses, plates, napkins, old dish towels. You name it. We needed it all.

Peg and Suze, the two biggest girls, were a big help. After that first night, Clarice took them with her to load up on what we needed to get by. I handed her a wad of cash and my checkbook as she walked out the door. She was determined, but weepy.

"Sally Lend, I love you, girl, I just love you."

She meant it and I knew that.

"I love you, too, Honey. I do."

Off she went with Peg and Suze. Three hours later, they came back with new underwear and socks, shoes, shorts, nightgowns, dresses and tee shirts. Peg and Suze needed training bras. We needed toothbrushes, bath towels and washcloths. Every Marks child got a new pillow with a clean pillowcase. Suze and Patty were beside themselves with what came out of the trunk of my car next: sleeping bags. Pink for the girls and a green one for Jules.

"We'll put names here on the bottom," said Clarice.

She already had the lid of a marker in her mouth.

"You won't be in sleeping bags forever, but for now, this will have to do the trick."

Peg and Suze came back through the door with more bags. The squealing that ensued was the sweetest sound I ever heard. There were brand new boxes of crayons and coloring books, blank paper, marbles, puzzles, jacks, bubbles, jump ropes and games. We had Twister, a set of Old Maid cards, Chutes and Ladders, Checkers, Bingo and a can of pick-up sticks. It felt like Christmas morning.

The last item out of the bag was a baby doll with long hair and her very own comb.

"Look what we found for Miss Kitty!"

Clarice handed the doll to that little child who had clung to me since the minute we picked them up from the police station.

Kitty was a wispy, little thing, a real snuggler. She was still not feeling great, but she took her medicine without a fuss. While the drug would do its work in good time, this baby in my arms needed something that would take longer to soak into her system, and she was hungry for it. She loved being held, laying quiet against my chest as she sucked her thumb and played with my necklace, taking it all in.

"I think you've got yourself a little friend," said Clarice.

"I sure do. Lucky me. I sure do."

Somehow, supper got made and consumed. The girls took turns having bubble baths, one by one, and came out in fresh nightgowns that had never been worn by another soul. I made popcorn, and we spent the rest of the night playing Bingo. Larry called the letters and couldn't keep from laughing each time a kid called out, "Bingo!"

The smile on his face and the way he sprang into action made me more than certain that the years I'd spent loving him and letting him love me back had not been frivolous. I loved everything about this man.

"You two look good together," he said, smiling at me and Kitty.

Even though she had a brand-new, pink sleeping bag waiting for her in my tiny living room, Miss Kitty liked it better sleeping right in between us. She was a kitten, that little thing, all fresh from a bubble bath with her thumb plopped in her mouth, drifting off in what was the safest set of arms she'd ever known.

"Thank you, Uncle Larry," I said.

"You're welcome, Auntie Sally."

He kissed my forehead and tucked us in a little tighter.

"Now go to sleep. We've got to get up in the morning and do this all over again."

I loved the sound of that.

Chapter Sixty-Eight

Larry

Earlier that day, I let Jules lead the way as we headed toward the trailer in Shakey's Half. I'd been there plenty of times, and taking in that air made me angry every time.

"Jules, Buddy, are you sure you need anything from here? You don't have to go in. We really don't. Anything you need, we'll get it for you. And the girls, too, man. What's in there is over. I mean it."

He believed me but still wanted to go inside. I wanted to get him over to Sally's to fill his belly and get some more ice on his puffy face. I quietly prayed for the chance to meet Lem Hauser in a back alley somewhere, so I could punch him in the face for Jules.

"Okay then, let's go on in," I said.

"No, you don't have to come with me," Jules said. "I think I want to do this by myself."

Chapter Sixty-Nine

Jules

We never locked the door to that place. We let it swing open and slam shut on its own. On windy days, it flew back and forth, begging for attention it never received.

I stood in the center of the room where our dirty, usually sheetless mattresses had been propped up against the wall. A cabinet hung open in the kitchen, revealing two cans of soup and a box of crackers. A jar of applesauce was stacked on top of a giant tub of creamy peanut butter. The refrigerator had nothing in it but a plastic pitcher and a single can of beer. An empty pack of Momma's cigarettes and an ashtray full of butts was on the kitchen table.

I walked toward the back room. Our toys were beat up and had lost parts and pieces. The girls had a collection of dolls in the corner. They all needed a good bath, too. Someone had shaven their rubber heads. I suspected this was Patty's doing. She was the realist among my girls. I respected her for it.

Our clothing was lumped in piles that got reshuffled and sorted from time to time. None of it was worth taking. There wasn't a thing here for us. There never had been.

I looked back one more time before I opened up the front door. I thought about Lem and Momma wearing handcuffs. I hoped seeing that hadn't scared the girls too much. I thought about Lem's bony fist and his nasty cackle. I thought about Mr. Bones and the way Violet's Dad put his hand on me like I was a man, a good man who had done a very good thing.

I *was* good, and I couldn't stop thinking about Vi. If she hadn't taken on Mr. Bones and been so eager to show me his teeth, we'd still be in Shakey's Half. How would I ever thank this girl? She was one tough customer. And just like me and my girls, she deserved rescuing.

"Got what you need, Jules?"

Uncle Larry smiled at me. He and Clarice had been trying to save me and my girls for as far back as I could remember. Any taste we ever had of something sweet or new came from them.

I hopped in the truck and shut the door.

"Yep. I have what I need."

We drove in silence toward his girlfriend's house. I had to see it for myself, this house and this woman who thought about my Uncle Larry in that kind of way. She had to be something special.

I took a deep breath as we pulled up. I couldn't wait to see Peg and Suze, Lolly, Patty, and Kitty in a fresh space that had its windows wide open. My uncle opened the door and motioned for me to step inside.

All four of the big girls came at me, rushing to get a piece of me with their clean arms. Patty ran into the kitchen and came back with an ice pack for my face.

"You're going to need this for a while, Jules."

I put it on the part of my cheek that hurt the most and took in my surroundings. The living room and dining room were small, but they looked enormous to me right then. Pictures hung on the walls, and they had a great big mirror in the dining room. I saw Jules Marks standing there. He looked like he might just know what he was doing.

"Where's Kitty?"

"Well, she's got herself a friend," said Larry. "Right now, they're in the bedroom having a snuggle. Come say hello."

I followed him as he opened the bedroom door.

"Look who I've got with me, Honey."

Sitting there propped up on the bed with my Kitty Cat in her lap was Miss Lend. My Miss Sally Lend.

"Hello there, Jules."

I'd managed to get through that day without crying. I didn't shed a single tear saying goodbye to Vi or taking a last look at the old place in Shakey's Half. I was proud to be on my way to being a man who could keep his tears to himself. But seeing Miss Lend, that sweet creature who remembered Jules Martin Marks, changed that fast. Seeing her with her arms wrapped around Kitty, planting a kiss on the top of her head, pulled out the little boy tears that lived inside me. I let them fall where they wanted.

Miss Lend smiled at me.

"You can call me Sally when we're here, Jules. I'm only Miss Lend when we're in class. Sound good?"

I nodded and smiled back. For that night and the next few days, Miss Lend was Sally. And Sally was holding my littlest sister the way she deserved to be held.

"We saved you boys a burger. Go have yourselves one, and there are two chocolate shakes in the fridge with your names on them."

We slurped those shakes like nobody's business. I wolfed down my cheeseburger in three bites. Larry laughed at me.

"Kid, I remember being able to eat fast like that. I bet you could eat another one, couldn't you?"

He pushed the bag at me and watched as I gobbled another burger.

"Jules, things are going to change now for all of us. And it's going to be good."

The big girls were settled on the living room floor, rolled into brand new sleeping bags. I had one, too, nice and green. I settled into it on Sally's soft couch and listened to my girls breathing. I knew that sound well, but on this night, my sisters breathed in the clean night air more deeply and exhaled peacefully in their new, safe space.

Their bodies knew that the shallow, careful breaths we used to take in Shakey's Half were no longer needed. The light from above the sink in Sally's kitchen threw a gentle beam across Lolly's face. She looked so relaxed and pretty. I hoped she was dreaming something sweet, her very own dream that she didn't need to share with anyone.

Chapter Seventy

Margaret Burns

There was no doubt about it. All the commotion next door was nothing but a saving. Dirty, scrawny kids coming inside and then emerging into the sunshine was a sure-fire way to see that.

The littlest scrawny one clung to the teacher for dear life. She was too big to have a thumb in her mouth, but there were bigger battles to wage. That little house wasn't going to hold that crew for long. They were going to need room to stretch, and soon. Their little love nest would never be big enough.

Watching the comings and goings from my kitchen window was soothing but thrilling. I knew this story. I knew it very, very well. What I understood about its beginnings gave renewed life to what I knew was unfolding in front of me.

All six kids had a Shakey's Half look about them. I imagined that they'd been bathed a time or two since they arrived next door, but if I got close enough, I'd catch that unforgettable scent. It clings to your skin, and no matter how hard you scrub, a Shakey's Half smell always comes back.

I knew the little one best of all. She was stringy and bird-like. She sucked hard on that thumb for good reason, and I figured she might still be a bed-wetter to boot. I could spot one. That's for sure. Poor little bird. That one would never cut her hair once it started growing. She'd become a tired, old woman with a long, gray braid down her back. And she would never miss an evening soak in the tub, even if she had to break her neck doing it.

What was happening right in front of me was a grander saving than my own. All those children being pulled out of the wreckage. This was a huge saving for the ages.

The day my aunt and uncle pulled me to safety was a day not to be forgotten. They'd come all the way from Kansas to get me. I'd been left alone for the day, and then a night. Another day went by, and then another. Hard knocks at the door followed harsh calls from the outside. Two men pushed the door in so hard that it broke off its hinges. The bigger man lifted me from a crib that was meant for a baby.

I'd wet myself and knew I was dirty. I must have smelled awful, but he held my head on his shoulder as he walked with force out into the sunlight. A big car was waiting, and inside it was an angel who pulled me right into her soft, lilac dress and petted my face like I was precious, a little girl not to be forgotten. She smelled wonderful.

As the months went by, I could name that smell. It was rosewater and jasmine—the perfume I watched my Aunt Helen daub onto her wrists and behind her ears each morning.

"Would you like some, Margaret?"

She pulled me to her and gave me little drops of the scent to place behind my own ears.

"That hair of yours is growing out nicely, little miss. Before you know it, Aunt Helen will be giving you a braid that goes all the way down your back."

The thought of that made me smile. It was another treat I'd never imagined would be mine to enjoy. I took baths every night. My clothes were crisp and clean. Cold milk was mine for the drinking. I had gloves and a matching hat. My Aunt Helen only got cross with me, in her own soft way, when she caught me with my thumb in my mouth.

"Oh, Miss Margaret. That will never do. No. I know it gives you comfort to suck on that old thumb, but your teeth won't be as pretty if you do."

She would distract me with some new thing, like paper dolls, a tiny cross necklace, an invitation to help her bake bread or Uncle Teddy's favorite, banana cream pie.

I saved my thumb sucking for under the covers, after she'd planted a kiss on my face and closed the door to my room. The sucks brought me comfort when I let my mind wander and imagined waking up to find I'd been left alone again, that my head was itchy and that I might not get another bath.

As the years went on, I needed my thumb less. My hair was allowed to grow all the way down my back, and I never went to bed without first lathering my whole body with soap and water.

I knew full well what a saving looked like. It had its own taste and landed on the tongue like hot baked potatoes with butter and salt, ice cream cones and fresh lemons. It smelled like honeysuckle and soap, jelly on toast and welcoming steam heat hissing from the radiator on a cold morning.

A saving takes you by surprise and lets you hold on as tightly as you like, until you meet a moment when you've surely soaked up more goodness than you'll ever need.

Once you get there, you can be generous. You know that your own saving served its purpose. It needs fresh soil, and your eyes start to see new places for the same goodness that landed on you to flourish.

Chapter Seventy-One

Gloria

Word travels fast in Poulson. Good stuff passes through at a fair clip. It's accepted begrudgingly, but only after being verified. Bad news is different. It's slippery and nimble. Anything from juicy gossip to something tragic or scandalous gets gobbled right up and swallowed as truth. No verification required.

News about Violet's tattoo and the whole sordid mess was common knowledge before Lee and Lem had even spent their second night in the Paradise County Jail.

The first call I received was from Ruth.

Did we need to have Richard come over to pray with us?

Could she send Jamie over with a meal?

Did I want to come over for hot tea?

Little sister was going through all the right motions. She had all the protocols of comforting down pat, like the seasoned pastor's wife she was, and she was authentic. It was no act.

As I listened to her chirp out one offer after another, I knew that there was no way we could stay in town and no way in hell I could share what happened between James and Violet with my husband or my sister.

Skip seemed satisfied with getting to the bottom of the tattoo. And hadn't I hurt Ruthie enough in our lifetime?

Chapter Seventy-Two

Clarice

Taking a day off from work was not easy. I didn't do the cooking, but I could. It didn't take a genius to fry an egg or slap a burger on the grill. Bacon and hashbrowns were easy enough and making toast was a no-brainer. Working the front took skill, though. You had to be nice for long stretches, which is not something many can pull off.

Keeping tabs on six booths and eight tables is no laughing matter. You have to care about how people want their eggs. Over easy is not the same as sunny side up. You need to be attentive enough to detect when someone's ready for the check but try not to hover or interrupt an important conversation. If a couple looks like they might be right in the middle of a breakup, then they don't want pie.

You need to keep just enough fresh coffee brewing throughout the day, so you don't run out, but you don't want a full pot to go to waste come closing time.

When the boss informs you that you're out of onion rings or fried chicken livers, you need to let customers know after you take their drink order but *before* you bring the drinks to the table. If there's too much time to let their hearts get set on something you can't deliver, it's bad for business.

Whatever that customer's second choice might be—toasted cheese, a BLT or even a chili dog with extra onions, it won't be as good as what they initially wanted and even the best Plan B will not matter.

You serve more regulars than newcomers in Poulson. They sit in the same spots, if possible, and they get miffed if their seats are taken. It's not that different than church.

Margaret Burns comes in on Wednesdays like clockwork. She brings her newspaper and camps out in her back booth for breakfast *and* lunch. She likes her coffee with two ice cubes, rye toast and one egg scrambled hard. For lunch, she'll have tuna salad on white toast with a slice of lettuce and a bowl of cottage cheese.

She needs to get home in time to watch her favorite TV shows and take a nap, so I have the cook make her lunch at the same time he preps her breakfast.

If there's a lunch rush, Margaret doesn't want to wait. She always leaves the same tip and pays at the register with a check.

Margaret doesn't care how busy you are, or that you have other customers ready to pay. Everyone can wait in line while she writes her check and records the amount in her register. Then, she's got to dig for her keys and put on her coat while time stands still for the rest of us.

"See you next week."

We got plenty of regulars at Slapp's, and I've been a fixture there, too, for quite some time. About two years in, I told my boss, Glen, that I needed Sundays off. Not for church. I just needed peace. Sissy, the back-up waitress, was okay playing second fiddle to me, but she was no queen bee. She couldn't manage the house on her own, so instead of hiring someone else, the boss decided Sundays would be take-out only. Sissy could do that.

"Clarice, I'm telling you, if you're going to be out, you got to give me more notice," the boss said. "If you're not here, things go to shit. And I mean straight to the shitter."

I would usually cave or reconsider if it was possible, but this time, I needed to be off the entire day. Yes, on a Wednesday, which I knew was smack in the middle of the week.

"What's the matter with you?" my boss said. "Are you sick or something? I don't know, Clarice. That's a big ask. I might as well shut down for all three shifts. I guess you're taking your Sunday, too?"

I *was* taking Sunday, too. I wanted to tell him that most Sundays, especially lately, I was hardly laying on the couch eating chocolates. There was always something cropping up for Lee's kids, but now, with Lee in the county jail, Larry, Sally and I were knee-deep caring for all six of her children.

Jules was fourteen and Kitty was six. The older girls could help, but things were tight at Sally's place. They needed to learn how to cook, clean and do laundry. Rinse and repeat. We were still figuring it out, and when I could, I was there, lending a hand.

"I know this is hard for you to imagine, Glen, but I have a life. Things *do* pop up. Every time I ask for a day off, you talk about hiring another waitress, a real waitress, not Sissy. But you never get around to it, so here we are again. If you'd get serious, it wouldn't be the end of the world every damned time your only full-time employee needed to take care of something."

Glen knew I was right. He was sheepish, as he should have been.

"Clarice, are you throwing sass at me?"

He knew he needed me.

"Yes, I'm throwing sass. Are you catching it? I'm happy to help you find someone, and I'll show her the ropes, but this week, on *Wednesday*, I will not be here, and I have a damned good reason."

Glen would learn what it was soon enough. When I missed a Wednesday, there would be all kinds of talk in the diner.

Where could she be?

Is she sick?

Why is the diner even open without Clarice?

Come to think of it, where the hell is Margaret Burns? Wednesday is her Slapp's day. Has been for years.

Not that it was any of our customers' business, but that particular Wednesday was a big day for me, my brother, and his Sally and all six Marks kids. Even Margaret Burns had something better to do than hang around at Slapp's Diner.

Chapter Seventy-Three

Ruth

As we grew up, grudges were never something we were allowed to hang onto for too long.

Once an offense was committed and the offender appropriately punished, we moved on. Pop insisted on this, and so did our mother. I think I'd only been swatted once or twice by Pop, and he never meant for me to feel it. Those smacks were just for show, to prove to my big sister that I wasn't the favorite. Both times he turned me over, I saw Pop give me a wink.

It was different for Gloria. She took it. We all agreed that her trips to the woodshed or the couch, or wherever Pop decided to dole out justice, were justified. No matter the size of the offense, the punishment always fit the crime. And afterward, whether we felt like it or not, a forgiveness session was forced upon us.

"Now, Red Ruthie, you forgive your sister," said Pop.

He grumbled as he pushed us to face each other.

"She's paid her price. Forgive her and go play, now."

Knowing the havoc Pop could do to someone's behind if he thought we deserved it, I wasn't about to argue. Gloria would sniffle and mutter "sorry" and we'd run off into the sunset until the next skirmish.

Gloria didn't seem to mind the beatings if she was caught in the middle of committing a crime. She always took those in stride. But the punishments that came her way after I'd tattled or cried too loudly were a different story. When I brought one of her slights to Mother or Pop's attention, there would be hell to pay later, and I'm not talking about Pop working on Gloria.

After the beating and an apology, Gloria would always find me alone and let me have it. We'd gone through the motions of an apology, but there was still a tax to be paid for tattling. I learned to pick my battles, cry more softly and try to be less bothersome to my sister.

"Ruthie, that big sister of yours is just jealous. She's jealous of your red curls and those precious freckles. We should have named you Dot. Gloria hasn't figured out how beautiful she is. Don't you worry, Ruthie. She'll forget one of these days, and the two of you will be the best of friends. You just watch."

Mother may have been onto something. I was nothing to look at, but I did get special treatment because I was ugly. Mother and Pop would never say so, but I could see the truth in the mirror.

Our scraps eventually subsided. Gloria turned beautiful, just like Mother predicted. To call us the best of friends would be a stretch. We reached an impasse that satisfied our parents, but my sister and I knew that deep down, our capacity to forgive and forget was tenuous, at best.

Chapter Seventy-Four

Richard Pullman

Skip and Gloria had a mess on their hands, that's for sure.

When my sister-in-law showed up at my office, I wasn't surprised. They would need prayer, and I'd already promised Ruthie I'd do that.

The tattoo business, with Violet getting tangled up with those dicey folks from Shakey's Half, was unseemly. They had to rein in that child of theirs.

Skip was a Catholic. His kind called on their patron saints for every request. We went through the requisite motions of attending Violet's First Communion, which was hard to watch. That child looked like a little bride, but she had no idea about what she'd been coached to recite. I kept those thoughts to myself.

"Gloria, come in," I said. "Here, now, Sister, come right in."

I expected Gloria to look pale from all the stress, but her face was full of color. It didn't appear that she'd been crying. Odd. She let me usher her into the office and took a seat in front of my desk.

"How's our Violet? We've been praying for your girl, *our* girl, of course. Ruthie just loved having her for a night or two awhile back. Jamie enjoyed it, too. We should do it more. But how is she? How are you and Skip doing? Are you hanging in there?"

Gloria took a deep breath.

"Well, Richard, thank you. That's why I'm here. I need to talk to you, and I thought it would be best if we talked without Ruthie. I also think, for everyone's sake, that it's best that Skip's not here, either."

I understood. We were family, and even though Gloria didn't attend my church, she did deserve discretion. Ruthie's big sister needed wise counsel that was also confidential. I owed her that.

"Of course, Gloria. Listen, I know that you and Ruthie had your squabbles growing up. I think that's water under the bridge. You could confide in her. She's very trustworthy, and I know she'd love to show you how much she loves you. Just know that. Now, if you're more comfortable talking with me, that's just fine, too. I'd be honored to do that for you. And anything you say, anything at all, will stay right in this room, just between you, me, and the Lord."

The next two hours tested my mettle.

What unfolded in that room was a test of some kind. Despite my training, it was difficult to determine the source of this trial. Was it a challenge sent from Heaven, or was it straight from Hell?

I was prepared to provide counsel, but that was not what was wanted or needed from me. The woman in front of me would seek counsel elsewhere, from someone less tangled up in the barbed-wire conundrum she laid at my feet.

There was no appropriate or good response. Was I shocked? Yes. Was I angry? Yes. Was I sorry? Certainly. Was I responsible? I needed to think about that. Was I sick, and sad, and disgusted, and ashamed and defensive? Was I all those things at once? The answer is yes, since the minute the message left Gloria's lips and was received by my ears. I needed to hear it again.

"Gloria, forgive me, but can you repeat that? I'm sorry, but can you? I can't believe I've heard you correctly. This seems impossible. There must be a misunderstanding."

She shook her head. The tears finally emerged. In that moment, I imagined that Ruthie's big sister was also managing wild emotions.

"Richard, there's no mistake. Violet has been through a lot, with the tattoo and all. It's a lot, and she's been difficult, but it all started after she came home early from staying with you, Ruthie and Jamie. Don't you remember that I had to come by and pick her up early? Now look, Vi is spoiled. There's no doubt about that. But she's never been a liar. Never. She has no reason to make up something like this. It's just not possible."

I could not say the same about Jamie. He mastered the dark art of lying early on. It was maddening. He would lie about the smallest, most inconsequential things, and only come clean if cornered. We punished him again and again, but he never learned. Instead, he fine-tuned his deception skills, leaving Ruthie and I to wonder if we could trust him with anything.

As Gloria explained the encounter for the second time, I knew she spoke the truth. James was capable of this. I could handle knowing such a thing. I could master this knowledge and contain the mess. Ruthie would not survive it, though. She could never, ever know.

"Richard, I don't want you to tell Ruth about this," Gloria said. "It would kill her, and I've hurt her enough. It would just destroy her."

I nodded, thankful that my sister-in-law felt the same way.

"What about Skip? Does he know?"

"Richard, let me be clear. Jamie should be in jail for what he did to Violet. If Skip knew about it, he'd see to that. That would be the very least he would do. He's now making sure that Lem Hauser and Lee Marks do time for putting that tattoo on Violet. They'll do time, and frankly, they'll be safer in jail. I can't promise that Skip won't take matters into his own hands with Lem if he gets the chance. But the tattoo never would have happened at all if it hadn't been for Jamie. He's a savage. I'd like to kill him myself. I'm not sure jail would be good enough for Skip if he found out about your boy. There is no way out of this that's good, Richard. This is the only path forward. We're leaving Poulson. We're leaving as soon as we can so Vi can have a fresh start. Nothing good will come of us staying, but you will stay. You will have to stay and stew in it. You and James, not Ruthie."

Everything Gloria said was true. Cleaning this up would need to be an ongoing project, held together with white lies and deceit. For that, I'd need to take pointers from James. Not doing so would ruin him, and us. We'd be *ruined*.

"What about Violet? Are you sure she understands this?"

"Richard, I'm not sure about anything. I don't like deceiving Skip or encouraging our daughter to do the same, but the alternatives aren't good. I'll get her some help."

"Does anyone else know, Gloria?"

"There's one other person who knew about this even before I did. He's a good kid, but he's been through hell himself. We owe him. Now, getting him to keep quiet is going to be your biggest challenge, and he's not leaving Poulson anytime soon."

"Who is it?"

"A kid named Jules Marks. He's from Shakey's Half, and he's the oldest kid of Lem Hauser and Lee Marks."

Shit. I had to think. I walked around my desk and moved Gloria toward the door. We were both shaking.

"Gloria, will you look at me? I am so sorry about this. I'm really, sorry. I know it will never be enough, but I am sorry, and I'm thankful, that you came to me first. And thank you for keeping Ruthie out of it. I won't forget this."

My wife's sister was really pretty. She wasn't as cute as my Ruthie, but she had that same stubborn streak.

"Richard, I know this isn't your fault, but he's *your* son, and he's done unspeakable damage to my daughter. *Unspeakable*. He deserves to be punished for this, but I know he's going to get by with it, and it's not fair. He's going to do more of it, too, if you don't get a handle on him. I'm furious. You need to get that kid in a room and work him over. Work him over *good*. You can tell him it's from Aunt Gloria. Trust me, you should be the one to take care of that. If I ever see him again, he won't be safe. Do you understand that?"

What else could I do but nod and watch her leave?

Chapter Seventy-Five

Ruth

Church weddings are usually Saturday affairs. When the decks are cleared of workaday burdens like deadlines, deposits and mail to be opened, the coast is clear to pull off the kind of wedding that makes headlines in the local paper.

Depending on how much the bride's family is willing to spend, a Saturday wedding in Poulson has been known to fill a full page with all the details that those uninvited are dying to know.

Dates, times and locations are much less important than what really matters: the bride, the groom and what they wore. Did the bride wear white, or some variation that was less blinding? How long was her train? Sweetheart neckline or one allowed to drape her shoulders? Silk? Organza? Brocade? What kind of lace, and exactly where on the dress was it situated? Long sleeves or arms exposed? And on her precious bridal head? Fingertip veil attached to a Juliet cap? Hat swathed in tulle and pearls? How many bridesmaids, and what were their names?

A full paragraph would be required to describe the confections these beauties wore gliding down the aisle. Readers expected details. Were their skirts burgundy, or was that shade best described as plum? The flora and fauna, details about the cake and where the bride and groom registered for china were details that needed recording.

Our wedding was like that. Mother and Pop insisted. Our nuptials were a full-page spread. They needed the rice, the gown, the flowers and a full registry at Kline's Department Store to prove to themselves, and to Poulson, that their red-headed little chicken of a girl, their homely Ruthie, could nab herself a decent man, a man of God.

Richard took part in these charades. He played right along, as was expected of a pastor, but he had his opinions.

"Ruthie, I know this is hard for you to hear, but most of the couples who come in for the bare bones of a ceremony, with just me, the bride and groom, and God—well, those are the most meaningful. There's no rice, no cake and no expense—just pure commitment. Those are the couples who have the right idea, Ruthie. Those are the ones that are going to last."

He'd just come home for dinner and let me know that he'd be busy the next day, and that I shouldn't plan on him being around for lunch. He had a Wednesday wedding to perform.

"Do I know the bride and groom? Are you sure we couldn't make them a little cake, something to celebrate?"

"That's sweet of you, Ruthie. Real sweet. I know you've done that before, but I don't think you need to this time. I bet you don't know these folks. They know what they want. I bet they have something real sweet figured out for themselves."

Chapter Seventy-Six

Richard

This fire could spread fast, so I needed to keep Ruthie in the dark. Gloria understood that, but Skip would be a problem. We never bonded like one might expect. We tolerated one another on Christmas, Easter and Thanksgiving, but never more than that.

Of course he'd want to press charges against my son. My brother-in-law would have Jamie's hide if he could. We would be ruined. I would be asked to step down from South Christian. Disgraced.

I could stand around and pray about it or I could use my God-given brains and body to start cleaning up the mess. I needed to find Jules Marks, but there was a young man who needed my immediate attention. God, help me, I wanted to throttle James.

Finding a private place to bellow at my son and throw him across the room, to scare the ever-loving shit out of him, and do so out of earshot would be a challenge. The church was off-limits, as was the parsonage. Committees, the quilting bee, custodians and Ruthie popped in and out too often. She didn't miss a beat.

There was simply no place to go for a pastor with the second largest congregation in town when he needed to have a come-to-Jesus moment with his devil of a son.

We needed to take a drive. Jamie and I didn't do that. We didn't play catch or fish or even collect baseball cards together.

As I pulled up to the high school to sign him out of his class on a Tuesday afternoon, I wondered if that was the problem, that I didn't really know my son.

He was surprised to see me waiting for him in the office. I greeted the principal and his secretary, but I did not extend a greeting to Jamie. He was a bright boy, so he noticed and said something as we walked out to the car.

"Dad, what's going on? Is everything okay? Is something wrong? Is Mom okay?"

"Your mother is fine, Jamie."

"So, something else is wrong. I can tell something is up. Why did you come to get me out of school?"

I chose silence as we drove past the football field and south on Highway T. Poulson was in the rearview mirror. We drove on further to avoid anyone who might recognize us.

We were just a man and his teenage son, taking an afternoon drive. What would we talk about? It was too late for the birds and the bees. The quiet between us was making James nervous. He could feel the gravity. Our son was a smart kid. He knew exactly what was on my mind. I was no priest. Our front seat was no confession booth, but a coming clean was about to happen.

I pulled off down a gravel road and stopped the car in a clearing.

"What happened with Violet?"

"What do you mean, Dad?"

"Son, let's not do this. I know something happened. And it wasn't good. Don't waste my time. If you're straight with me, I can help you, but if not, I guess we'll have to do this the hard way."

The boy wouldn't look at me. He was a liar and a coward. A beast.

I couldn't stop thinking about his poor mother. Ruthie had done everything for this kid.

"You have five seconds to face me, James. If you don't look at me like a man by then, we're heading back to town. You hear me? We're heading back to Poulson, and we're not going home. We'll go straight to the police station. If you think I'm kidding, think again."

I didn't need to start counting. The whites of Jamie's eyes were already red. Good. He was scared shitless. Balance of power adjusted. Now we could get down to business.

"Aha. There he is. There's the big man. You're really something, aren't you? Huh? Right now, I don't want to hear one fucking word come out of your mouth. You got that? What? Is James surprised that his pastor father knows that word? Get over it. Right now, I'm asking the questions and you're nodding *yes* or shaking your head *no*. Got it?"

He nodded.

"Oh, one more thing, James Pullman. If I think you're lying to me, I'll do things you won't fucking like."

I could see him sweating.

"Did you assault Violet when she stayed with us? Yes or no?"

His head moved in the affirmative.

Next question.

"Was she bleeding?"

Yes.

"Did Violet give you any indication that she was inviting you to engage with her physically?"

No.

"Did you stop to think that this girl is your cousin?"

No.

"That she's considerably younger than you, and smaller?"

Yes.

Oh, good. He factored that in.

"Was Violet upset?"

Yes.

"Have you spoken to her since?"

Yes.

"What? You've spoken to her?"

Yes.

"Were you trying to apologize?"

No.

"Have you shared this with anyone else?"

No.

"Okay, you careless, thoughtless piece of shit. Violet shared it with your Aunt Gloria. That's how I know. And your cousin shared what happened with one other person. Do you care to take a guess?"

No.

"We'll come back to that. I'm going to take pity on you, James. I'm going to extend you a kindness you don't deserve. Are you ready?"

Yes.

"It's not your mother. Thankfully, she doesn't know, and your Aunt Gloria doesn't want her to. She's not telling Uncle Skip, either. Lucky you. You're damned lucky, because he's got every right to skin you alive first and then press charges. You hear that, James? Charges!"

Yes.

"What you've done is a sin. It's also a *criminal* act. You understand this? You realize you belong in jail, don't you?"

Yes.

He was crying and his body shook. Good.

"Did it ever cross your mind what this would do to Violet? Aunt Gloria? Your mother? Me? Did you ever think about what this might do to us?"

Before he could shake his wretched head, I pulled James toward me with more force than I intended. Then, I pushed him hard against the car door, with my arm lodged under his neck.

I shook my son, smacking the back of his head into the glass. We were both crying. I released him and fell back against the seat.

What had I just done? And what was I about to do to save this boy, to save us and to save myself?

We sat there, miles from Poulson, thinking about what needed to happen once we rolled back into town. Ruthie would wonder where we'd been. She'd be curious about why we looked so disheveled. We needed to tidy ourselves.

We'd need to avoid Violet and definitely Skip. I might need a final check-in with Gloria to get our stories straight and I needed to find that Marks kid.

I turned the car around and we headed back. There wasn't much left to say.

"Dad?"

"What is it?"

"I'm sorry. I am. I know I messed up. I know it. I won't do it again. I won't. I promise. I know I've caused a lot of trouble. Thank you for fixing this mess."

He looked sheepish and sorry, at least in that moment, but I wasn't sure I believed him.

I did not pray that night, or for many nights after that. What did I need to ask for? Patience? Forbearance? Forgiveness for James? For myself? A chance to make this right, but protect what was mine at the same time?

Once I started talking to God again, I was ashamed what I brought with me. Could Violet and Gloria forgive or forget? Could the Marks kid keep his mouth shut? Could we keep Ruthie in the dark? Could James learn from this and find his way to the straight and narrow, like a good pastor's boy? Could the Lord let me take care of my business, just this once, the way I needed to?

Surely there were greater sins from bigger sinners than us on which our Maker could fix his gaze.

I negotiated all of this into a tidy box. This was family business, what any father would do, even a pastor. Of course it was.

Chapter Seventy-Seven

Sally

As a little girl, I always dreamed of a big, fluffy wedding with guests throwing rice, church bells ringing and champagne flowing.

I never dwelt on who might be my husband. That seemed like a cumbersome detail. He was a vague, fuzzy figure who was only needed for the vows, the kiss and cutting the cake.

As a teenager, I had a handful of boyfriends, or *beaus*, as my mother referred to them. They were fine enough for the homecoming dance or frantic necking at the movies.

Mother found two toads from the country club who she considered suitable. The Fogarty twins were nearly neckless and all sweaty with pimply faces. I didn't want to hold hands with them or even sit next to them with our parents at the club, but I did consider offering to work on their faces. All I needed was their cooperation, about an hour per face and my two nimble hands. I'd start with anything that presented white or yellow, then go to town on those blackheads. It was hard not to stare and think about which twin needed the most help.

College offered many more choices. Since Mother was three hours away and not breathing down my neck, there were several possibilities to consider that held promise, including frat boys, a football player, and a brief dalliance with a professor.

They all wanted sex, and so did I. Even then, I chose carefully. No need to be reckless. I opted for the professor. He was a safe bet, and skilled. He introduced me to American literature and then took off his glasses for more memorable lessons. He was married, so he wasn't a viable candidate for formal dances, football games or other settings for conventional mating rituals.

When graduation time arrived, nearly all my sorority sisters were either pinned or flashing diamond rings. I had a diploma, but no ring. Another imaginary husband had slipped through my ringless fingers. I guess I wasn't trying hard enough to catch someone.

I taught, dated here and there and the years added up. I had my tiny house, my students, teacher friends and Bootsie.

A fluffy wedding seemed ridiculous. I could buy an inexpensive bottle of champagne whenever I wanted. I was willing to look past all that and just find a good man, someone to love. He didn't need to turn into a husband. In fact, deep down, I'd come to love my spinster status as a weapon.

The fact that I was a schoolteacher and still single kept my parents, especially my mother, up at night. My singular state made her fret. In the beginning, I let myself fret along with her until the conversation no longer interested me.

I stopped watching the horizon for prospects that weren't coming. My knight wore no suit of armor. He pulled up in the school truck, popped open my hood and gave me a jump. We gravitated to each other, Larry and I, and settled into the most comfortable, secure love. It was soft and strong, and so was he.

Larry always joked that one day he was going to present me with the smallest speck of a diamond he could find in Poulson. He said he was even willing to cross Paradise County lines if it meant there was something smaller that still had a twinkle.

Once we were feeding and clothing six kids within the confines of my little cottage, we lowered our standards even further. Simple gold bands would have to do.

I love the weight of mine on my finger.

Larry and I got married in a church.

It was a small affair, no champagne needed. We had ginger ale, so the kids could take part in the toast back at the house. I did not wear white. I did spring for something pretty from Kline's, though. Larry insisted, pressing cash into my hand as he pushed me out the door to pick something out.

"Don't you come back empty-handed Miss Lend. You hear me?"

I loved his wink. That was twinkle enough for me.

Chapter Seventy-Eight

Clarice

I often wished that Mama could be here with us, even for a day.

Once she got over the shock that Lee was in jail and had six kids she couldn't take care of, she'd be so happy to see Larry take this step in his life.

Mama would eat Sally right up. She looked good most days, but on her wedding day, she was the angel my little brother deserved.

Cornflower blue was her color. The dress went below her knees and had sleeves to her elbows. Her hair was gathered in a bun at the base of her neck. She wore pearl earrings.

That was it. The way Larry looked at her made the world feel right.

Little brother didn't look so bad himself. He was doing things grown men do—taking a wife, six kids and then some. He embraced it with his eyes wide open. He was no lamb to the slaughter. He knew exactly what he was doing, and his smile took over his handsome face. I really wished Mama was there to see it.

I showed up to Sally's place early on Wednesday. Getting six kids cleaned up and looking decent enough to enter South Christian was no joke. It wasn't a formal situation, but Larry and Sally deserved to have Jules tuck in his shirt and for the girls to wear skirts.

It was a wedding, after all. I was nearly wiped out, scrubbing faces and helping kids find something clean to wear. They were excited. It was a party atmosphere.

Then came a knock at the front door. One of the kids ushered Miss Burns into the living room. She was dressed up with gloves and a fancy looking purse.

"Well, hello there, Clarice! My word, it's a madhouse over here! Good, Lord, how are the bride and groom going to not lose their ever-loving minds cooped up like this?"

I shrugged and surveyed the space.

I'd gotten used to it, but Margaret wasn't wrong. This couldn't last, not like this. Sally's place was way too small for two adults, six kids and a cat.

"Knowing my brother and Sally, they'll figure something out. All I know is, I'm happy to get home to my quiet little place after I spend too much time here!"

Margaret let out a loud laugh that came from her belly.

"Oh, yes, Ma'am! You've got that right. I like watching from my window, and popping over now and then, but I know what you mean! Good Lordy, this place hops like it never did before!"

I was glad that Larry and Sally included Margaret. Whenever she came over with cookies, the kids gobbled them up before she could put the plate on the kitchen table. They invited her to their new Saturday night tradition—roasting wieners and marshmallows over a fire in their little backyard.

Margaret liked it so much that she brought the marshmallows every Saturday night. I watched her move to a chair to watch the antics while the whole gang finished getting ready for the wedding. Kitty found her and walked over to show off her brand-new party shoes.

Yes, Margaret Burns was the perfect guest for this wedding.

Chapter Seventy-Nine

Richard

Well, I'll be damned. I started the day ready for the Downs wedding to be over.

This was a no-frills ceremony. Still, it was a sacrament. Vows were being exchanged. God was invited. It was legally binding, too. I'd be signing the wedding certificate. I wasn't sure what the bride and groom would be wearing. I wore a suit and tie. Ruthie ironed my shirt, as usual.

Jamie was still asleep. He was pretending to be sick, and Ruth bought it. She put the kettle on the stove to make an unnecessary cup of hot lemon tea and had the thermometer in her hand. If anyone could fake a fever, it was our son.

I imagined that he felt like shit. Our road trip had rattled us both. Nothing would ever be the same.

"Well, you better get on over there," Ruthie said. "This is old hat for you, but a big day for the couple."

The happy couple looked eager, waiting at the office door for me. They had a whole crew with them: an old lady I'd seen here and there around Poulson and Clarice from Slapp's. Everyone knew Clarice. I'd seen the groom before, too. The bride, Sally Lend, was a teacher up at the school. I wasn't sure, but she might have been James' kindergarten teacher way back. I'd need to ask Ruthie about that.

The bride's something blue was her dress. She had a pint-sized friend holding her hand, a fragile little girl wearing black patent shoes.

"Reverend Pullman, this is Kitty," said Sally.

"Hello there, Kitty. Are you happy now about your mama getting married today?"

The bride and groom looked at one another and smiled.

"And who are the rest of these good-looking guests?"

I asked because it was the polite thing to do. I made my way down the line, meeting four other girls and a gangly teenage boy. He looked younger than James, and a little scroungy.

"Young man, do all these girls belong to you?"

He smiled. I could tell he was from Shakey's Half. Those teeth.

"Yes, Sir. They are my sisters, all of them."

"You're a good man. Oh, my, I don't think I caught your name."

"I'm Jules. Jules Marks."

Chapter Eighty

Margaret Burns

What a glorious day it was. My Lord, it was a good one.

The wedding was short and sweet. My neighbor and her man had finally tied the knot. After the groom and bride kissed, we all whooped, hollered and headed out to pile into Larry's truck and Sally's car. It was a real circus, and I loved it.

Back at the house, Clarice snuck in a little wedding cake, and we all enjoyed a piece washed down with ginger ale. We played bingo and laughed ourselves silly. Kitty was getting pretty good at the game. Later, Sally made tomato soup and grilled cheese for dinner.

By that time, the night was closing in for me.

"Well, my neighbors, it's time for Margaret Burns to head over yonder. It's past this old gal's bedtime."

Kitty thought that was funny. I gave Sally and Larry a squeeze and waved goodnight to Clarice. The poor thing was staying over so the newlyweds might stand a chance of being left alone that night without precious Kitty or the real cat insisting on celebrating with them.

"Margaret are you sure you don't want to stay and sleep on the floor with me?" said Clarice.

She was a funny one.

"Not on your life, lady. Not on your life. Let's just see how much sleep you get tonight!"

I shuffled across the lawn. My house was even smaller, but it felt expansive and filled with stillness. I hung up my coat and pulled off my shoes and hose right there in the living room. I peered out the kitchen window toward the crowded, happy place I'd just left. The lights were still on. My waitress friend was probably in her nightgown and starting to shush everybody down.

It had been a very big day and I'd been part of it. My cuckoo clock clucked out a gentle reminder that it was time to take a bath.

The janitor had finally made it back over to fix my icebox and to fortify my slippery tub.

My nightly baths were less risky after that. I slipped out of my skirt and drew the water as hot as my wrinkled skin could stand it. I held on to the new handle Larry had rigged up and eased myself into the water. My braid, completely wet, looked like a long, slithering snake coiled against my legs, all the way down to my gnarled feet.

I soaked until the water turned cool and pulled myself out of the tub. That handle was handy, and I needed to thank him again.

When I saw my reflection in the mirror, it no longer startled me. I'd been around a long time, and you don't hold onto that many minutes and hours and days without a good deal of weathering.

I slipped into fresh drawers and an old flannel robe that had seen better days but still did the trick.

Falling into my featherbed, the one Aunt Helen left me, was easy that night. The next day would be busy. I'd need to catch up on reading my paper and make a grocery list. Thursday was the best day to shop. I'd need to get a big bag of marshmallows for Saturday night.

I hoped the newlyweds had four walls to themselves for at least one night. The next morning, the sun would rise, and I presumed that the bride and groom would both need to get back to work at school.

It wasn't my problem to chew on, but the children couldn't sleep like they were camping forever. Those scrawny scamps, all six of them, must have felt like they were staying in a five-star hotel, compared to where they came from. I knew this was so.

Even eighty years later, I still wake up in the middle of the night and marvel at my soft and safe surroundings. I touch my nightstand and graze the pretty lamp with my fingertips. I feel the flowers embroidered along the edge of my pillowcase and sigh with relief that my saving wasn't all just a dream that someone had forgotten to snatch from me.

My aunt and uncle made sure that I'd never return to Shakey's Half. Even as an old woman, when I thought about that place, I was nothing but a trembling kitten of a girl, a child again, afraid of the daylight as much as the dark.

I'd been saved, and meticulous steps had been taken to ensure I would never be without. What more could a wet kitten from Shakey's Half possibly want?

Chapter Eighty-One

Gloria

I think Richard felt real shame. The news I gave him brought him back down to Earth, which is the least we deserved.

He was sorry about what happened to Vi. He even touched my arm in a brotherly way, which was his natural impulse to comfort. But I knew that when I told him the whole story, he would rescind his initial gesture. I was sure of that.

The story of Violet and James was a tale of prey and predator.

Richard, as the father of the predator, needed to know that.

On my way over, it occurred to me that Reverend Pullman might not believe me. I needed to prepare for that possibility. I had dates, times, behaviors and descriptions of what took place that were rooted in truth by all of their details. This kind of information was not easily conjured up by a young girl without being anchored in the ugly truth. It was impossible that Violet made this up and I was ready to stand by every word.

To my surprise, Richard didn't challenge me. His eyebrows raised slightly, and he watched my face intently as I pulled him directly into the problem. We sat there together in his office as the gravity of the situation was made clear.

In that quiet space, an unexpected sense of grace bubbled up in me for my brother-in-law. I actually felt sorry for him. Being the mother of the victim allowed me a wide berth of emotions. A mama bear could claim righteous anger, rage, outrage, shame, helplessness and the desire for exacting sweet revenge.

The man sitting across from me needed a more expansive space to hold what he had. Outrage and anger and shame could be his in equal measure. But as the father of the criminal, Richard needed elbow room for much more. His burden was heavier, and its stink would be harder to contain.

From that minute forward, he would not rest. He was responsible and would forever hold the knowledge that his son was a beast who deserved to be in jail. Still, he was forced to contain it, bury it, create untruths and track their trails. He would do this because it was his job, and his job alone, to champion his vile child.

Chapter Eighty-Two

Skip

My family was thrilled we'd be leaving Poulson and coming closer to the Sellers fold. Once we made the decision to get the hell out of there, our moving forward clipped right along.

Vi, Gloria and I could think less about the tattoo and more about what was on the horizon. Vi had started playing the piano again. I'd forgotten how much I'd missed hearing that sound fill the house.

"I guess this means we're taking the piano with us?"

Gloria smiled.

"Yes, Skip. Let's take the piano. But we're leaving all of the stuff we don't need."

News of the tattoo had spread far and wide. It made school difficult for Vi, and daily life was hard for me and Gloria, too. At the bank, people looked at me differently. What kind of a banker lets his daughter get a tattoo? Who was steering that ship over there at our house?

Violet's tattoo was nasty, for sure, but the gossip in Poulson gave it expansive proportions. In this town's telling, the tattoo changed from a skull and crossbones on her panty line to a full-scale pirate ship that covered her whole belly. Word got around that Vi shelled out $200 to Lem and Lee instead of $35, and that she'd made three trips to his shithole encampment to get it worked on.

We needed a fresh start. If Lem Hauser and Lee Marks did serious time, that was fine with me. Our work was done in Poulson. It didn't take me long to get another job closer to my folks. When I turned in my resignation, I noticed the board was a little relieved. All this tattoo talk wasn't good for business. They didn't say so, but their eagerness to stand up and shake my hand told me that's what they were thinking. I'd close a handful of commercial loans, and then the Sellers family would get out of Dodge.

The only thing left to do was sell the house. It was one of the bigger homes in town and should have been an easy sell, but we had one little problem. A house like ours didn't have too many eligible buyers in Poulson. We were only the third owners. Whoever built this place had meant to stay. It had gleaming hardwood floors, high ceilings and stained-glass windows in the living room and dining room. There were more bedrooms than we ever needed, and baths, too.

Our family of three didn't fill this house to the brim. It needed more people and a dog or a couple of sneaky cats. I could imagine a pack of playful children being shooed out to the backyard. The front porch swing was begging to be put through its paces with carnival-ride gusto during the day and a measured, creaking calm come nightfall.

We might have to sit on the place for a spell. At least that's what I thought. Then I found Margaret Burns waiting for me when I got back from lunch on Thursday. She had her paper tucked under her arm and didn't want to talk to anyone but me.

Margaret had grown on me since I'd come to Poulson. She was crusty on the outside and seemed to think she knew your business. At first, that bothered me, but I had to admit she was right most of the time. For someone who could be all up in everyone else's business, she was fiercely protective of her own.

Most people in Poulson didn't know that Margaret had a pile of money and never spent much of it. She lived in a tidy cracker box of a place with no liens. She paid her property taxes in cash and lived close to the bone. She wasn't foolish with her money, but she did like to keep tabs on it with me a few times a year.

"Miss Burns, what are you going to do with all this money? You need to throw yourself a party or start shopping at Kline's. Get yourself a beau and set sail for someplace fancy."

She'd shake her head at my teasing and smile.

"That's just nonsense, Mr. Sellers. Pure nonsense. I'm saving it for something. I don't know what it is just yet, but when something worth doing comes along, I'll know it. I'll know."

We'd been bantering like that for years, but time had changed the two of us. That braid of hers got longer and whiter. It was a wonder she didn't trip over it. She was shrinking, while I was expanding. I had gray at my temples and a paunch. I needed to start laying off the pie and whisky sours.

"Mr. Sellers, it looks to me like you're putting on, Sir. You're getting rounder."

Her wrinkled finger pointed right at my midsection. I'd never need to hop on the scale as long as Margaret Burns was around. She could be counted on to let me know if I was getting too big for my britches.

We started that Thursday visit with her usual assessment.

"You're getting fat, aren't you?"

"Miss Burns, I suspect you're right about that. I do like my dinners. One of these days, I'm going to do something about that. What can I do for you this afternoon?"

She sat down and motioned for me to do the same. She slapped her newspaper on my desk.

"I'm here to get some of my money. I'm going to buy a house."

"A house? Miss Burns, you already own a house. It's a nice little space, just the right size for you. Why on Earth would you need to buy another house?"

"I hear you're moving, Skip Sellers, and I think I'm going to buy your house. In fact, I'm sure of it. Now, I've got three questions for

Violet *is* Blue

you. How much do you want for it? When can you leave? And can I come over and see it today?"

I sputtered.

This was hard to take in, but a welcome surprise. I probed further. She had the cash. There was no doubt about that. It would sure solve our problems. We could hit the road.

"Miss Burns, that's mighty nice of you. We need to sell our house, and I'd like to do it quickly, but we'll figure something out."

"Listen to me, Skip Sellers. I'm sorry for all your troubles, and I'm happy this offer helps you, but that's not why I'm here. I want that house sooner rather than later. Take me over there so I can look it over, and let's make ourselves a deal."

Gloria had taken Violet out of town for the day, just to get some relief. The house was empty. I grabbed my keys—and Margaret—and we took a drive.

I held the front door open for her.

"Miss Burns. Let me show you around."

Gloria had already started packing. Boxes were stacked all over the place and labeled. She'd been busy.

"No need, Skip. No need. I know every inch of this place. Every last inch."

Chapter Eighty-Three

Violet

Jules didn't know I could play the piano. Now that he could come inside, I had more to show him than Mr. Bones.

"That's really good, Vi. How did you get so good like that?"

I shrugged and kept on playing.

"Hours and hours of practice, and lessons, I guess."

My friend watched me play. His hair was growing out.

"I guess you'll take your piano with you to your new house, huh?"

"Of course. It cost a fortune. Gloria has already found me a new piano teacher and everything."

"You're pretty lucky, Vi."

"I know. I'm lucky, and you are, too. At least now you're lucky. Do you like things better, now that you and your sisters are with your aunt and uncle?"

He nodded but closed his eyes. It was a ridiculous question.

"Jules, do you miss Lee and Lem? Do you miss them just a little bit? Even the tiniest bit? I would understand it, if you do."

"Well, you don't need to understand it, Vi, because I don't miss them, and neither do the girls."

"Okay, okay Jules. Don't be so touchy."

I could tell he wanted to go outside. All this time inside, with my mother hovering around, cramped our style. There wasn't any privacy for cutting up, and we still both craved a sting now and then, just like old times. I gestured with my head toward the porch.

Once outside, we found our spot on the steps. Gloria could pop in anytime, so we needed to make short work of it. My friend came fully prepared. He pulled out a small pocketknife I'd never seen before.

"Uncle Larry gave it to me."

"That was nice of him. I bet he was thinking you'd use it to cut string and stuff like that, not to slice yourself open."

"Yeah, and that seam ripper of yours sees all kinds of seams, Vi."

Jules challenged me, and I liked it.

"Jules, I'm sorry I asked about Lee and Lem. That wasn't nice to bring up, was it?"

"That's okay."

He was going quiet on me. Jules and I held onto quiet together. It was just something that came natural for us.

I was going to miss him.

"I wish you didn't have to leave, Vi. I really wish you could stay."

"Me, too."

Jules put his hand on my arm.

"Who are you going to cut up with once I'm gone?"

"Nobody, Vi. Nobody. Aunt Clarice is asking all kinds of questions about my scars. She's not letting it go. I'm going to cut one more time, with you, then I'm done, Vi. And you should be, too. Nice girls like you don't do this. I never should have shown you how to do this. And if it weren't for Lee and Lem, you wouldn't have that nasty Mr. Bones. We've marked you up, good, Vi. You need to get as far away from me as you can."

"No, Jules. No! Don't say that. Don't you say that. You're my friend. I'm your cutting queen, and I have one last command for you, then we'll have a slice. You'll be rewarded for obeying me."

Jules said yes with his soft, brown eyes before I said another word.

Chapter Eighty-Four

Ruth

Why would Skip and Gloria leave Poulson? It didn't make sense. It was a rash move that they would soon regret, and I wasn't shy about telling her that.

"Gloria, talk about the tattoo will die down. It's on people's minds now, and they're gossiping about it plenty, I will give you that, but it will pass. Something else will come along for people to chew on. You just wait and see."

My big sister didn't want to hear me.

"Ruthie, we're doing this. It's what's best for Violet, and for us, too. Skip's already accepted an offer, and we're leaving."

"But Poulson is your home, Gloria! You've never left this place. What about Mother and Pop? What about them? They aren't getting younger, Gloria. And Vi? Moving when you're in high school is hard. Everybody's already made their friends. It's hard to fit in. This tattoo news will die down. What about Vi and Jamie? They are just starting to get to know each other. They had a really good time when she stayed over. And you and me? I think we're getting closer, too, aren't we? Aren't we? What can I do to help you reconsider?"

I meant every word I said, but I also knew how my words landed. They sounded whiny and pleading, in the little sister way that my big sister didn't appreciate. We were kids again. One of us earnest and wanting, the other rejecting and resentful. She didn't give me her old pinch and nip. Instead, she put her hand on my arm and spoke gently, like I'd always wanted her to. It took me by surprise, that Gloria felt this kindness for me.

"Ruthie, look at me. I love you. I do. And I love Mother and Pop, and Poulson. But trust me when I tell you that this is the best thing for all of us, even you. I've given you no reason during our lifetime to trust me. I know that. I'm sorry for not being a better sister, the sister you deserved. But now, I'm asking you to trust me on this. We are leaving, and we're not coming back. Trust me, Ruthie. It's better this way."

Gloria hugged me tighter than she ever had. Stunned, I hugged her back. I followed her to her car and watched her climb in.

As I wiped my face, she brushed away her own tears.

"Gloria, can our families get together before you leave? For dinner or a lunch?"

She shook her head.

"No, Honey, I don't think so. We've got to get packed. Vi and I will run by to give Mother and Pop a goodbye, but that will be it. I'll send you our new address. Don't cry, Ruthie. This really is what's best. Bye-bye, Ruthie."

I was weepy the rest of the afternoon and night. Richard tried to comfort me as best he could, patting my back as we settled into bed.

"Ruthie, your sister has always had a mind of her own. She'll do things her way. You know that. Now, come on. Wouldn't we do the same if Violet was our girl? Wouldn't we? It's hard. I know it is, but this might be for the best, my Ruthie. It might be for the best."

Chapter Eighty-Five

Clarice

Everything happened so fast it was hard to believe.

My brother and I were good at cleaning up other people's messes. If I had a nickel for every time I'd swooped in and spiffed things up, I could stop waiting tables and put my feet up. Larry, too. That man was a fixer. He could sniff out a problem like nobody's business, think about it for a minute, and then make things right.

Both of us were dependable.

Once the sexy parts of a crisis are under control, the average person can move along. They don't look in the rearview mirror. The back half of a cleanup can't be left flapping in the wind. The soapy rag needs to be squeezed. The mop needs to be wrung out and the bucket emptied, rinsed out and filled again for the next calamity. The trash needs to be emptied. Broken pieces must be swept up and discarded. Nobody ever sticks around for that.

Sally and Larry were married. It was about darn time. Jules' face was healing. All six kids were out of Shakey's Half. Sure, they were sleeping on the floor in Sally's living room, but they had clean pillowcases to rest their patchy heads on and were getting dunked in the tub on a regular basis. They had clean clothes and were eating hot meals.

They were all back at school during the day, holding their heads just a little higher. Kitty was clingy, still sucking her thumb. Jules and the older girls were still seeking comfort. You could see it in their eyes. Jules had taken to cutting himself. I'd need to ask him about that. Lolly was a nail biter, and Patty liked to take whatever was on her plate, wrap it up in a napkin and keep it in her pocket.

Violet *is* Blue

"Sugar, I want you to look at Aunt Clarice. Come on, look at me. You don't have to do that. Not anymore. Sally's making dinner tonight, and breakfast after that. We'll make sure you get plenty. And if you're still hungry, I will bring you something from the diner. Do you believe me, Sugar?"

Keeping these kids fed and loved was a day-in, day-out proposition. It was going to cost more money than my head janitor brother could make. Even with Sally teaching, it would be a stretch. I could help. There would always be an expense that required me reaching into my tip jar. These kids were my responsibility, too. Leave it to me to start thinking about wringing out the mop instead of looking at the shining floor that gleamed beneath us.

After the wedding, I worked on Thursday, Friday, and Saturday. I'd promised to come help Sally with laundry and cooking on Sunday, but there was a matter we'd left hanging.

It was time to visit Lee. I hadn't seen her since she was arrested. Mama would want me tending to Lee. I knew that, and I dreaded the visit, but this was the vegetable on my plate that needed to be eaten before I could have dessert.

Paradise County Jail was nothing special. It had an institutional smell, like the way the school building smells in the morning before Larry unlocks the doors to let the students and teachers rush in and start stinking the place up. It was a far cry better than Shakey's Half, though.

I wondered if Lee even noticed.

I signed myself in and waited to get a spot inside the visitor's room. I hoped nobody would recognize me. A cold metal folding chair in the corner looked like the best place to sit and think about what I was going to say to Lee.

What *was* I going to say? I was damned mad at her. She would know this version of me well. Since Jules had come along, I hadn't shown her much else.

I had the makings of a good big sister. She could ask Larry. But with Lee, there wasn't much goodness to spare. We always had her bullshit to get out of the way first. She was always doing something wild and stupid, and I stood by with my hand on one hip and my finger wagging at her.

I made warnings, suggestions, and even laid out guilt trips, offered in exasperated tones that took their toll on her and me. I wasn't her mother, but we shared one. I tried to tell myself that our mama would give her much of the same business.

Lee wasn't easy to love. And those kids of hers upped the ante. If she couldn't do better for me or Larry, I had one question.

Could she snap out of it and do right by her children?

Wasn't this an instinct of a mother? Of course it was.

Thinking about Lee was hard on my head. I'm pretty sure she was the source of all my dark brown headaches. The aches she caused to my heart were deeper, though. I'm not sure what color to give an ache that haunts your heart.

Chapter Eighty-Six

Margaret Burns

Things were buzzing over at the hive. The teacher and the janitor hadn't quite figured out how to get that brood all dressed up and ready for church on a Sunday morning, but they'd get there.

On Sundays, Clarice usually stopped over to help. She was good to them. I'd made up my mind to get over there as soon as Clarice got herself settled. She could hold down the fort while I took my neighbors to see their wedding present.

I knocked on the door and was ushered in by the little one. It was hard not to be in love with that sweet thing. She walked me into the kitchen. Sally was making a big old pot of soup and there were cookies cooling on racks on the table.

"It smells mighty darn good in here. Let me guess. That's chicken noodle, isn't it?"

Sally beamed at me with her happy face. She looked good standing over that oven and swatting kids away from the cookies.

"Hello there, neighbor! You've got that right! It's chicken noodle soup, and I'm making a pot big enough to feed this crew two suppers. I bet we could spare a bowl for you if you'd like to join us."

"I might just take you up on that, but I'm wondering where your mister has got himself to."

Larry was in the yard with the boy.

"Oh, we can get him. You got something for him to do? He could bring Jules along to assist."

"Well, no, nothing's broken, at least not today. I was hoping I could show you and Larry your wedding present today. I never did give you a proper gift."

"Oh, Margaret, that is the sweetest thing. You don't have to do that though. How lovely. I'll call Larry in to help me open it."

"Oh, I'm afraid I didn't wrap it, and it's too big for me to carry over here. We'll have to take a drive for you to see it."

"Miss Burns, what are you up to?"

"You'll have to come with me to find out."

"Clarice, do you mind if we take a drive with Margaret? The girls are folding up the laundry and by the time we get back, the soup will be ready."

Clarice wasn't her usual sassy self that day. Something must have been bothering her. Poor thing worked herself to the bone.

"Sally, it might be the only time you get some peace and quiet for the day, maybe the whole week. Pick up some of that for me, too, while you're out. I could sure use some. So, go for your Sunday drive, and enjoy it!"

Five minutes later, the three of us were squished into Larry's truck.

"Are you sure we don't have any stowaways?"

I laughed as Larry looked into the bed of the truck and smiled.

"I think we're good. We'd better get out while we can! Miss Burns, you've got me curious. Where are we headed?"

We rode across town, past the high school, past the row of churches and on past the cemetery to the nice side of town.

"Turn here," I said.

"Margaret, we're headed to the other side of the tracks. You must have gotten us something really fancy, neighbor!"

"You'll have to wait and see, Larry. Keep driving, now."

"Yes, Ma'am."

We turned the last corner and there was the house.

"Stop here. Right here."

"It's the Sellers place," said Sally. "They're moving, aren't they?"

Skip had agreed to have his family out of the house for a while so we could look around. I had the key all snug in my pocket.

Sally didn't understand.

"Margaret, what is going on here? Are they selling their furniture or something? What is this surprise?"

"You two come on. Don't you love this great big porch?"

"I know this place," said Larry. "I've been here a few times."

The teacher and the janitor didn't know what to think.

"Let's go inside," I said.

"Are you sure this is okay, Margaret? This doesn't feel right. Are these folks home? They might not want us snooping around their house like this. The For Sale sign isn't even up yet."

"There won't be any need to put up a sign. It's already sold."

Sally was still making sense of it as we walked inside. The entryway had not changed at all. The light was streaming through the stained-glass windows in the living room, making the same patterns on the floor I remembered. It was so pretty and sacred, we might as well have been in church.

Larry held his hand up, as if to stop the proceedings.

"Miss Burns, this is a very nice place, and of course I know we need something bigger, but a place like this would never be in our price range. We'll have even less money next year because we're thinking it's best for Sally to stay home with all these kids. We need someone running the ship."

"I know that. I know all of that. But I want you to listen to me. I bought this place. Yep, I did. I bought it as soon as I knew this family was moving. I paid cash, too. I bought it with you two and that baseball team of kids you've picked up in mind. I want you all to live here."

As soon as Sally and Larry picked their jaws up off the floor, they protested. Sally started crying and walked into the kitchen.

No, I said. I will not accept rent. No, they cannot pay taxes. Yes, they *can* pay for water and heat.

Yes, I was sure. Yes, I had the money. No, I didn't have any kids or relatives to think about. No, I didn't care if they brought their damned cat.

"You can get a dog, for all I care! Please. You just have to let me come over to enjoy those wiener roasts on Saturday nights. I'll bring the marshmallows."

Now, the janitor was crying, too. They hugged me and I hugged them right back.

We walked around the whole house together, from room to room, and I told my happy and good young friends all about a little girl named Margaret Burns.

Chapter Eighty-Seven

Clarice

I was glad Mama wasn't there when Lee walked through the door. It looked like she was drowning in her gray uniform. Her hair looked clean, as if it had been combed by someone else.

She scanned the room looking for me. She knew I was coming. I stood up and gave a little wave. I wanted to hug her, then shake her until her teeth rattled. She did not offer a smile but tossed me a wave and headed over to where I was sitting.

Lee looked like a criminal. She fit right in with the other inmates. Just like a tough one, she sat down and folded her arms.

"I guess you're happy, aren't you?"

Jesus Christ. Here we go.

No greeting. No thanks for stopping by. Spending my Sunday to see her was not appreciated. She wanted a visitor, but not me. We were fresh out of soft landings.

"Lee, I won't take any of your sass. You hear me? I'm not happy about this, not one bit. You might try being grateful that I came here in the first place. I'm pretty sure that I'm the first one to come see you and I'll probably be the only visitor you get. You've been in here for six weeks, and I'm the first one to swing through to check on you. What does that tell you?"

She shrugged.

"What took you so long? Where the hell have you been?"

Where the hell had I been the last six weeks? Hmmm. Where to begin? I gave her my watch-your-mouth look.

"Listen up, Sister. I've been a little tied up and so has your brother. We've got ourselves a project, a great big to-do list to clean up another one of your messes. Those children of yours, all six of them, need a place to stay. And they need to be cleaned and fed and loved. They need all kinds of help, Lee, thanks to your shit. And Lem's. We're happy to take over, and this time, Lee, we're making it permanent. You don't get another chance. Nope."

"That's not up to you, Clarice."

I moved in closer. I didn't mind making a scene.

"Listen to me, Lee. Listen good. You've been skating by for too long, and this time, everybody's onto you. Shame on you and shame on Lem. Those kids of yours were filthy and scrawnier than I've ever seen them. What's the matter with you? And what the hell are you and Lem doing, giving a kid, Violet Sellers, of all people, a tattoo? Are you wild animals? You both deserve to be in here."

She gave me another shrug.

"We needed the money, Clarice. You wouldn't know about that."

"Oh, stop. You always need money, Lee. You need money every time I turn around. When you're not getting cash from me, you're working on Lem and Larry. You make the rounds with your hand out. Larry and I always pour money into you."

She started to say something, but I cut her off.

"You hush, Lee. I'm not finished. I want to know why the hell you thought it was a good idea to put a tattoo on anyone, and as soon as you knew your customer was Violet Sellers, why didn't you bow out and ask Lem to bow out, too? What has Violet ever done to you, Lee? Do you remember all that her mother did for you? Gloria gave and gave and gave, until she saw you for the taker you are and sent your ass packing. I told you that would happen. That's what happens when you're ungrateful and wild and foolish. You look at me, Lee, and you tell me you didn't do this to get back at Gloria."

Another shrug.

"Lem did it. I just helped. I held her down."

"What is the matter with you? Tell you what, Girl. You've got all kinds of time to think about that, don't you? Let me tell you something. You know what? I'm glad you were in on the tattoo. And I'm glad Lem gave Jules his big black and blue face. You know why? Because it opened up the whole nasty works. It made room for someone to save your kids. And let me tell you, they deserve saving."

"When are you bringing them by?"

I laughed out loud. It was an ugly laugh that drew attention from everyone else in the room, but I didn't care.

"You have got to be kidding. We won't be bringing them by. Ever. And when you get out of here, whenever that is, you won't be seeing them either. I'll make sure of it. Count on it, Lee. But I'll give you a quick run-down. Nobody has head lice this week. They're all wearing clean clothes and sleeping with their heads on clean pillows. They eat breakfast every morning. They eat lunch on yellow tickets at school, then come home with Larry and his new wife, Sally. They eat dinner every night. Jules' face is healing up nicely, but he's got cut marks all up and down his arms. We'll be getting to the bottom of that. Kitty's still sucking her thumb, and clinging like a baby doll to Sally, who loves on her and kisses the top of her little old head."

Finally, tears started streaking down Lee's face. I teared up, too. Why did she have to be like this? I hugged my little sister, and she hugged me back. I whispered in her ear.

"You can't have these babies back, Honey. Nope. They aren't yours anymore. We're going to give them something better, something much, much better."

Visiting hour was over. I stood up and so did Lee. I was still mad as hell at her. She didn't come from trash. She had good people. We were decent. There was no excuse for all this. Mama would have been happy to know that despite all my hard feelings, I still felt sorry for Lee.

"Honey, I got to go now. I'm going over to Larry and Sally's place to help, so they're ready for Monday morning and the rest of the week."

"Will you come again?"

She was pitiful.

"Yes. I'll come next week. I'll see you next week."

Lee curled up her lip at me and walked out the door. That was the closest thing she had to a smile.

Chapter Eighty-Eight

Sally

I don't look too pretty when I cry. My face gets all red and blotchy. Larry's seen me like that and says I still look good even when my face is a mess. He's an awfully handsome liar.

I cried and sniffled the whole time we walked through the Sellers house. Margaret assured me that we were all doing the right thing.

"When I was a child, this was called the Burns House. This place has changed its appearance but still has the same soul and bones. This is a good house, my friends. You need this place, and it needs you."

The kitchen was warm and quite large. We'd need a big table to fit everyone. Larry could rig up something. He would love doing that.

There were built-in bookshelves in the living room. We had a nice, growing collection of children's books, and plenty of board games and puzzles that could live there.

I smiled at Larry.

"We can put the Christmas tree in that corner. And stockings. We'll need six stockings."

"Nine. Let's not forget me and you. And Clarice."

We hugged and wept. My husband looked even more handsome after a good cry.

There were five bedrooms. Five! One for us, and four to divvy up between the kids.

"I think Jules deserves his own room," said Larry. "He's a young man now. He needs space from his sisters."

We talked our way through the rooms as Margaret told us more about living there long ago.

"I was just about Kitty's age when my Aunt Helen and Uncle Teddy pulled me out of Shakey's Half and brought me home with them to this house. It felt like a castle back then, and it still feels that way!"

"We didn't know you were a Shakey's Half girl."

"Oh, yes. I know all about coming from that part of town. It's a different, hard world over there. The minute those kids piled out and followed you single file through your front door, I knew they came from there. I could see it in their eyes and from those raggedy heads of theirs. I had my head shaved a time or two. Why do you think I'm sporting this ridiculous braid that nearly reaches the floor? Once I got out of that dark place, and then when I knew for sure I'd never go back, I vowed to never cut my hair again. And I haven't, except for a trim now and then to keep from tripping over myself!"

We continued walking through the rooms until we reached one at the end of the hall, closest to what would be the master bedroom.

Margaret flipped on the light.

"Well, will you look at that? This room is still pink. Still pink! This was my room. My bed was right there by the window. Aunt Helen put a throw rug right by the bed, so when I woke up in the morning, my little feet wouldn't get a shock from the icy cold floor. She was so good to me. My uncle, too. They slept in the next room and Aunt Helen would run to me in the middle of the night when my nightmares got bad, or I'd worry out loud about getting sent back to Shakey's Half. She'd cuddle up with me and whisper sweetness at me until we both fell asleep."

Margaret looked back at us both. Her eyes were glistening, too.

"They saved me. They really did. They saved me and brought me here. That's what I want for those kids. The two of you are saving six children. Six! And you're doing it so well. I just want you to have a comfortable place to do it. That's all. This is worth doing. Nobody knows that more than yours truly. So, let me help you."

Margaret wiped her face with her coat sleeve and then turned off the light.

"Maybe this room here would be a good spot for that little one. She'll be right close to you, Sally, and she needs that."

We walked out onto the porch and let Margaret lock the front door.

"I think the Sellers will be on their way next week. Then, you can move your family in here."

We were still stunned as we got back in the truck. Larry's hand delivered tight, sweet squeezes to my thigh as we drove across town. I let my head rest on his shoulder, and he planted kisses all the way home. We didn't mind if our sweet old neighbor saw us. She was looking out her window and smiling, too, watching the late Sunday afternoon sun try its best to catch up with us.

That night, hot chicken noodle soup warmed our hands as we held our bowls and filled our bellies. Six kids and four adults can make a dent in a pot of soup. There wasn't a noodle left at the bottom of the pot. We made short work of the cookies, too, and I made hot cocoa for anyone who wanted it. Everyone did.

We decided to wait until the next day to share our good news with the children. That night, we made sure to hug Margaret and thank her and hug her some more.

Larry walked her home while the big girls and I tackled the dishes. Finally, everyone was settled down for the night, even Kitty.

I sank into our bed and let my husband take me in his arms. We talked quietly in the dark, making plans. We were tired, but too excited to sleep. We found one another and made quiet, thunderous love that made us laugh.

"Shhh," said Larry. "We don't want to wake the kids up."

I finally drifted off to sleep, wondering what my dreams had in store. They would have to work hard to best what Margaret dreamed up for us that day.

Chapter Eighty-Nine

Richard

Keeping the Marks kid quiet was going to be tricky.

For one thing, I didn't know him. He looked like a good kid when he popped up at the Downs wedding, but a bit skittish. Poor boy. I knew that this young man was better behaved than my own son. Jules Marks could teach James Pullman a thing or two about decency. And knowing what he knew about Jamie, this wild card boy had all the power. I just needed to find out if he understood that.

I'd need to find my way in through the back door. The best I could do would be to reach out to his uncle, Larry Downs. He was a nice enough fellow. Maybe he could be reasonable. He and that new wife of his were taking on plenty. It made me tired just to think about it. They wouldn't let Jules get tied up in something messy like what happened with Jamie and Violet. A heart-to-heart with Larry, who was essentially a stranger to me, and to Jamie, would allow another person to know the truth. It wasn't worth the risk.

Normally, I could call on Ruthie for help. She was sharp as a tack, and always picked up on things most people missed, including me. But this time, I could not lean into my wife. I'd have to stand on my own and come up with a plan. Praying about it seemed inappropriate, but I wanted this cup to pass my lips.

The Lord must have been eavesdropping. Gloria dropped by my office for one last goodbye.

"Hello there, Richard. Do you have a few minutes?"

Of course. Anything for Gloria. We both knew that anytime she wanted, she could change her mind and bring Skip and Ruthie into the mess. It was possible.

I waved her in.

"How's the packing going?"

"Fine. Moving is a good time to throw away things we don't need. There's a lot that won't come with us."

"And Vi? How's our Violet? I do pray for her, and for Skip. I hope you know that."

Did she believe me? She didn't need to know that God and I hadn't been on speaking terms the last few weeks. If I was in a praying mood, I'd sure add the Sellers family to the agenda, right after my own hide, and Jamie's, of course.

"Vi is doing the best she can. She's sleeping better and playing the piano again. We're glad to hear that sound in the house. I think the fresh start will be good for her, and for us."

"You know, Gloria, I've been thinking about our situation. I'm still not sure about how to get the Marks kid onboard. I don't know him that well, and there isn't a good reason to meet privately with him without people getting suspicious."

She nodded.

I needed her to be a little bit more concerned. If Jules decided to spill the beans, things wouldn't be good for her, either. In fact, we'd both be in much more trouble for hiding something so enormous from our spouses.

This was a deal-breaker and had the makings of justifiable divorces for both of us. On top of that, my career would be over, and my son would be in jail.

"Gloria, I was thinking that Violet and Jules must be close. He's a boy and she's a girl. She's been raised right, and he hasn't. Are they romantically involved?"

"No. I asked, and they are not. I think Jules has his crush on Vi, but I don't think she's sweet on him. They're good friends. He's been very good to her."

"I wonder if he'd listen to Violet. Do you think she might be able to convince him to keep this mess to himself? I hate to ask her, after all she's been through, but I think she might be our only option."

"Richard, you know that I've already asked my daughter to keep this from her father, right? Do you know how I did that? Let me tell you. I told her that I was afraid Skip might kill Jamie, and that he'd end up in jail. Jail! She's fourteen, and fragile enough for now to buy that. I've encouraged my child to be dishonest with her father. I've asked her to accept that your son's beastly actions will go unpunished so that all the adults involved can keep their shit together. Remember, Richard, I'm protecting Ruthie, too. I've hurt her enough, and I'm holding this one. It might be wrong, all of it. I suspect it is, but this is where we are."

"Gloria, I know that. And I'm thankful to you. I really am. I know this is impossible. I'm lying to my wife, too. This would surely break her, but if she ever finds out that I'm covering my tracks, it's over for us. She'll walk out on me. I'm asking now, what I can do for you, and for Violet, to get this young man on board. What will it take? We're running out of time, Gloria. Every day that goes by without locking this down is dangerous."

"Dangerous? Richard, my dear brother-in-law. Reverend Pullman. *Dangerous* is not a word you get to use to describe anything or anyone but your own son. He's dangerous. Let's remember that. So, I would say that every day that goes by without locking down Jules will be inconvenient. That's right. *Inconvenient* is the better word. I like that word better."

Oh, Jesus. We didn't have time for this. This visit needed to get back on track.

"Gloria, listen to me. I know that James did a monstrous thing. I'm sorry, and he is, too. But that's not what we're talking about right now. Today, we're trying to figure out how to lock this down. Can Violet help us convince Jules to keep his mouth shut? Yes or no?"

I was shaking. Ruthie's sister had never seen me like this. She was very still, thinking, I hoped, about meeting me half-way.

"Yes, Richard. Don't worry. I will talk to Violet, and I'll ask her to stress to her friend that it's best for everyone if they *both* keep the rape to themselves. You have my word."

Rape.

When she said that word, I couldn't say any more.

Gloria left my office, closing the door behind her. Rape? What James did to Violet was violent. Unwanted. Uninvited. Since I learned the truth and cautiously considered the details with Gloria and James, I hadn't allowed myself to consider the word.

Rape.

Our futures were in the hands of a woman who despised us for good reason, and two wounded, unpredictable kids.

Chapter Ninety

Gloria

After all the fallout, Jules started coming around again. It took a few days for things to settle down. When he did show, there was no waiting on the porch.

He looked more scrubbed up and less hungry. Still, if cookies or sandwiches were offered, he took them. After all, he was a teenage boy with a hollow leg.

As I packed the good china in the dining room, I could hear Jules and Vi chatting, sometimes teasing, sometimes so soft I couldn't make out what they were saying. Were all their secrets revealed, or was there more they held between them?

I wondered what Jules thought of me. After Lee was in jail, Clarice and Larry took their nephew aside and shared the sticky, complicated history that Lee and I shared. I hoped they included my good intentions and glossed over my raw, nagging need, the times I poured myself for no good reason on Jules and his mother. At the very least, did they tell this kid how ignorant and grasping his mother was? That she was a taker? That she never said *thank you*? That she was negligent on a good day, and worse when it was bad? Did he need to be told such things? I suspected not.

I owed Violet the backstory, too. She was going to find out from Jules, anyway. That's what all the whispering was probably about in the next room. They were comparing stories. Those whispers were about her parents and his parents, and how we let the two of them fall. None of us minded our ships properly.

I wanted to curate the story that Violet knew and believed. I was generous with Lee, to a fault, just trying to help, and she took advantage of me. My sweet nature was not borne of a deep need to make things right with the universe for all the torments I unleashed on my little sister over the years. I'd fallen down on the job. My good deeds came back to bite me.

To do right by Ruthie this one last time was going to cost me more than all the fine goods at Kline's I'd forced on Lee's doorstep. I wanted to help, but I also drew pleasure from showing this poor girl the finer things in life she would never have.

It was a power move and wicked of me. And there was more. A skilled psychiatrist armed with all the facts would only need five minutes to clarify what took me years to even face.

In the beginning, instead of making authentic amends with my own sister, I chose a convenient proxy: Lee Marks. How much easier all this might have been if I'd only had the courage to look Ruthie, Pop's Little Red, in the eyes, and apologize. Searching my soul too deeply on it made me red in my face.

I didn't want Vi in on that, too. She already knew that I expected her to keep what happened between her and James a secret. I expected her to join me in deceiving Skip. I offered her no alternative. How long would that hold? Had it occurred to my girl that she could, perhaps even should, deny me?

I required just a bit more. She and I needed to take a prisoner with us. Jules owed me nothing. To ask this of him was presumptuous and unfair, coming from me. Hadn't this urchin endured enough? And wasn't it honesty and a compass pointing north that brought him to my door to help Violet? How many lies had Jules ever told? I guessed not many. But coming from Violet, I was willing to wager he'd leap at the chance to please her. It was a bitter tonic to swallow, but if served up by Vi, it could still go down sweet enough.

This young man had already proven he'd go to great lengths to do right by Violet. Even in its initial puppy stage, love can be so strong in a way we long for it to always be.

Chapter Ninety-One

Jules

Vi and I had a little time left before she left Poulson, and I wasn't going with her. Waiting for the loneliness that would come hurt me worse than any slow cut.

She needed to go. We knew this. Word about Mr. Bones had spread fast. Luckily, Vi had the option to run far away from the mess and take her tattoo with her. A fresh start would be easy enough for someone like her. I didn't hold it against her, not after all she'd been through at the hands of Lem, Momma and that nasty cousin of hers. I'd seen that smug son-of-a-bitch around. I knew exactly who he was.

People like Vi and James had choices that people like me never have. Those of us with no leg up are tethered like dogs to spikes in the yard. We can strain and pull, but that will only make us tired. After a while, we accept the circle that has been drawn for us. Inside that circle is where we get to exist. We must eat in the same place we shit, love in the same places we hate and die in the same circle where we live. To stray beyond where the world wants us is not possible.

It wasn't worth sharing with Vi, but the tattoo story would stay in Poulson. Vi would be long gone, but not me. It was my people, Lee, and Lem, who did this. I was tied to its stink forever, no matter how good I was. And so were my girls. We could live with it. We would have to.

I couldn't hold anything against Violet. I could never stay mad at my cutting queen. I could make peace with the mess Mr. Bones left behind, but there was something harder to stomach.

James Pullman's crime would go unchecked. He had a leg up, too. What he'd done to Vi was far worse than Lee and Lem's handiwork. They were still in jail. They'd come up for air in time. I could wait.

If I thought too hard about James hurting Vi, the sting was strong. My eyes burned and I wanted to deliver punch after punch, even worse than I did to Lem. I wanted to make him bleed. My face, finally less tender from my father's sucker punch, could take whatever James could deliver. I wanted more than a fight. I wanted justice.

"Vi, why don't you and your mother want to see him punished? What he did was a crime! You wouldn't even have Mr. Bones without your cousin's shit happening first!"

Vi was very still. Her calm angered me and frightened me, too.

"Jules, listen to me. I think we both know something else that never would have happened, don't we? Don't we both know that I'd never have found *you*?"

My God, she was right. No girl like Vi would ever find her way to a boy like me unless she was badly wounded. There was no denying this. Still, my face burned as she watched me digest this deep down for the first time.

What were we without our wounds to bind us? If I broke free from where the world wanted me and followed my friend and Mr. Bones to their fresh start, what would we find there?

"Jules Marks, you look at me. I'm glad I know you. I'm glad you are my brave friend. Tell me you believe me."

"I believe you. I do. I'm glad you're my friend, too. I'm gonna miss you, Vi."

"I'll miss you, too. Do you promise to keep quiet about James? Even though it's hard?"

"I don't understand it, but if that's what you really want, I'll keep it to myself. I promise."

"Thank you. Thank you, Jules. It's just better this way."

My heart hurt as it thumped for my friend.

I kept what I was thinking to myself.

Get on out of here, Violet Sellers. Get as far away from this place and that beast as you can. Let your family keep its peace, fancy girl. Jules will stay right here and keep watch for you. I'll watch him come and go like nothing's ever happened. I'll watch him smile and charm his way through it. I'll remember what he did to you every time I see him, so you don't have to think about it so much. I can't do much for you, Vi, but this I will do.

Chapter Ninety-Two

Violet

As we pulled away from the house, I watched my mother wipe away a tear. We were both weepy, but for different reasons. Each of us was leaving behind our childhood, and my mother looked like her memories were too big to bear. So, like she usually did with complex feelings, she avoided them for the moment and focused on other more tangible matters.

"Vi, are you sure about the piano? It's really expensive, Honey. I'm not sure Jules and his sisters will appreciate it."

"Mom, I think they'll love it, and who knows? Maybe one of the girls will really get into it. Maybe even Jules will, too."

By then, I had decided to stop calling my mother Gloria. Saying Mom again felt nice.

"But Violet, it's a *grand* piano! Couldn't we find them one that's less expensive?"

I insisted that we leave our deluxe version in the living room. Jules deserved a grand gesture, and I figured Margaret Burns would love it, too when she came by to visit.

Skip, who was now Dad again, even got onboard with the idea.

"Oh, for Christ's sake, Gloria. Leave the piano here. If Vi wants to take lessons in Rock Hill, we'll buy a new one. Honestly, it's a small price to pay for getting out of here. This is no time to look back."

I wish Dad was more gentle with Mom, but he loved us, for sure, and the piano was a small sacrifice. Mom wasn't weeping about the piano, or the stained-glass windows, or the front porch swing she loved so much.

My mother had never lived outside of Poulson. Rock Hill wasn't a stone's throw away, either. It was nearly a three-hour drive away from Paradise County, far enough to put meaningful distance between us and the sinkhole we were leaving behind.

My father still didn't know the full story, but he was relieved that we were leaving the tattoo story in the rearview mirror, along with all of Poulson's chatter. Mr. Bones had rattled this good man, and he was more than ready for all of us to wash our hands of the whole mess.

Thank God he didn't know about that rainy afternoon I spent in the parsonage, under the savage weight and stink of James Pullman, how my entire body revolted as he did his best to batter and bruise me. Had my father known, he would have cried harder than me and my mother.

If I had run to them first, everything would have been different. Mr. Bones would never have surfaced, and James would have been spared handcuffs, but not because his father was a pastor. None of that would have mattered to my dad. He would have gone straight to the parsonage and beat my cousin to a pulp right in front of Aunt Ruthie and Uncle Richard. He might have killed him. My mom knew this, and I believed her. Neither one of us wanted to see our protector spend the prime of his life in jail. So, my mother and I held this secret between us and agreed that the piano could stay.

How long could we hide such a heavy truth before it eventually broke our backs?

The moving truck pulled away and we followed close behind. Dad had things to wrap up at the bank, so he would meet us at the new house later that night. We drove through town, past Slapp's and then Phelps Fabrics, where Jules and I had found our gleaming seam ripper, and headed toward the outskirts of Paradise County.

My mother stopped the car at the top of the street where she lived for so long with her parents and Ruthie. She shuddered and sighed and smiled at me as we kept driving past the parsonage and my school. My teachers wouldn't miss me, and I was ready to move on.

As we whizzed on past the gravel road that led to Shakey's Half, it was my turn to cry. I was ready to be anywhere but Poulson. Jules wasn't leaving anytime soon. My dirty, brown-eyed boy was staying behind to keep our secrets safe and to grow into a strong man who might just visit me one day.

I hoped he would not forget his cutting queen.

Maybe, just maybe, Mr. Bones had served his purpose after all. Without him, Jules and those sisters of his would still be scratching themselves in the dusty, dirty clutches of Shakey's Half, stuck with Lem and Lee.

Maybe my gatekeeper had done something good for all of us.

Chapter Ninety-Three

Margaret Burns

Watching those kids run up onto the porch and go screeching through that great big saving place I knew so well made me want to take off my shoes and dance.

I'd sure miss watching them come and go from my kitchen window. I could get to them when I wanted. This patched-together crew would no longer be my neighbors, but they were now friends.

Sally was one of those strangers that got herself mixed up with a lifer. And they had kids and a house. She was in deep, but this stranger was going to work out just fine. She was a real mama bear ready to protect the cubs she'd collected overnight. She would stay and fit right in with barely a scratch.

I knew that by the time I went over there with my marshmallows ready to roast, the house would be warmed up and wild with life. It would remember what it could provide when given just the right bodies and full hearts.

Healing would happen in ways big and small. Wounds would be tended, and bellies filled. Games would be played and lost or won. Spilled milk would be wiped up and spilled again, puzzles solved, and gifts opened. Tears would be shed now and then, but those would be noticed and wiped, their source given due respect, then shown the door. People would rest in this space and wake up refreshed for a new day, filled with everything it was meant to hold and then some.

I thanked God for all of it.

The newlyweds were already inside watching all their kids shake the space awake as they explored their new home. The grand piano had been left behind at the Sellers girl's insistence. Someone was already plucking out chopsticks with skill that surprised me.

Jules, the oldest, already knew the place well. He'd stayed behind with the little one. They walked onto the porch and through the front door together, holding hands, like they belonged there. They *did*.

I watched him as he stooped down to whisper something into Kitty's ear. The gentle way he cupped his hand to protect their sweet secret tugged at this old gal.

I didn't know their secret, but I knew a thing or two about how a heart soars again and again, as a saving settles into its goodness.

About the Author

Since she first fell in love with writing in high school, Anne Shaw Heinrich has been a journalist, columnist, blogger and communications professional. Her first article appeared in *Rockford Magazine* in 1987. She's interviewed and written features on Beverly Sills, Judy Collins, Gene Siskel, and Debbie Reynolds.

Anne's writing has been featured in *The New York Times* bestseller *The Right Words at the Right Time, Volume 2: Your Turn* (Atria) and Chicken Soup for the Soul's *The Cancer Book: 101 Stories of Courage, Support and Love*.

Her debut novel, *God Bless the Child*, was the first in this three-book series.

Anne and her husband are parents to three grown children. Anne is passionate about her family, mental health advocacy and the intrepid power of storytelling.

Upcoming New Release!

ANNE SHAW HEINRICH

HOUSE OF TEETH
The Women of Paradise County
Book Three

House of Teeth, Wendy's parents were yoked together by three kids, bad habits and personal indulgences they could not afford. Many of her mother's sentences began with "When he goes," spurring a smorgasbord of miseries, indignities and slights she planned to smash with relish as soon as he took his last breath. But Wendy's bitter mother "went" before her father, leaving him to master his many regrets with his daughter's help. She's the only one left with him there in Poulson, working through her own brand of forgiveness as she sees her old man in a brand new, revealing light.

**For more information
visit: SpeakingVolumes.us**

Now Available!

ANNE SHAW HEINRICH
The Women of Paradise County
Book One

"...a captivating book that touches your heart and leaves a lasting impression. This beautifully crafted story will deeply resonate with you emotionally, as its characters will leave a lasting impression."
—*Midwest Book Review*

"...the tale plays out in addictive alternating first-person chapters, individually narrated by a vivid collection of primary and pivotal secondary characters." —*Kirkus Reviews*

**For more information
visit:** SpeakingVolumes.us

Now Available!

JACQUE ROSMAN

The Academic Mom Mysteries
Book One – Book Two

If you like amateur female sleuths in academia, moms struggling with work-life balance, relatable characters, high stakes and the backdrop of the nation's Capital, then you will love The Academic Mom Mysteries.

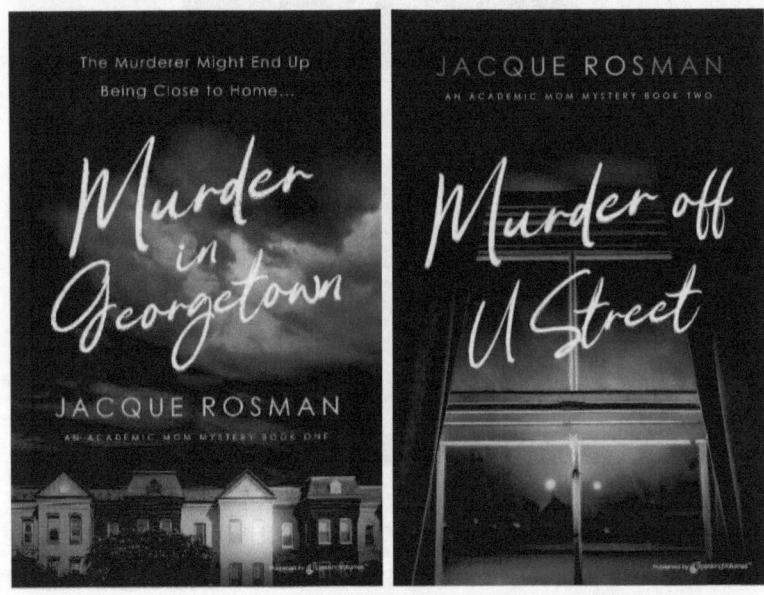

**For more information
visit: SpeakingVolumes.us**

www.ingramcontent.com/pod-product-compliance
Lightning Source LLC
LaVergne TN
LVHW091622070526
838199LV00044B/898